Under the Counter and over the Border
Aspects of the Contemporary Trade in Illicit Arms

Edited by

MARK PHYTHIAN
School of Languages, Humanities and Social Sciences, University of Wolverhampton, UK

KLUWER ACADEMIC PUBLISHERS

DORDRECHT / BOSTON / LONDON

A C.I.P. Catalogue record for this book is available from the Library of Congress

ISBN 0-7923-6593-3

Published by Kluwer Academic Publishers,
P.O. Box 17, 3300 AA Dordrecht, The Netherlands.

Sold and distributed in North, Central and South America
by Kluwer Academic Publishers,
101 Philip Drive, Norwell, MA 02061, USA

In all other countries, sold and distributed
by Kluwer Academic Publishers,
P.O. Box 322, 3300 AH Dordrecht, The Netherlands.

Printed on acid-free paper

Printed in the Netherlands

Table of Contents

Editorial

Over the last few years the illicit arms trade has begun to attract the kind of attention it has always deserved. Increased media exposure and the growing attention of campaigning and human rights groups have informed public opinion and contributed to the issue rising up the policy agenda. In addition, another development has been crucial to this rise; the end of the Cold War has created the political space required for the international community, primarily through the United Nations, to begin to tackle the trade for the first time.

As I outline in the opening article in this collection, the nature of the illicit arms trade has changed significantly since the Cold War ended. During the Cold War, study of the illicit arms trade was eclipsed by the study of the high politics of the East-West nuclear balance and developments in nuclear strategy. It was also made problematic by the fact that both sides in the Cold War viewed recourse to the illicit arms trade and the establishment of illicit arms pipelines as a policy option. In this context, the business of arriving at an acceptable definition of what constituted the 'illicit arms trade' became a political act. Given the negative connotations of the term, governments declined to see their involvement in clandestine arms flows (whether, for example, to the PLO or UNITA) as constituting participation in the illicit arms trade. In this, the contest over definitions was similar to the contemporaneous debate over definitions of terrorism. Brian Jenkins' observation regarding the use of the term 'terrorism' applies equally to the term 'illicit arms trade':

> What is called terrorism thus seems to depend on one's point of view. Use of the term implies a moral judgement; and if one party can successfully attach the label terrorist to its opponent, then it has indirectly persuaded others to adopt its moral viewpoint.[1]

Hence, acceptance of the term 'illicit' could carry with it the connotation that not only was the means of supply illegitimate, but that so too was the cause being pursued by the recipient group.

One solution to this definitional problem was to make a distinction between the 'black' and 'grey' arms markets. The black market was that populated exclusively by privateers, without governmental involvement or acquiescence. The grey market was still characterised by a covert, under-the-counter, trade that did not enjoy the hallmarks of the licit trade – i.e. open delivery, official export licences, genuine end-user certification, delivery to recognised governments. Neither was it necessarily consistent with declared government policy. However, it was officially sanctioned; it represented, at some level, government policy. Hence, the black market was the covert arms trade when outside the scope of state influence or control; the grey market referred to the covert arms trade when utilised in pursuit of policy or broader state interests.

While this distinction was useful, it clearly ran the risk of conferring a kind of legitimacy on 'grey' transfers that was absent from 'black' transfers. Given the extent to which the application of the Reagan Doctrine relied on covert arms transfers to non-state actors involved in efforts to overthrow governments (of varying legitimacy), one effect of this separation of 'grey' from 'black' was to elevate Reagan Administration-related involvement in covert arms flows above non-governmentally sanctioned arms flows, and to bestow on the former a greater degree of legitimacy. For example, the distinction could be taken to imply that arming UNITA ('grey') was a more legitimate act than Iran's contemporaneous search for arms and spare parts ('black') during the war with Iraq.

Another problem with this distinction was that it implied a clear division between 'black' and 'grey' markets when, in practice, it was unclear exactly at what point that separation occurred. In reality there was a significant degree of overlap and, as William D. Hartung has argued, a symbiotic relationship, where, 'as the case of Iran/contra forcefully demonstrates, the private practitioners engaged in the secret arms trade almost invariably got their start in the business in government military or intelligence agencies', and where officials 'may need to turn to a Richard Secord or an Adnan Khashoggi for a favour at some point down the road.'[2] When 'black' market actors can cross over into the 'grey' market and then back again, and vice-versa, the utility of the distinction is diminished.

As Owen Greene outlines, in the post-Cold War environment, as part of its move to make the illicit arms trade a priority issue, the UN has made progress towards an inclusive definition of 'illicit arms trafficking', with Article 2 of the 1999 draft International Firearms Protocol, for example, defining it as:

> The import, export, acquisition, sale, delivery, movement or transfer of firearms, their parts and components and ammunition from or across the territory of one State Party to that of another State Party without the authorisation of or in violation of the legislation or regulations of any one of the States Parties concerned.[3]

Against this background of increased international focus and determination to tackle the illicit arms trade, the current volume is designed to offer an overview of some of the key contemporary issues and debates regarding the illicit arms trade, now that it co-exists at the top of the UN agenda and is being debated alongside the issues, such as nuclear disarmament and proliferation, that in the past tended to eclipse it. Following an overview chapter intended to outline the changed character of the illicit arms trade in the post-Cold War era, and which thereby highlights the barriers to control, the volume proceeds with Alan Block's incisive re-assessment of the origins of the Iran-Contra affair. This is followed by John Berryman's assessment of the scale, forms and consequences of illicit transfers of conventional arms from the Russian Federation, and of the risk of illegal diversion of nuclear, chemical and biological materials. Mel McNulty offers a detailed account of French complicity in the 1990s' Rwandan genocide and the 1998 Quilès Commission report into it. Gerry Cleaver deals with a related issue of growing international concern – the growing use of private security companies in post-Cold War Africa, in particular focusing on the activities and structure of Executive Outcomes and Sandline International, two of the most prominent companies in the sector. Finally, Owen Greene gives a detailed overview of the recent surge in international efforts to tackle the illicit trade in small arms and light weapons, analysing and assessing developments at sub-regional, regional and international levels.

Notes

1. Brian Michael Jenkins, *The Study of Terrorism: Definitional Problems* (Santa Monica, RAND Corp., 1980), p.10.
2. William D. Hartung, *And Weapons For All* (New York, HarperPerennial, 1995), p.184.
3. See Owen Greene, 'Examining International Responses to Illicit Arms Trafficking', in this issue.

Mark Phythian
Guest Editor

Contributors

John Berryman is Principal Lecturer in European and International Studies in the School of Languages, Humanities and Social Sciences and a member of the Russian and East European Research Centre at the University of Wolverhampton. He has written widely on Russian foreign policy and security issues.

Alan Block is Professor Administration of Justice, Professor Jewish Studies, Director Jewish Studies Program at The Pennsylvania State University. He has written widely on organized crime and National Intelligence Services.

Gerry Cleaver teaches in the School of International Studies and Law, Coventry University. He has written widely on African security and peace-keeping issues.

Owen Greene is Research Director and Senior Lecturer in International Relations and Security Studies at the Department of Peace Studies, University of Bradford, UK. He has authored or co-authored some 10 books and numerous articles on arms control issues. He was Consultant to the UN Group of Governmental Experts on Small Arms, head of the 1999 EU Fact-Finding Mission on small arms in Cambodia, and closely involved with the recent development of regional programmes in Europe and Africa.

Mel McNulty is Lecturer in French Area Studies at Nottingham Trent University, and has published a number of articles on French policy in Africa.

Mark Phythian is Principal Lecturer in Politics, University of Wolverhampton, UK. He is the author of *Arming Iraq* (1996), *The Politics of British Arms Sales since 1964* (2000) and numerous articles on aspects of the arms trade.

Crime, Law & Social Change **33**: 1–52, 2000.
© 2000 *Kluwer Academic Publishers. Printed in the Netherlands.*

The illicit arms trade: Cold War and Post-Cold War

MARK PHYTHIAN
*School of Languages, Humanities and Social Sciences, University of Wolverhampton, Castle
View, Dudley, DY1 3HR, UK*

Abstract. This article considers the principal changes that have occurred in the illicit arms
trade across the Cold War and post-Cold War periods. It discusses the changed nature of
demand and the sources and means of illicitly supplying arms to areas of conflict. Through a
number of case studies it highlights the declining use of illicit arms supply as a foreign policy
tool, and the extent to which involvement in the trade is now determined more by profit than
policy considerations, with all the implications these changes have for control initiatives.

Introduction

The intention behind this article is to illustrate the shifting nature of the illicit
arms trade in the post-Cold War era. Simply stated, it argues that changes
in the international system have impacted on producers and markets so as
to fundamentally alter the nature of the illicit arms trade. During the Cold
War years, but especially in the 1980s, utilization of the illicit arms trade, its
methods and personnel, were instruments of Cold War foreign policy. In the
post-Cold War era states still support and engage in the illicit transfer of arms,
but where they do it is more likely to be out of an ethnic, religious, or tribal
affinity, rather than as part of an ideologically-based competition. Utilization
of the illicit arms trade as an instrument of great power foreign policy is no
longer one of the defining features of the trade. To a significant extent the
trade has been depoliticized since the end of the Cold War, with involvement
now motivated more by profit potential than policy considerations.

George Bush's optimistic 1991 proclamation of a "new world order' has
since given way to a world of increased regional, ethnic, and religious conflict, as the Cold War permafrost which helped hold these tensions in sus-
pension quickly melted, creating fresh markets for illicit arms. At the same
time, developments in eastern Europe – a weakening of state authority and
control over arms production, the collapse of domestic and traditional (Cold
War) overseas arms markets, concerns about arms-related employment and
the future viability of the defence sector, the apparent ease with which officials can be bought and false paperwork secured, and so on – have made
the sourcing, transportation, and passage of arms somewhat less problematic
than was previously the case.

This change has encouraged another; an increase in what might be termed the "amateurisation' of arms trafficking. The ease with which arms can be sourced, often through one of a growing number of companies offering to broker[1] deals, has attracted to the trade a number of individuals who see it as a way of getting rich quickly, and who operate by circumnavigating restrictions which may exist in their country of operation by sourcing arms in states like Bulgaria, and flying them to their destination on leased aircraft, with hired crews, and bundles of forged paperwork. These new entrants operate in parallel with the detritus of the Cold War – former covert operatives who served their apprenticeships, for example, servicing CIA arms pipelines, or destabilizing front-line southern African governments on behalf of apartheid-era South Africa – whose services are no longer in such demand from government agencies in the post-Cold War world.

The cases presented here are intended to be indicative rather than exhaustive. They are designed to give something of an indication of the scope and nature of the contemporary illicit arms trade and the different levels at which it operates, and in so doing indicate some of the problems which control initiatives must be capable of overcoming if they are to stand any chance of being effective.

The illicit arms trade: The Cold War years

Notwithstanding concerns during the inter-war years about the merchants of death syndrome and associated bribery and corruption, and the existence of the US Senate Munitions Inquiry (Nye Committee) from 1934–36, and the Royal Commission on the Private Manufacture of and Trading in Arms in 1936,[2] the trade in illicit arms is largely a product of the post-1945 world order. The demand for arms through illicit channels at a state level is a consequence of the application of either embargoes or restrictions on the flow of certain categories of equipment to target states. The Cold War era witnessed the widespread use of embargoes or restrictions as tools of Cold War foreign policy. In 1949, the Western powers established the Co-ordinating Committee for Multilateral Strategic Controls (Cocom) which restricted the export of broad categories of military and related equipment to the Eastern Bloc. The 1950 Tripartite Declaration gave birth to the Near East Arms Co-ordinating Committee – an ultimately failed attempt by the US, UK and France (and later Italy) to restrict the flow of arms to the Middle East. Up to this point the trade in illicit arms was largely confined to light arms. Moreover, the zero-sum nature of Cold War calculations meant that the vacuums into which illicit arms would flow rarely emerged. However, with the application of international arms embargoes against South Africa and Rhodesia, and the outbreak of the Biafran War in the 1960s, a growing trade in illicit arms, components, and technology developed.

Arms were a valuable currency in the Cold War competition, strengthening rebel groups and, where they had no chance of seizing power, allowing them to continue to act as a thorn in the side of the target government. Hence, the US supplied arms to Chinese nationalists in Burma after 1949, many of the supplies dropped by Air America aircraft. Elsewhere, Chinese nationalist rebels were supplied with arms via the front company Western Enterprises Inc. Arms were also funnelled to anti-Sukarno forces in Indonesia in the late 1950s.[3] As well as east European arms smuggled into Africa, Egypt (itself a useful transit point for these arms) supplied arms and training to rebel groups. Algeria passed on east European-origin weapons to rebel forces in the Congo which, during and after the government of Patrice Lumumba, became the focus of Cold War competition on the continent. Porous borders allowed arms to be smuggled easily from states such as Uganda, Zambia and Tanzania to rebel groups in the Congo and Mozambique.[4]

With regard to South Africa, United Nations Security Council (UNSC) Resolution 181 of 1963 introduced a voluntary arms embargo (with western states successfully resisting calls for it to be made mandatory) which was to prove far from watertight.[5] In response, South Africa began to focus on developing an indigenous military base, initially producing small arms but gradually extending the scope of the production which the Armaments Corporation of South Africa (Armscor) undertook. Increasingly, rather than seeking to import the finished product, South Africa sought technology, components, and individuals with a particular expertise to work in South Africa. This strategy meant that when the 1963 voluntary embargo was supplanted by UNSC Resolution 418[6] in November 1977, bringing a mandatory embargo into force, the impact on South Africa was only ever likely to be limited. As well as importing technology, South Africa enjoyed the full co-operation of a small number of states in weapons development. In particular, from the mid-1970s Israel – as isolated in the Middle East as South Africa was in Africa – allowed South Africa to produce equipment under licence and helped in the establishment of a defence electronics sector.[7] In addition, there was collaboration on nuclear weapons issues. "Why?", Seymour Hersh quotes a former Israeli official as asking: "One: to share basic resources. South Africa is a very rich country and Israel is poor. Two: the supply of raw materials. Three: testing grounds. Try to do a [nuclear] test in Israel and all hell breaks loose. In South Africa it's different. Four: there is a certain sympathy for the situation of South Africa among Israelis. They are also European settlers standing against a hostile world."[8] In addition to Israel, other military support came from the pariah military governments of Pinochet in Chile and Stroessner in Paraguay.

It is also clear that elements within the executive branch of the US government encouraged an under-the-counter military trade with South Africa in the 1970s, in defiance of the UN embargo. Artillery design *wunderkind* Gerald Bull was one prominent player in this trade. Through his Space Research Corporation, and with the active encouragement of the CIA, then backing South Africa and their joint creation UNITA (União Nacional para a Independência Total de Angola) in the war against the MPLA (Movimento Popular para a Libertação de Angola) government in Angola, Bull exported extended-range 155 mm shells to South Africa (initially via Israel), and subsequently passed on his expertise in 155 mm self-propelled gun design to South Africa. The South Africans used this to produce their own variant – the G-6 Rhino, the so-called "Kalahari Ferrari". When an out-of-the-loop US Customs investigation uncovered Bull's activities and he was charged with violating the embargo, the Justice Department offered a plea bargain which resulted in him serving four and a half months of a twelve month sentence. Bull would go on to do the US government's under-the-counter bidding with regard to China before going on to work for his final customer, Saddam Hussein's Iraq.[9]

In addition to Bull, there is also the case of James Guerin and his company International Signal and Control (ISC). In 1991 Guerin was sentenced to fifteen years in prison on multiple fraud and illegal arms export charges after he sold ISC to British defence electronics company Ferranti, only for Ferranti to discover that its US$700m purchase was almost worthless, its accounts filled with bogus orders. Investigation revealed an elaborate pattern of front companies, financial fraud and money laundering. For example, in Panama alone Guerin had created 38 front companies which between them controlled 51 Swiss bank accounts. Amongst the multiple charges laid against Guerin was one of aiding:

> Armscor in evading the United Nations arms embargo by selling United States made arms, munitions and weapons technology, as well as other restricted commodities, to Armscor and its related entities in order to build the arms and weapons industry of Armscor, so that Armscor could enhance its military capabilities and market weapon systems to third world countries.[10]

In practice, this was a governmentally-sanctioned relationship, initially aimed at allowing South Africa to acquire the technology that would enable it to monitor Soviet naval and submarine traffic off the Cape of Good Hope. Indeed, on the eve of Guerin's sentencing, Admiral Bobby Ray Inman, a former deputy director of the CIA, wrote to the judge in the case seeking leniency for

Guerin on the grounds that he "displayed patriotism toward our country",[11] adding weight to Guerin's oft-repeated contention that he was operating at the behest of the CIA.[12]

To give a flavour of Guerin's enterprise; through one of his front companies, Gamma Systems Associates, he exported over US$10m worth of military technology to South Africa. This included components for air-to-air, ground-to-air and ground-to-ground missiles; components for night-vision equipment; components for inertial navigation systems; and 40mm grenade technology. In another case, ISC collaborated with South Africa on a proximity fuze. In 1988 this was sold on in the form of fuze assembly kits to Industrias Metalurgicas Estrategicas de Contrabia (IMEC) in Spain, a subsidiary of Industria Cardoen of Chile. At the time, Cardoen was involved in providing a proximity fuze production capability to Iraq. In return for supplying 300,000 of its PF-1 fuzes to South Africa for onward delivery to IMEC, ISC was to receive over US$33 m via South Africa, once it had been paid by Iraq in crude oil.[13]

In addition to the demand generated by South Africa, in the early-mid 1970s various anti-colonial struggles and civil wars were fuelling demand for illicit arms among sub-state actors, the most notable cases being those in Angola, Mozambique, Ethiopia, and Somalia. In the case of Angola, in mid-1975, with independence set for November, the CIA began to funnel millions of dollars worth of arms into the country in support of UNITA and the FNLA. The former Chief of the CIA Angola Task Force, John Stockwell, left a detailed memoir outlining how this was initially achieved:

> The CIA maintains prepackaged stocks of foreign weapons for instant shipment anywhere in the world. The transportation is normally provided by the US Air Force, or by private charter if the American presence must be masked. Even tighter security can be obtained by contracting with international dealers who will purchase arms in Europe and subcontract independently to have them flown into the target area. Often, the CIA will deliver obsolete American weapons, arguing that World War II left so many scattered around the world they are no longer attributable to the US. In the Angola programme, we obtained such obsolete weapons from the National Guard and the US Army Reserve stores. Initially, US Air Force C-130 transports picked up weapons from the CIA warehouse in San Antonio, Texas, and delivered them to Charleston, South Carolina. US Air Force C-141 jet transports then hauled twenty-five ton loads across the Atlantic to Kinshasa. Inevitably, the air force billed the CIA for the service, $80,000 for each flight.[14]

While intra-state conflict in Central America from the late 1970s provided a further spur to the illicit arms trade, its phenomenal rise in the 1980s was essentially due to two other conflicts, one in Afghanistan, the other in the Gulf.

Arming the Mujahedin

The Reagan Administration's recognition, encapsulated in the emerging Reagan Doctrine, that arms were "an indispensable component of its foreign policy"[15] led to the arming of the anti-Soviet Mujahedin guerrillas with state-of-the-art Stinger missiles. Already, days after the December 1979 Soviet intervention in Afghanistan, President Carter had signed a finding authorizing the supply of lethal weapons to the Mujahedin. In the first instance this translated into small arms, largely .303 Enfield rifles.[16] In addition, a number of other states were drawn into the operation. For example, Pakistan played a leading role in supply, Saudi Arabia contributed financially, and Egypt provided Soviet-origin arms. Although assistance increased in the first years of the Reagan Administration, at first no US-origin arms were used so as to maintain deniability. As former CIA operations officer Vincent Cannistraro recalled; "the CIA believed that they had to handle [the Afghan operation] as if they were wearing a condom."[17]

This changed in 1986 with the introduction of the US Stinger anti-aircraft missile, a move in line with the changed emphasis of NSD 166, signed by President Reagan in March 1985, and aimed at forcing the Soviet Union out of Afghanistan by "all means possible". Although the Pentagon opposed the supply of the Stinger, on the reasonable grounds that it could, "fall into Soviet hands and thus compromise our technology, or be sold to Third World terrorists for use against American targets",[18] the move had strong supporters such as Secretary of State George Shultz. DCI William Casey was particularly enthusiastic.

The Stingers were introduced through Pakistan in September 1986 and had an immediate impact, reportedly bringing down up to one aircraft or helicopter gunship per day. Overall, it has been estimated that between 1,000–1,200 missiles were transferred together with around 250 launchers.[19] However, once the Soviets became committed to withdrawal, the problem anticipated by the Pentagon materialized. The missiles were hot property and the Administration had been unable to control their distribution. In the first instance, Pakistan imposed a "missile tax" in return for its role, skimming-off a number which were subsequently offered for sale on the black market.[20] Iran either captured or was sold a quantity, while Soviet forces certainly captured some. Moreover, once the conflict ended, Stingers became available from the Afghans themselves to any insurgent or anti-American groups who could meet the asking price. Edward Juchniewicz, CIA director of covert operations during the Reagan Administration, was philosophical about this turn of events, explaining that: "One makes the assumption when one goes to battle that one's equipment will be captured by the enemy. So unfortunately, we lost some Stingers, and now our enemy has one of our best weapons."[21] This somewhat misrepresented a situation in which the group the US had armed was now prepared to sell US weapons to anti-US groups. Consequently, Stingers are now widely dispersed:

> Reportedly, Stingers already have shot down aircraft twice in Bosnia and once in Tajikistan. In 1987, an Iranian boat fired a Stinger that reportedly hit a US helicopter in the Persian Gulf but failed to explode. Tunisian fundamentalists are reported to have used a Stinger in a failed 1991 assassination attempt. Stingers also reportedly have been acquired by Kashmiri militants, Indian Sikhs, the Iranian drug mafia, Iraq, Qatar, Zambia (most likely from Angola), North Korea, Libya, and militant Palestinian groups. In addition, authorities reportedly have broken up plots to acquire the missiles by the Irish Republican Army, the Medellin Cartel, Croatian rebels, Armenia, Azerbaijan, Chechen secessionists, and Cuban exiles.[22]

The threat posed by this under-the-counter proliferation has led the CIA to spend over US$65 m – over twice the missiles' original value – in an attempt to buy-back the remaining Stingers. This effort has been a failure. Although it is impossible to put a precise figure on the number of Stingers unaccounted for, of the 1,000–1,200 supplied, 340 were used prior to the Soviet withdrawal, leaving approximately 660–860 unaccounted for. Of these the CIA has reportedly managed to buy-back approximately 60–70.[23]

Once purchasers have been identified they have been reluctant to give them up. In March 1988 American Embassy officials in Bahrain, watching an official military parade in Qatar on Bahraini television, were surprised to see a Stinger missile being openly displayed. Qatar readily admitted buying 12, but was more reluctant to reveal either the seller or serial numbers, and even less interested in returning them to the US.[24] In sum, it would appear that well over 500 are in existence and outside US control. And although the battery packs which power them may well be run-down by now, it is not beyond the bounds of the possible that buyers could engineer a replacement battery pack. Meanwhile, airlines have had to adopt contingency measures, so that any "flight from Islamabad to Europe heads south before heading west, and flights between south-east Asia and Europe now avoid Pakistani and Afghani airspace, adding two hours to their journey."[25]

In addition, the end of the Afghan war left a reservoir of unwanted arms which has had the impact of transforming north west Pakistan into a regional centre for arms trading, "attracting customers from all over the country in search of unlicensed weapons."[26] Once there, potential buyers could choose, for example, between ex-US-pipeline weapons (ranging from Chinese and east European arms, to arms supplied from Israel and Egypt), stocks of Soviet arms captured by the Afghans (for example, rocket-propelled grenade launchers and AK-47s), and locally-produced arms (cheaper and inferior versions of weapons such as the AK-47).[27] In addition, Pakistani intelligence agencies have reportedly stored a large number of light weapons. As regards the Taliban, Tara Kartha has noted how their:

> supply and communication lines run directly into Pakistan, thus keeping alive a web of smuggling networks that sustains the clandestine trade in weaponry. Among the poor and illiterate Pashtuns who make up the bulk of the Taliban's "work forces" are many ex-convicts with links to these smuggling networks. One of the Taliban coterie is Mullah Rocketi – so named because of his reported arsenal of shoulder-fired weapons – who was once a arms dealer of note. Though portrayed as a moralizing, "clean-up force" for Afghan society, the Taliban have increasingly been implicated in both weapons smuggling and narcotics production along the Central Asian border.[28]

The Iran-Iraq war and the illicit arms trade

Even more important than the Afghan war in stimulating demand for illicit arms, in September 1980 Iraq invaded neighbouring Iran, marking the beginning of a bloody eight-year long land war – the First World War transplanted to the 1980s' Gulf. Neither side had the capacity to indigenously produce the range or quantity of matériel required to sustain their positions. At the same time, most of the international community responded to the outbreak of war by imposing restrictions on the type of arms which could openly be sold to either side. However, the strategic interests of suppliers gave them an interest in encouraging or turning a blind eye to the trade in illicit arms operating in or through their boundaries. The war would expose the fiction that the international system of end-use certification was an effective way of regulating the international arms trade – something which was already well known within the arms industry. For example, Chris Cowley, the project manager for Gerald Bull's Iraqi supergun project, found that:

> European countries that are flexible in their approach to the issue of certificates include, Belgium, Spain, Portugal, Yugoslavia and Austria.

Virtually all South American countries sell them, at rates of commission ranging from 10 per cent to 200 per cent. "Quickie" end-user certificates are available over the counter in Pakistan or Thailand, while there is a standing joke that Singapore would long since have sunk had it kept all the arms that its nationals had signed for.[29]

While both Iran and Iraq turned to the illicit arms market to meet their substantial needs, the Iranian turn was marked by a greater urgency than that of Iraq. Having inherited an impressive inventory of state-of-the-art US arms from the Shah, the Iranians found themselves denied spares by a US administration so anxious to ensure it was not victorious in the war that it launched Operation Staunch to encourage or pressurize allies into not supplying it with arms, and to stamp down on illicit networks as and when they were exposed.

Hence, while Iraq was able to take advantage of the benign attitude most "neutrals" displayed towards it, and was able to receive notionally prohibited equipment via neighbouring allies who acted as willing conduits, Iran had more difficulty in securing the means by which it could continue to prosecute the war.

Following the outbreak of war, both belligerents developed an almost insatiable appetite for explosives/ammunition. The Bofors affair revealed the extent to which Iran was meeting this demand with the assistance of a network of major European explosives manufacturers which had formed a European propellant cartel[30] involving companies in Austria, Belgium, Britain, Finland, France, Italy, Netherlands, Norway, Spain, Sweden, Switzerland, and West Germany. Companies in these countries illicitly supplied propellant to Iran during the 1980s through the tried and tested methods of utilising false end-users, funnelling arms through conduits, and mis-labelling consignments of (dual-use) explosive as being for industrial rather than military use.

Belligerent demand for gunpowder was so great that it could not be met by individual manufacturers alone, and so the companies comprising the European Association for the Study of Safety Problems in the Production and Use of Propellant Powders (EASSP)[31] began to use the organization as a forum for allocating orders and devising means of delivery. The cartel's head office in Brussels, from where EASSP's official business was conducted, also acted as a centre for the cartel's unofficial business (although meetings tended to be rotated in hotels across Europe). The unofficial nature of the cartel makes it difficult to say with any certainty how many companies were involved. In addition to the seven members identified by Swedish Customs and the Swedish Commissioner for Freedom of Commerce – Bofors (Sweden); SNPE (France); Dyno (Norway); Biazzi (Dinamite) (Italy); Nobel Explosive (ICI) (Scotland); PRB (Belgium); and SSE (Switzerland) – a number of other companies were identified as having participated in discussions and contracts.

These included Rio Tinto in Spain, Muiden Chemie in the Netherlands and Royal Ordnance in the UK.

Documents obtained by Swedish Customs suggest that the cartel performed three major functions. Firstly, it reached price-fixing arrangements. Secondly, it arranged "splits", the parcelling out of large orders among the member companies. In this regard, a Swedish Customs official described how: "Cartel members in Sweden, France, Holland and Belgium would meet regularly to eat and drink together and plan how they would keep Iran and Iraq supplied with munitions. They knew that no single company would produce enough gunpowder to meet the enormous demand, without raising production quotas and attracting attention so they decided to spread the work around."[32] Finally, the cartel also kept an eye on the activities of competitors outside the cartel, and any information obtained by one cartel member would be passed on.

In the case of Sweden, investigations uncovered a major operation by Nobel Kemi and Bofors – both subsidiaries of Nobel Industries, Sweden[33] – to supply Iran through several conduits, prominent amongst which was Singapore, in contravention of Sweden's prohibition on the export of arms to warring states. The scandal that resulted from this revelation gathered further momentum when Admiral Carl-Fredrik Algernon, head of the Swedish War Materials Inspectorate (KMI), apparently fell to his death in front of an on-coming train on the Stockholm underground in January 1987, only days before he was due to give evidence to a special prosecutor. A number of senior Bofors officials subsequently resigned, including managing director Martin Ardbo, and an internal Nobel Industries inquiry confirmed that Bofors had made illegal shipments bound for Iran through conduits. However, Ardbo claimed government complicity in the exports, saying that the KMI knew of the exports and had recommended that Bofors route them through conduits like Singapore in order to avoid attracting attention.

As Chris Cowley's anecdote suggests, Singapore was a much-favoured conduit. Bofors notionally sold artillery shells, 155-mm guns, 40-mm naval guns and at least 714 RBS-70 laser-guided anti-aircraft missiles to Singapore. These were then shipped on to Iran. So extensive was the use of Singapore that by 1985, on paper at least, Singapore had become the second-largest importer of Swedish arms in the world, accounting for 14.4% of Swedish arms exports.[34] Another useful route was via Portugal and Spain. Spain was a channel favoured by SRC for getting arms to Iraq via Saudi Arabia, while Portugal is estimated to have sent at least US$150 m worth of arms to Iran between 1984 and 1987, as well as arms to Iraq. As well as favoured conduits, the cartel also had favoured modes of delivery. One was to use Danish cargo ships – Swedish Customs investigations came up with a list of 19 that had carried military equipment to Iran during the 1980s.

A crucial link between the Swedish companies, other cartel members and Iran and Iraq was provided by Karl Erik Schmitz's Malmo-based company, Scandinavian Commodity (SC). In 1983, SC received an order for 4,340 tonnes of 105 mm and 155 mm ammunition from Iran, which was originally to be supplied by South Africa. However, when South Africa began to supply Iraq in 1984, it cut off supplies to Iran, leaving 1,400 tonnes still to be produced. Hence, Schmitz (described as "one of Iran's most capable arms brokers"[35]) turned to the state-owned Yugoslav company FDSP (Federal Directorate of Supply and Procurement) which could supply 500 tonnes itself, and was persuaded by Schmitz to buy in the remaining 1000 tonnes from Bofors, Muiden Chemie, Kemira, Raufoss, ICI-Nobel and Expro in Canada to complete the Iranian order. When an order placed with the cartel via PRB and SNPE with Italian company Tirrena fell through because of the Italian Government's tilt towards Iraq, Schmitz took over this order, routing it through Yugoslavia. The powder would be loaded at various European ports like Nordenham and Zeebrugge, from where it would sail to Bar in Yugoslavia. The powder would then go through the Suez Canal to Bandar Abbas in Iran, complete with false Kenyan end-user certificates so as to avoid the close attentions of the Egyptian authorities. As Schmitz explained to Swedish Customs investigators:

> **S**: When we pass through the Suez Canal they want to know the destination of these goods and the Yugoslavs then say we need basic documentation to avoid being left naked. Here therefore an EUC-confirmation has been made on Kenya against Y. This is what they wanted for each contract. There are ships destined for Iran that have been sequestered. All contracts receive a document from Kenya – not that we've deceived them – all cargoes need a document that can be produced at the Channel so that that product is not stopped.
> **Q**: We have encountered a number of EUCs issued by the appropriate Kenyan authority.
> **S**: These certificates are issued to all and sundry. You merely go to the embassy and say that you need one.
> **Q**: The embassy in Stockholm?
> **S**: No it is the President himself. Count them all and you have an army on par with the Russian. But the documents are for the canal only.
> **Q**: Do you pay Kenya for this service. A rhetorical question perhaps?
> **S**: Of course, US$10,000.[36]

In 1987, the *Wall Street Journal* reported that Schmitz had delivered two consignments of explosives to Iran in 1985 via St. Lucia Airways – a CIA-linked company which Oliver North was using just three months later to ferry US

missiles to Iran. The first flight occurred on 24 July 1985, carrying explosives
from Muiden Chemie and PRB, complete with false Yugoslav and Greek end-
user certificates, the second on 14 August from Israel to Lille and then on to
Iran.[37] In May 1987 Schmitz was indicted on 42 separate counts concerning the illegal sale of explosives and gunpowder with a value of 74,800,000
kronor between 1981 and 1985.[38]

At the time the entire Iranian procurement operation in Europe – one part
of Iran's global reach in the search for arms[39] – was being co-ordinated from
offices at 4 Victoria Street, London, under cover of the National Iranian Oil
Company (NIOC). This was not a particularly well-kept secret, and the Iranians were under surveillance, with those who entered and left the building
being photographed. According to author James Adams, via GCHQ, MI5,
"was able to routinely listen to all telephone calls, intercept all telexes and
facsimile messages and, using other systems, observe and listen to conversations between arms dealers and the Iranians."[40] When Britain closed this
office in September 1987 Iran shifted the operation to Frankfurt.

Austria also sold arms to Iran and Iraq, despite the existence of a re-
strictive arms export regime similar to that of Sweden. It did so through the
state-owned arms manufacturer Voest Alpine, to which Gerald Bull had sold
designs for a towed 155 mm gun (designated GHN-45) in 1978 for a one-off
fee of just US$2 m. To get around Austrian neutrality laws which prohibited
the sale of arms to states at war, Voest Alpine funnelled the Bull-designed
155 mm guns through Jordan. As a consequence, on paper, between 1981
and 1990, Jordan was Austria's largest market for arms, importing US$320 m
worth of major weapons. The company reported sales of 200 GHN-45s to
Jordan in 1982 alone. On paper, Jordan was a formidable military force.

The US acquiesced in the Voest Alpine sales to Jordan (i.e. Iraq), but when
Austria began to sell to Iran as well, the US, under Operation Staunch, moved
to prevent such sales:

> In an unusual move in early April 1986, CIA and State Department
> officials showed Austria's ambassador to Washington classified satellite
> photographs of 15 GHN-45s at Iran's Isfahan artillery training center. A
> CIA narrative stamped "TOP SECRET – SENSITIVE" with the photos
> declared, "we believe that significant amounts of the extended-range
> full-bore ammunition were purchased along with the guns." But the
> Iranians got an estimated 180 GHN-45s anyway.[41]

Iran-Contra

The Iran-Iraq War also provided the immediate background to the Iran-Contra affair. The Reagan Administration's desire to free US hostages held by pro-Iranian factions in Lebanon drew it into agreeing to sell arms to Iran, the illicit demand for which had been partly generated by Operation Staunch in the first place, in return for the hostages' release. The profits from the inflated price of these arms would then be used to secure a further imperative of Reaganite foreign policy – the funding and continued arming of the anti-Sandinista Contras.

Exposure of the Iran-Contra affair opened an invaluable window on the illicit arms trade, exposing a cast of characters who illustrated well the symbiotic relationship between politics and arms trafficking which developed in the Reagan White House. These included retired CIA official Theodore Shackley; Israeli arms dealer Yaakov Nimrodi; Iranian middleman Manucher Ghorbanifar; Saudi Arabian middleman Adnan Khashoggi; Richard Secord, the retired US Air Force Major General; his business partner Albert Hakim; retired US Army Major General and Chairman of the World Anti-Communist League, John Singlaub; Miami-based arms dealer Ron Martin; Iranian middlemen and arms dealers Cyrus and Jamshid Hashemi; retired CIA agent Thomas G. Clines; and Marine Lieutenant Colonel Oliver North. The proceeds from the illicit arms transfers went into a network of 21 Swiss bank accounts, controlled by North, Secord, and Hakim. The accounts were held in the name of front companies that have since become almost household names – Lake Resources Inc, Stanford Technology Corp, Udall Research Corp, and so on.

Flights of arms in the main relied on four private companies: Eagle Aviation Service and Technology, a company operated by retired US Air Force Lieutenant Colonel Richard Gadd; Southern Air Transport; Amalgamated Commercial Enterprises Inc, a Panamanian corporation set up by Southern Air Transport; and Corporate Air Services.[42] For Secord and Hakim at least, this was a highly lucrative business. For example, in addition to other payments, in 1985 and 1986 Secord received cash payments of over US$1 m, while Hakim received cash payments of US$550,000. As William D. Hartung suggested: "With all the front companies, questionable characters, and easy money floating around, it was hard to tell how much of North's 'enterprise' was motivated by misguided patriotism and how much was sheer profiteering by a band of veteran arms sales operatives who felt that the US government owed them one."[43]

Unfortunately for North, formal administration policy sometimes interferred with his initiatives. In one case North, keen to locate a source of surface-to-air missiles with which the Contras could attack Nicaraguan HIND helicopters, sought to acquire UK-manufactured Blowpipes via Chile, only

for administration criticism of the Pinochet regime to get in the way. As a
March 1986 e-mail from North to Robert McFarlane explained:

> we are trying to find a way to get 10 BLOWPIPE launchers and 20
> missiles from Chile thru the Short Bros. rep. The V.P. from Short Bros.
> sought me out several mos. ago and I met w/ him again in London
> a few weeks ago when I was there... Short Bros., the mfgr. of the
> BLOWPIPE, is willing to arrange the deal, conduct the training and even
> send U.K. "tech reps" fwd if we can close the arrangement. Dick Secord
> has already paid 10% down on the delivery and we have a Salvadoran
> EUC which is acceptable to the Chileans. Unfortunately, the week all
> this was going to closure we decided to go fwd in Geneva w/ our human
> rights paper on Pinochet. The arrangement is now on ice...[44]

Just over a week later, McFarlane was in touch with North, telling him: "I've
been thinking about the blowpipe problem and the Contras. Could you ask
the CIA to identify which countries the Brits have sold them to. I ought to
have a contact in at least one of them."[45]

Iran-Contra and subsequent investigations also shed light on the symbiosis
which can exist between arms and drugs traffickers. As the Kerry Report
concluded: "Covert war, insurgency and drug trafficking frequently go hand-
in-hand without regard to ideology or sponsorship." General Paul Gorman,
told the Committee that: "If you want to move arms or munitions in Latin
America, the established networks are owned by the cartels. It has lent itself to the purposes of terrorists, of saboteurs, of spies, of insurgents and
subversions."[46]

Nicaragua's southern neighbour, Costa Rica, offered a large number of
unmonitored small airstrips near to the Nicaraguan border, and these represented an important supply route for the Sandinistas during the anti-Somoza
insurgency. After this succeeded in 1979 trafficking via northern Costa Rica
continued, with surplus weapons originally stored for use by the Sandinistas
being sold on the regional black market, some to the Salvadorean rebels.
When the southern Contra front was established in 1983, Costa Rica remained
ill-equipped to deal with the threat posed by the Colombian drug cartels.
Without its own military, with only limited law enforcement resources, and
with a limited radar system, Contra supply aircraft were able to fly in and out
of the clandestine strips with something approaching impunity. As the Kerry
Report noted, this meant that: "Colombian and Panamanian drug operatives
were well positioned to exploit the infrastructure now serving and supplying
the Contra Southern Front. This infrastructure was increasingly important to
the drug traffickers, as this was the very period in which the cocaine trade to
the U.S. from Latin America was growing exponentially."[47]

Werner Lotz[48] confirmed that Contra operations on the southern front were funded by drug operations. According to Lotz, weapons destined for the Contras were shipped from Panama on small planes which contained mixed loads of both arms and drugs. Once the pilots had unloaded the weapons for the Contras, they would refuel and fly on north toward the U.S. with their drugs cargo. These pilots were American, Panamanian, and Colombian. Sometimes it was even known for uniformed members of the Panamanian Defense Forces to act as pilots. Once this route and method had been established, it was a short and almost inevitable step to the drug flights using the Contra airstrips to refuel when there were no weapons to unload. They knew that aircraft using the airstrips were immune from serious searches, Lotz explained, because the nature of the war and US involvement rendered them "protected". As the Committee concluded, in practice: "To a significant degree, the infrastructure used by the Contras and that used by drug traffickers was potentially interchangeable, even in a situation in which the U.S. government had itself established and maintained the airstrip involved."[49]

Angola

The case of Angola provides a clear illustration of some of the major differences between the Cold War and post-Cold War illicit arms markets. Following the collapse of the 1991 peace agreement, UNITA's refusal to accept the outcome of the 1992 multi-party elections, and a return to the Hobbesian status quo ante across much of the country, stemming the flow of arms to UNITA and securing compliance with UNSC Resolution 864 of September 1993 became UNSC priorities. However, as recently as the late 1980s, Angola was a central pawn in the Cold War game, and US and South African arms, support, aid, and encouragement of UNITA were largely responsible for a situation in which hundreds of thousands of Angolans were killed, tens of thousands maimed by landmines, and the country's mineral wealth sold off to buy arms.

Angola represented a most suitable case for the Reagan Doctrine treatment. In part this suitability was based on an understanding of events in Angola which lay somewhere between the naïve and the perverse. During the 1980 presidential campaign, candidate Reagan had explained with regard to UNITA:

> Well frankly I would provide them with weapons. It doesn't take American manpower. Savimbi, the leader, controls more than half of Angola. I don't see anything wrong with someone who wants to free themselves from the rule of an outside power, which is Cubans and East Germans. I don't see why we shouldn't provide them with weapons to do it.[50]

In a similar vein, Republican congressman Mark Siljander told the House Foreign Affairs Committee Subcommittee on Africa in 1986: "Jonas Savimbi... is a true liberation fighter, and he deserves US support... As long as we do not have a military option, Angola will remain a Cuban colony. Freedom in Africa will never be a reality."[51] With the repeal of the Clark Amendment the Administration was free to covertly arm UNITA, which it set about doing from late 1985. In December 1985, DCI Casey, as enthusiastic about arming Savimbi as he was contemporaneously regarding the Mujahedin, flew to Zaire where he met with President Mobutu, who agreed to funnel US arms to UNITA. A UNITA supply and training base was set up in Kamina in Zaire, with a contract company, Santa Lucia Airways, ferrying arms from the US via Kinshasa at a rate of four-to-five C-141 flights a week by 1987.[52] Amongst the items shipped were Stinger missiles. By 1988 this covert operation was being funded to the tune of US$40 m a year.[53]

The routes established during the Cold War push of the 1970s and 1980s are still being utilized by privateers today. The sheer range of neighbouring supply routes and endemic difficulties in policing and monitoring the embargo on arming UNITA (the absence of monitors, highly permeable national boundaries, difficulties in monitoring unauthorized air traffic, relatively rich rewards stemming from supply, etc.) make enforcing compliance highly problematic.[54] In addition, arms continue to pour into Angola legitimately, purchased by the government. In recent years, Angola has received arms or military assistance from Russia, Belarus, Brazil, Bulgaria, China, Poland, Portugal, South Africa, the Czech Republic, India, Israel, Kazakhstan, Slovakia, Ukraine, and Zimbabwe. This flow represents one potential source of arms for UNITA – captured government equipment. For example, in 1999, UNITA claimed to have captured T-55 and T-62 tanks, mortars, rocket launchers, and artillery, alongside a range of other equipment.[55]

UNITA has also acquired arms from a range of external sources, which it pays for via the illicit sale of diamonds mined and smuggled out of UNITA-held territory. The hundreds of millions of dollars this pipeline has netted UNITA has sustained its operations. As an indication of something of the range of weapons it has acquired, the Angolan government claims, since December 1998, to have captured SAM-16s, anti-aircraft weapons, rocket launchers, and a range of artillery. It also claims that UNITA possesses a range of other equipment, including 155 mm artillery, M-60 grenade launchers, and RPG-7 rocket launchers. There have even been independent claims that UNITA has six MiG-23 aircraft, six MI-25 combat helicopters, and a significant number of tanks and armoured personnel carriers, supposedly sourced via the Ukraine, although there does not appear to be any corroborating evidence for these claims.[56] Whatever the truth of specific allegations, there is no doubt that UNITA used its diamond revenue to arm heavily in advance of the most recent outbreak of violence. According to the government, UNITA also employed Serb, Israeli, South African and Ukrainian mercenaries to help maintain its weapons.[57]

In the mid-1990s UNITA was still receiving weapons via Kinshasa's airports. This route received unwelcome publicity in an article in the *Washington Post*,[58] although a number of plane crashes during 1995 and 1996 involving aircraft thought to be destined for UNITA-held territory (one of which, involving an aircraft suspected of trying to ship petroleum products in defiance of the UN embargo, killed approximately 350 people), had already attracted some attention.[59] However, the end of Mobutu's rule has led UNITA to shift its operation to the Republic of Congo (Congo-Brazzaville). It also receives arms from a range of other neighbouring countries. Post-apartheid South Africa has been one source of willing carriers,[60] with privateers able to bypass the lax controls at airports like Gateway International at Pietersburg, often by the simple expedient of setting-up foreign-registered companies which are beyond the scope of South African law. Zambia has represented another useful transit point. In July 1997 the Zambian government responded to Angolan pressure by grounding two planes owned by a South African company Metex International and expelling Metex personnel after uncovering evidence that the company was funnelling arms from South Africa to UNITA via Ndola airport, using two vintage Sierra Leone-registered Hawker Siddeley 748 aircraft.[61]

In addition to air, UNITA has also utilized arms routes which involve shipping by rail and boat. For example, by rail from Dar es Salaam to Kigoma, Lake Tanganyika, from there by boat to Zaire, and on by plane to UNITA-held territory. Other countries thought to have been involved in arming UNITA are Uganda, Togo, Burkina Faso, and Côte D'Ivoire. Whereas in a previous era its arms came via the US and South African governments, UNITA's arms are now sourced in eastern Europe – the home of its supposed ideological enemies just over a decade ago.

More recently, in addition to receiving arms, the regionalisation of conflict in Africa has seen UNITA itself supply arms and training, for example, to Burundian Hutu rebels between 1995–96. In other words, one consequence of the regionalisation of conflict is that the same weapons are being circulated from conflict to conflict.

The illicit arms trade today

While there are clear differences in the nature of the illicit arms trade Cold War and post-Cold War, there are also a number of insurgencies – mainly separatist in character – which transcend the divide and still require arms to be sourced on the black market. For example, going into the peace process in Northern Ireland, the Provisional IRA retained an arsenal which included an estimated three tonnes of Semtex, 600 assorted detonators, 600 AK-47s, 40 RPG launchers, 6 flame throwers, and two SAM-7 anti-aircraft missiles.[62] The bulk of this came from the 150 tonnes of arms smuggled from Libya between August 1985 and October 1986, when the Panamanian-registered *Eksund*, carrying a cargo which included 20 SAM-7 missiles, 1,000 AK-47s, and 120 RPG launchers, was intercepted by French customs officials.[63] However, break-away Republican groups opposed to the Irish peace process have continued to attempt to acquire arms. The Continuity IRA reportedly smuggled MAC-10 rifles and Uzi sub-machine guns from the US, utilizing a source used to smuggle arms to the Provisional IRA in the 1970s.[64] Members of the same group reportedly travelled to Libya in an attempt to re-open the Libyan arms pipeline, something which a foiled bank robbery in the Irish Republic in May 1998 may have been intended to finance.[65] Indeed, Libya is claimed to have supplied the IRA itself with a fresh cache of arms following the end of the IRA's first cease-fire, marked by the 1996 London Docklands bombing.[66] In another case, in July 1999, three people were arrested in Florida and charged with attempting to smuggle arms to republican groups in Ireland. The arms were to reach Ireland by the simple expedient of posting them from Florida. Unfortunately for the smugglers, this post first passed through the UK mainland en route to Ireland, and as a result a number of parcels were intercepted by police in Coventry.[67]

For their part the Liberation Tigers of Tamil Eelam (LTTE) continue to utilize a sophisticated international network of offices and front companies, through which they raise finance from the Tamil diaspora with which to buy arms. The group also boasts a fleet of small vessels registered under various flags of convenience (e.g. Panama, Liberia) and formally owned by LTTE front companies. Arms have been sourced via Cambodia, Burma and Thailand, and more recently through the Ukraine. In one 1994 case, a consignment of explosives from Ukraine was arranged via Carlton Trading, a front company based in Bangladesh, complete with false Bangladeshi end-user certification, and shipped on the LTTE-owned vessel *Swanee*. The explosives were used in the beginning of 1996 in a truck bomb attack, killing 91 and injuring more than 1,400 others.[68]

Notwithstanding these continuities, the nature of the illicit arms trade has changed in the post-Cold War era. This change is in part a reflection of the changing nature of war itself. The Center for Defense Information has listed 38 ongoing major conflicts at the beginning of 2000,[69] while SIPRI counted 27 major armed conflicts in 1998.[70] The majority of these have little in common with the clearly-defined inter-state conflicts of previous eras. These current conflicts, termed post-modern wars by some commentators,[71] and "New Wars" by Mary Kaldor involve; "a blurring of the distinctions between war (usually defined as violence between states or organized political groups for political motives), organized crime (violence undertaken by privately organized groups for private purposes, usually financial gain) and large-scale violations of human rights (violence undertaken by states or politically organized groups against individuals)."[72] They also "involve a myriad of transnational connections", blurring the boundaries between "internal and external, between aggression (attacks from abroad) and repression (attacks from inside the country)".[73]

The impact of this new type of war has been most acutely felt in sub-Saharan Africa, where the "combination of weak states and rich natural resources has resulted in a dangerous structural environment fuelling conflicts Natural resources have become a cause for war as well as a necessary source of wealth for keeping the conflicts going... In several parts of sub-Saharan Africa semi-political actors are fighting for the control of natural resources without any wider political ambitions."[74] The regionalisation of sub-Saharan African conflict (see Table 1), especially around the Great Lakes region, in the greater Horn and in southern Africa, has exacerbated already existing levels of violence. It has also made the application of arms embargoes problematic, in practice rendering them extremely porous. To illustrate the point, at least six African states – Angola, Chad, Namibia, Rwanda, Uganda, and Zimbabwe, have been directly involved in the military conflict in the Democratic Republic of Congo (DRC),[75] offering an embargo-beating variety of routes by which arms can reach the combatants.

Surplus Cold War vintage small arms are now the staple arms import into sub-Saharan Africa, flown into airfields in Entebbe, Goma, and Kigali, and so on. It has been said that so great was the increase in arms flows after the Ugandan military involvement in the DRC conflict began, that "at least five East African-based commercial air carriers (Air Alexander International, Busy Bee, Sky Air, Planetair, and United Airlines)", along with "Sudanese, Ugandan, and possibly other regional military aircraft transported weapons and other military supplies" into the territory.[76] Small arms have also been sent by sea, via ports such as Aseb, Beira, Conakry, Dar-es-Salaam, Djibouti and Mombasa, to complete their journeys via road, rail, or air.

Notwithstanding the fact that regionalisation of conflicts in Africa has diminished further the effectiveness of arms embargoes, the international response to the upsurge in post-Cold War conflict has been a proliferation of arms embargoes, mandated by the UN and other international bodies, and intended to restrict the flow of military equipment to affected areas. For

Table 1. Ongoing major African conflicts as of 1st January 2000

Main Warring Parties	1st Year	Cause(s)	Other Foreign Involvement
i) Algeria vs. Armed Islamic Group (GIA) and Islamic Salvation Front (FIS)	1991	Religious vs. Secular rule.	UN
ii) Angola vs. UNITA	1975	Economic & Ethnic	UN, US, South Africa
iii) Burundi: Tutsi vs. Hutu	1988	Ethnic	None
iv) Democratic Republic of Congo vs. Rwanda, Uganda & indigenous rebels	1997	Ethnic	UN, Namibia, Angola, Chad, Zimbabwe, France, Organization of African Unity (OAU)
v) Ethiopia vs. Eritrea	1998	Territory	OAU, UN, US
vi) Guinea Bissau vs. former army rebels	1998	Power	Economic Community of West African States Monitoring Group (ECOMOG)
vii) Rwanda: Tutsi vs. Hutu	1990	Ethnic	UN, US
viii) Sierra Leone vs. Revolutionary United Front	1989	Ethnic	Guinea, Nigeria/ECOMOG
ix) Somalia: factions	1978	Ethnic	UN (humanitarian aid)
x) Sudan vs. Sudanese People's Liberation Army	1983	Ethnic Religious	& Iran, Uganda
xi) Uganda vs. Lord's Army	1986	Power	Sudan

Source: Center for Defense Information: www.cdi.org/issues/World_at_War/wwar00.html

example, in 1999, the British Government applied UN arms embargoes on Angola, Liberia, Rwanda, Sierra Leone, Somalia, Sudan, the Federal Republic of Yugoslavia, and Iraq. In addition, it implemented a non-binding embargo on Ethiopia and Eritrea, two OSCE embargoes on Armenia and Azerbaijan, and a national embargo on Iran.[77] This combination has created the necessary pre-conditions for the illicit arms trade to thrive. Embargoes are the life-blood of the illicit arms trade. Effectively barred from openly buying the arms they require, warring factions or states must instead rely on the black market in weapons.

However, the illicit arms trade operates at a number of levels, and it would be a mistake to simply equate it solely with the smuggling of light weapons to areas of conflict. Concurrently, there exists a trade in attempting to smuggle nuclear, chemical, and missile-based technology to states seeking to acquire these technologies, but denied open access by the existence of a series of multilateral export regimes and groupings, such as the Missile Technology Control Regime and the Australia Group. The states seeking to acquire such technology about which concern is most frequently expressed are those which former Clinton Administration National Security Advisor, Anthony Lake, labelled the "backlash states".[78] The source states of most concern are those of the former Soviet Union and eastern bloc.

At the same time as creating the pre-conditions in which the illicit arms trade could thrive, the end of the Cold War also helped create the political space required to begin to tackle the trade. With the zero-sum calculations which underpinned superpower assessments of Third World conflict a thing of the past, and with a decline in political manipulation of and state involvement in the illicit arms trade, the possibility of genuine international co-operation aimed at achieving a degree of control was opened up. The OAS, EU, G8 and UN all began to address the issue. Since 1991, the UN has passed a number of Resolutions calling on governments to take measures to curb the trade. For example, Resolution 48/75F from December 1993 noted the link between illicit arms transfers and threats to international peace and called on member states to "give priority to eradicating the illicit arms traffic associated with destabilizing activities, such as terrorism, drug trafficking and common criminal acts." The 1996 Report of the Disarmament Commission called on states to co-operate in combating illicit arms transfers, comply strictly with UN embargoes, and regulate private arms dealers. Since then a Panel of Governmental Experts on Small Arms has also reported. In particular, with the end of the Cold War and superpower involvement in its internal politics, the upsurge of violence across sub-Saharan Africa has been met by a general agreement that something must be done to curb the illicit arms trade which fuels its conflicts.

However, as the following cases suggest, the successful implementation of measures emanating from international bodies face enormous obstacles in relation to a trade still dominated by the transfer of small arms and components. This trade is characterized for the most part by the movement of weapons or components in quantities that can be easily housed in mis-labelled freight containers, flown to small non-official landing strips on private aircraft, sent via small ships, or on trucks, and where innovations and ingenuity in brokerage appear to be keeping pace with control initiatives. As the State Department points out:

> Monitoring state-to-state weapons transfers is relatively easy because there normally is only a seller and a buyer. The grey and black arms trafficking businesses are significantly more complex operations involving African and non-African, corporate, and individual suppliers and an array of transshipment points, brokers, and financiers throughout the world. African states or insurgents interested in obtaining weapons can choose from numerous manufacturers whose headquarters span the globe. A single weapons purchase can involve several nations, corporations, or brokers.[79]

Control initiatives must confront additional supply-side problems. Many states are too weak or have inadequate resources to enforce international agreements or resolutions on illicit arms, while many have little or no interest in so doing because public and enforcement officials regard payments emanating from them as constituting a regular supplement to their often low official salaries. In addition, notwithstanding the decline in political manipulation of embargoes, there clearly remain instances where geopolitical considerations dictate that embargoes should be undermined.

Cases: The contemporary illicit arms trade in operation

Rwanda

One of the difficulties involved in tackling the illicit arms trade lies in unravelling the often intricate trails which even amateurs construct to conceal illicit arms activity. This process is well illustrated by the case of Mil-Tec and its supply of arms to Rwanda. In 1996 it was revealed that Mil-Tec Corporation Ltd, a British company registered in the Isle of Man, with a correspondence address in Hove, links to a travel agency in north London, and whose directors operated from the Channel Island of Sark, supplied over US$5.5 m worth of arms to the former Hutu-led Rwandan Government during and after the 1994 genocide.[80]

On 17th May 1994, five weeks into the genocide, the UN imposed an embargo on arms sales to Rwanda, but both before and after this Mil-Tec was delivering arms flown in from Israel and Albania (having sourced the arms in Bulgaria and the former Yugoslavia) via Goma in neighbouring Zaire, complete with Zairois end-user certificates. Documents discovered abandoned in a bus near Goma revealed a series of flights to Zaire both before and after the imposition of the embargo. For example, on 17th April 1994 an aircraft chartered to a company called Jet Lease, based in the Bahamas, flew out US$753,000 worth of ammunition from Israel. Five days later, a further flight carrying US$681,000 worth of ammunition left Israel. On 9th May, 2,500 AK-47s, ammunition and mortar bombs were flown in from Tirana. Almost two months after the UN embargo came into effect, flights from Tirana were continuing. On 13 July 1994, ammunition, 2,000 mortar bombs, and over 100 rockets for RPG-7 launchers left Tirana.

The manager of Mil-Tec was one Anoop Vidyarthi, a Kenyan Asian who ran a travel agency situated above an aromatherapy salon in Hendon, North London. Mil-Tec itself was a shell company registered in the Isle of Man, a Crown dependency, in February 1993. Its original directors were both partners in the Isle of Man branch of accountants BDO Binder, whose address was used by Mil-Tec in registering. As Helen Hatton, the head of enforcement for the Isle of Man's Financial Supervision Commission explained: "Binder act in a general way as company formation agents. They keep a stock of companies 'on the shelf' so that, if someone wants to set up a company quickly, they can respond immediately."[81] The original directors were replaced in June 1993 with two nominee directors, the father and son combination of Trevor and John Donnelly, based on the Channel Island tax haven of Sark. According to Helen Hatton, they were on the boards of "literally thousands of companies" in the UK, the Channel Islands, Ireland, and the Turks and Caicos Islands.[82]

Mil-Tec officials were never prosecuted for their arms trafficking activities, as the UK Government had failed to extend the UN embargo to crown dependencies such as the Channel Islands and Isle of Man. In fact this was only done in mid-December 1996, one month after the Mil-Tec story broke. An Inter-Departmental Committee on Trafficking in Arms set up to investigate governmental shortcomings in the affair reported that, "there had been a lack of consistency in implementing embargoes in the UK, the Crown Dependencies and the Dependent Territories", and that "there were no structured arrangements for ensuring the timely and accurate imposition of embargoes."[83] However, any prosecution would have been problematic, even if the government had acted efficiently. No British arms were involved and none of the arms were transshipped via the UK, so no UK export licences were required. Moreover, even though arms were still being exported after the UN embargo came into effect, the arms were being shipped to neighbouring Zaire rather than directly to Rwanda. Although Customs officers did interview Anoop Vidyarthi once he returned from a hastily-arranged trip to Kenya, and raided the offices of a number of air freight companies implicated in the arrangement, including Jetlease International (based in Windsor), Treasury Solicitors reportedly overruled their intention to bring charges.[84] Ironically, given that he was to experience a similar problem over Sandline and Sierra Leone, then shadow foreign secretary, Robin Cook said the case had exposed the fact that the government "can't control . . . what is happening here, which is a company registered in Britain, drawing its profits into Britain, providing the planes and acting as middleman for somebody else selling the arms and taking them on to Zaire."[85] Despite his embarrassment over the Sandline affair, the loophole over the activities of arms brokers remains.

Sierra Leone

Hot on the heels of the Mil-Tec scandal came another, this time involving the private security company Sandline and its supply of arms to ousted President Kabbah of Sierra Leone.

In 1997 and 1998, Sandline International Ltd., a private military company set up by former British Army officer Tim Spicer OBE, arranged and supplied arms sourced in Bulgaria and flown via Nigeria to Sierra Leone in contravention of UN and UK arms embargoes. Sandline's involvement was underwritten by the financier Rakesh Saxena in return for diamond concessions in Sierra Leone. Saxena was described by Foreign Secretary Robin Cook as, "an Indian businessman, travelling on the passport of a dead Serb, awaiting extradition from Canada for alleged embezzlement from a bank in Thailand."[86] While the Sandline affair highlights the role played by private security companies in Africa, it also offers a useful guide to the complexities involved in drawing up UN embargoes and the need to avoid ambiguity in doing so.

Formal British policy with regard to Sierra Leone was to support by peaceful means the restoration of President Kabbah's government, overthrown in a May 1997 coup led by Major Johnny Paul Koroma.[87] Concurrently, however, ECOWAS, the Nigerian dominated Economic Community of West African States, which also controlled the ECOMOG forces, was adopting an approach which combined diplomatic negotiation with economic sanctions and the use of force. UNSC Resolution 1132, passed on 8 October 1997, was supportive of ECOWAS, and while it did not authorize the use of force to restore the status quo ante, it supported the ECOWAS effort – one prong of which was to do just that. Further ambiguity arose from the section of UNSC Resolution 1132 which dealt with the arms embargo, and which was unclear as to exactly whom it applied. It mandated that:

> all States shall prevent the sale or supply to Sierra Leone, by their nationals or from their territories, or using their flag vessels or aircraft, of petroleum and petroleum products and arms and related matériel of all types, including weapons and ammunition, military vehicles and equipment, paramilitary equipment and spare parts for the aforementioned, whether or not originating in their territory.[88]

What precisely did "Sierra Leone" mean in this context? Was it a reference to the military junta alone, or did it extend to any force operating in Sierra Leone? Did it include President Kabbah, who was still recognised as the democratically-elected Head of State of Sierra Leone but was no longer in the country? Moreover, what about the ECOMOG forces in Sierra Leone? Did the embargo apply to them?

The British government's interpretation was that the scope of the embargo was geographic, and as such applied equally to all forces inside Sierra Leone.[89] In contrast, the UN Assistant Secretary General (Legal Affairs) argued that ECOMOG had to be partially exempted, because "any other interpretation would lead to a paradoxical situation in which the Council, while entrusting ECOMOG with important responsibilities, at the same time deprived it of the means to carry out those responsibilities."[90] To complicate matters further, Sir John Kerr, Permanent Under-Secretary at the Foreign Office, told the investigating Foreign Affairs Committee (FAC) that the "geographic" interpretation was shared by "a large majority of members of the Security Council", and that "it is the Security Council that is responsible for the reading of its own Resolutions."[91] For his part, President Kabbah thought that the Resolution did not apply to his government in exile. Adding to this spiral of ambiguity, British government statements about the embargo referred to it as a ban on arming the military regime, the absence of a reference to Kabbah's government-in-exile offering the implication that it did not apply there.[92]

However, when the UN embargo was implemented in British law via an Order in Council, this clearly defined Sierra Leone as being:

(a) the Government of Sierra Leone;

(b) any other person in, or resident in, Sierra Leone;

(c) any body incorporated or constituted under the law of Sierra Leone;

(d) any body, wherever incorporated or constituted, which is controlled by any of the persons mentioned in sub-paragraphs (a) to (c) above; or

(e) any person acting on behalf of any of the persons mentioned in sub-paragraph (a) to (d) above.[93]

Hence, where the UN Resolution was ambiguous as to what constituted "Sierra Leone", British law was not. President Kabbah was recognised as the lawful head of state, but any supply of arms to him or his supporters in Sierra Leone by British citizens or from British territory would be a criminal offence. However, the Order in Council was not accompanied by any public announcement, so that, "most of the main players… had either no, or only a vague and very general, awareness of the existence of the Order, and still less of the fact that it expressly prohibited the supply of arms, without a licence to or to the order of President Kabbah."[94]

This was the background to Sandline's involvement. Sandline describes itself as having been "established in the early 1990s to fill a vacuum in the post cold war era", and its purpose as being, "to offer governments and other legitimate organizations specialist military expertise at a time when western national desire to provide active support to friendly governments, and to support them in conflict resolution, has materially decreased, as has their capability to do so."[95] It aims to provide, "the best possible military services in order to assist them with solving security issues quickly, efficiently and with minimum impact." In addition, Sandline states that it will only undertake projects for:

> Internationally recognised governments (preferably democratically elected); International institutions such as the UN; Genuine, internationally recognised and supported liberation movements – and which are – Legal and moral, Conducted to the standards of first world military forces, Where possible, broadly in accord with the policies of key western governments; Undertaken exclusively within the national boundaries of the client country.[96]

In July 1997, following an initial contact with Rakesh Saxena, anxious to see a restoration of order that would safeguard the interests of his Jupiter Mining Company, Spicer flew to Conakry and produced a situation report for a fee of US$60,000 plus US$10,000 expenses.[97] Spicer then flew to Vancouver to meet Saxena, on bail over an alleged US$88m fraud in Thailand. Saxena also underwrote the cost of acquiring the necessary arms. Spicer sourced these – 35 tonnes comprising 600 AK-47s, 36 rocket-propelled grenade launchers, 750,000 rounds of ammunition, 30 light machine guns and 800 rocket grenades – in Bulgaria, from where, in February 1998, they were flown to Kano in Nigeria, to be taken from there to Sierra Leone by Ibis Air, in which Sandline had an interest. Ironically, once it arrived at Freetown's Lungi airport on 22nd February, the shipment was impounded by the Nigerian-led ECOMOG forces (the Nigerian commander, Brigadier Maxwell Khobe, explained that: "We were mandated to seize any weapons brought into the country under the terms of the embargo. We did that."[98]), and so played no role in the restoration of the Kabbah government on 10th March 1998.

Fundamental to Spicer's case was his claim that he was unaware he was breaching the UN embargo in flying arms to Freetown. Officials seemed sceptical of this claim (Sir John Kerr thought that, "if one is in the business of supplying arms it seems that the natural first thing one would do is to look at the law of the land and establish whether what one was doing was legal or illegal", and pointed out that, "Mr Spicer... operates with a firm of solicitors about him"[99]), while the FAC concluded that if he "truly was not aware of the Order in Council, then his firm and their advisers are guilty of professional incompetence."[100]

However, Spicer had made Peter Penfold, the British High Commissioner in Sierra Leone, aware at a 23 December 1997 meeting that he had an arrangement with President Kabbah which involved the supply of military equipment, a copy of which he gave to Penfold who had already been shown a draft of the relevant contract by President Kabbah himself four days previously. As the Legg Report into the affair noted, "although the contract did not expressly mention arms or weapons, Mr Penfold says that he immediately assumed that it included them, because of the size of the sum involved."[101] Penfold saw nothing wrong in this because, just as Spicer claims to have, Penfold believed the embargo to be aimed at the military regime and Sandline's activities were not inconsistent with the British government's policy of returning Kabbah to power. Moreover, Penfold was unaware of the Order in Council translating the UN embargo into UK law, and hence of its terms.

On 28 January 1998 Penfold visited Sandline, was taken through their plan, given a copy of a strategy paper outlining "Project Python", and had the difficulties Sandline was facing in sourcing weapons and arranging transportation explained to him. Hence, as the FAC reasoned, Spicer by now "had every reason to believe that the FCO was aware of the nature of his business with President Kabbah because of his dealings with Mr Penfold. It would have been entirely reasonable of him to assume that Mr Penfold was acting with full authority of HMG. As Mr Spicer pointed out, the High Commissioner was the representative of Queen and Government in Sierra Leone. If the FCO machine was working properly, once a matter had been reported to Mr Penfold, it had been reported to the Government."[102] Although Spicer had discussions elsewhere in the FCO, the substance of which is debated, it is clear that the ambiguity in UNSC Resolution 1132 and general ignorance about the terms (or even existence) of the Order in Council created a corridor of opportunity which should not have existed and which Sandline were able to exploit.

Notwithstanding the debate on mercenaries, the element of the Sandline operation which breached the UN embargo was not the supply of personnel, but of arms. While the Major government had agreed that a "considered assessment of the advantages and disadvantages of primary legislation to prohibit arms trafficking"[103] should be undertaken, the current Labour government have not considered controls on brokering arms to be enough of a priority to find time to bring in the primary legislation necessary to create them.

Other Africa

Elsewhere in Africa, the pattern of extensive small-scale trafficking in illicit arms across large, porous, inadequately policed borders, has been repeated. Take the case of Air Atlantic Cargo, a British company based in Kent. The major shareholder in the company is Air Atlantic Nigeria, based in Lagos, in whose name Air Atlantic Cargo's aircraft are registered. In October 1997, an Air Atlantic Cargo Boeing 707 was spotted unloading at Pointe Noire airport in Congo, just north of Angola, for the third time in a matter of weeks. There, UNITA troops met the flight and unloaded its cargo. In August 1998 one of the company's aircraft delivered arms to both sides in the civil war; a consignment of 38 tonnes of arms to Goma in DRC one week, followed by a delivery of 21 tonnes of arms in Namibia the following week. The aircraft then flew on to Botswana to off-load armoured cars.[104]

In another case, in October 1998 Belgian Customs officials seized a shipment of assorted military equipment en route to Eritrea. The shipment – 80 engines for Soviet T-54 and T-55 tanks, infra-red sights, thermal imaging equipment and periscopes - "bought in Germany, brought together in the Netherlands and moved by rail to Antwerp for loading", was reportedly organized by London-based JMT Charlesworth Ltd, trading as Global Services. The cargo had been listed as building equipment and water pumps. The company's owner said he was unaware that infra-red sights, thermal imaging equipment, or periscopes were among the cargo, and claimed that the engines were for Russian-manufactured bulldozers.[105]

In yet another case, in the late 1990s, Christopher Barrett-Jolly – who had previously courted controversy with his live veal export business – turned to arms trafficking. After buying a small freight aircraft, he flew to Ostend and placed it on the Liberian register, forming Balkh Air, under the cover of which he flew arms from Bulgaria to Afghanistan.[106] In 1998 he leased a Boeing 707 and reportedly flew arms to southern Africa (possibly to UNITA), from Bulgaria to anti-Kabila forces in DRC, and by late 1998 was flying arms to the Sudanese army (with end-use documents for Chad) in breach of the 1994 EU embargo – for example, in one flight carrying 42 tonnes of arms from Hermes, the former Slovak state-run arms producer based in Bratislava.[107] This particular channel was only exposed when the aged and over-loaded Boeing crashed on take-off from Bratislava in February 1999.

Arms have continued to flow into the civil war in Burundi. While Rwanda and Uganda have been sources of arms (conduits) for the Burundian government and Tutsi militias, Hutu insurgents have been armed via Tanzania, Angola, Zambia, Zaire, and South Africa. In Sudan, a range of external actors have been involved in arming the government during the ongoing civil war, including China, east European states (e.g. Russia, Bulgaria, Ukraine, Kazakhstan), South Africa, and Iran. Human Rights Watch also found evidence of the supply of Chilean cluster bombs.[108] As with Burundi, most of this trade is best explained by reference to financial incentives, although elements of it – the support of Iran, Iraq, and Malaysia – stem from political support for Khartoum. The opposition National Democratic Alliance receives arms from neighbouring Uganda, Ethiopia and Eritrea. It also enjoys tacit US support. Given that, as Human Rights Watch notes, the region remains awash with

Cold War-era arms (from the time when the area "mattered"), even the imposition of an arms embargo which is strictly adhered to by all external actors is, in isolation, unlikely to bring a halt to the fighting:

> The US alone provided successive Khartoum governments with close to $1 billion in arms in the late 1970s and 1980s, usually in the guise of fighting Soviet influence, after pouring hundreds of millions of dollars of arms into Ethiopia from 1952 through 1977. For its part, the Soviet Union provided arms to Sudan in the early 1970s and then supplied Ethiopia with over $12 billion in arms between 1977 and 1991. As the Horn of Africa lost significance to the departing superpowers, Sudan was allowed to wither in arms-bloated poverty, but many of the cold war-era arms are still present throughout the region and are in use by forces on all sides of the conflict.[109]

With regard to Congo-Brazzaville, former President Pascal Lissouba implicated French oil company Elf-Aquitaine in the 1997 coup that removed him. It has also been claimed that Turkish-born Lebanese arms dealer Sarkis Soghanalian re-emerged from his spell in a Miami prison to be "linked with the supply of arms and assistance" to the man who overthrew Lissouba, General Denis Sassou-Nguesso.[110] Elsewhere, it has been claimed that the missiles which brought down the plane carrying Rwanda's late President Juvenal Habyariman had been seized from Iraq during the 1991 Gulf War from where the US passed them on to Uganda, which in turn passed them on to those responsible (both Hutu extremists and Tutsi rebels have been accused). In another case, in February 1998 it was announced that elements in the Guinea Bissau military were trafficking arms to the Movement of Democratic Forces of Casamance, Casamance separatists conducting a campaign in neighbouring Senegal.[111] The Guinean chief of staff was sent on indefinite leave and 13 other officers were arrested and detained.

In 1994 the South African Cameron Commission provided an insight into the milieu of the illicit arms trade while investigating the circumstances surrounding a consignment of South African arms, supposedly destined for Lebanon, but instead bound for prohibited Yemen, then in the midst of a civil war. It found, "a world of freewheeling and idiosyncratic characters; of intrigue, deception and subterfuge; of lucrative and often extravagant commissions and of high living; of deliberately disguised conversations; of communications shrouded in complex documentation and cryptic notes; of deals structured to conceal their true nature; a world with its own rules and code of conduct, in which intimidation, threats and actual peril are ever present; a world, also, of unpredictable allegiances and loyalties: the world, in short, of arms dealers."[112] Although it was a description that Eric Ambler would have been proud of, it described a real rather than a fictional world.

Eastern Europe

Post-communist eastern Europe remains the prime source for black market small arms. Controls are weak and easily evaded, corruption is rife, and the financial rewards are far in excess of the meagre salaries of most east European munitions workers or officials. Poland is a case in point. To take one case from many; in March 1992 future Polish Senator Rajmund Szwonder, then a deputy production director of the Lucznik factory, was one of six Polish businessmen arrested in Frankfurt and charged with attempting to sell 105,000 AK-47s, 1,000 anti-aircraft missiles, 5,000 rocket-propelled grenades, not to mention two MiG-29s, to Iraq[113] – charges which were dismissed by a New York court which ruled the businessmen had been entrapped. In November 1993, British Customs officers uncovered a shipment of 300 assault rifles aboard a ship at Teesport docks, destined for Ulster Loyalist terrorist groups, and which, they claimed, were manufactured at the Lucznik factory. The consignment had been labelled as Polish ceramics. Szwonder denied that the company was responsible, explaining that: "The West is trying to create this image of Poles as gun-runners. It is absolutely not true. Nothing whatsoever has been proved. And in any case, other countries do this sort of thing all the time... America and the West are simply trying to eliminate us from the market."[114]

Poland also faces a problem in policing its borders and preventing the influx of former Soviet arms destined for the Warsaw organized crime gangs which control drugs trafficking, prostitution, and various other rackets. To take a recent example, in October 1999, Polish police intercepted a consignment of explosives, 120 hand grenades and a rocket, at Rzeszow, near the Ukrainian border, arresting six Moldovans and one Ukrainian.[115]

Although controls over arms sales from the Czech Republic have been stepped up in recent years, for example, over what was formerly its most infamous export, Semtex, there are indications that comprehensive control of the arms sector has proved illusive. In 1997, the US government successfully pressured the Czech government not to go ahead with the planned sale to Iraq of five of its Tamara stealth-detection radar systems. It was earlier suspected that these had been used by Bosnian Serbs in helping to bring down a US F-16 aircraft over Sarajevo in 1995 and, later, that one loaned from Russia to Yugoslavia had helped bring down a US F-117 Stealth aircraft in March 1999 during the air war over Yugoslavia. Two months later, in May 1999, it was revealed that Azerbaijani officials had intercepted six dismantled MiG-21s on board a Russian Antonov aircraft at Baku. Reports that these had originated from the Agroplast company in northern Bohemia, however, appear to have been inaccurate. The shipment had arrived in Azerbaijan via Kazakhstan, from where it was apparently bound for North Korea, part of a much larger order for MiGs which North Korea had attempted to secure through the lax controls of Kazakhstan.[116] However, the Kazakhstan Ministry of Foreign Affairs ended the attempt, rejecting an unconvincing attempt to pass off the jets as being destined for Sierra Leone.

Bulgaria

> You must keep the true faith of the armourer ... To give arms to all men who offer an honest price for them, without respect of persons or principles: to aristocrat and republican, to Nihilist and Tsar, to Capitalist and Socialist, to Protestant and Catholic, to burglar and policeman, to black man, white man and yellow man, to all sorts and conditions, all nationalities, all faiths, all follies, all causes and all crimes.
>
> Andrew Undershaft in George Bernard Shaw's *Major Barbara*[117]

The east European source of illicit arms of greatest concern in the post-Cold War era is Bulgaria. As Human Rights Watch summarized: "Bulgaria has earned a reputation as an anything-goes weapons bazaar where Kalashnikov assault rifles, mortars, antitank mines, ammunition, explosives and other items are available for a price – no matter who the buyers are or how they might use their deadly wares."[118]

During the Cold War Bulgaria was a front-line Warsaw Pact supplier to both the Communist world and non-state actors such as the PLO. It has compensated for the post-Cold War decline in demand from these markets with a willingness to supply areas of conflict, including destinations embargoed by the UN. Despite becoming a signatory to the Wassenaar Agreement in 1996 and agreeing to abide by the EU Code of Conduct on Arms exports in 1998, Bulgarian arms continue to flow to the world's trouble-spots, particularly in Africa, raising questions concerning the Bulgarian state's enthusiasm for enforcing compliance with embargoes, and about the role of officials in by-passing them. Involvement in wars has not been a barrier to purchase of Bulgarian arms. For example, towards the end of 1998, Bulgaria shipped a consignment of tanks to Uganda, then involved in a civil war at home, fighting in the Democratic Republic of Congo, and supporting rebel forces in both Sudan and Angola. In addition, displaying the "true faith of the armourer", since 1993 Bulgaria has armed both sides in both the Angolan civil war and the Ethiopia-Eritrea conflict.

Why is Bulgaria such an "Aladdin's Cave" for arms brokers? There are a number of reasons. Firstly, enforcement of Bulgaria's arms export regulations – themselves hardly watertight[119] – has been weak, with relatively few resources allocated to monitoring. Hence, the authorities have a limited capacity to confirm that arms have reached their stated destination. Human Rights Watch found that, for Bulgaria:

> Direct physical inspection is prohibitively expensive, particularly as Bulgaria has few overseas embassies or trade missions, and is therefore rarely performed. This is particularly true in Africa, which is the destination for a substantial portion of Bulgaria's arms exports. . . Most of the information [the Bulgarian authorities have] received about suspected illicit arms trade activities. . . has been provided by foreign governments.[120]

However, the extent to which the political will exists to tighten up these procedures must be open to question as, allied to the weakness of monitoring, turning a blind eye to dubious exports seems to have been a source of income for some officials. Moreover, Bulgaria must aggressively export arms in the post-Cold War world if it is to maintain those jobs dependent on arms production. Traditionally, little of Bulgaria's arms production, the core of which has comprised small arms and ammunition (including a range of Kalashnikovs), has been for domestic use, while the end of the Cold War closed most of its traditional export outlets. At the end of the Cold War, in 1989, Bulgaria's arms industry employed over 100,000 people, and at its height generated annual earnings of around US$1bn. However, with the end of the Cold War, the Warsaw Pact folded, proposed sales to states of the former Soviet Union, such as Georgia and Estonia, were abandoned under pressure from Moscow, other markets, such as Iraq and Libya, were proscribed as a result of UN embargoes, while Bulgaria was not well situated (for a variety of reasons) to compete effectively in the increasingly competitive buyers' market of the licit arms trade. This meant that whereas leading western governments had the advantage of seeing the impact of the post-Cold War fall in demand cushioned by a post-Gulf War arms bonanza, east European exporter states like Bulgaria had no such luxury. On the contrary, the end of the Cold War brought an end to state subsidy and left east European exporters faced with unrecoverable debts from states like Iraq and Syria.[121] This left a combination of growing debts, unsold arms, and mounting pressure to safeguard employment in the arms sector.

These forces have combined to generate a culture where the destination of arms is less important than the fact of their export, especially where falsified documents or circuitous delivery can provide officials with a degree of deniability. This culture is exemplified by comments made by Bulgarian government officials to Human Rights Watch. One informed them that monitoring was "an international problem" rather than a Bulgarian responsibility, while another offered the view that there "had been no cases of Bulgarian involvement in illicit arms deals, and that diversion always took place outside Bulgaria's borders and without the foreknowledge of Bulgarian arms trading companies."[122] Faced with conclusive evidence that in February 1998 Bulgarian arms were flown to Sierra Leone in defiance of a UN embargo (the Sandline affair), Prime Minister Ivan Kostov issued a flat denial, saying that: "Bulgaria has not exported military supplies to Sierra Leone; we find it implausible that a large shipment of arms can be loaded and exported behind the back of the customs authorities."[123] This culture could harbour the seeds of future illicit arms dealing, as membership of NATO, which Bulgaria aspires to, requires a standardization of military equipment. This means that as well as buying Western arms to comply with this standarization, Bulgaria will be rapidly ditching its Warsaw Pact-era equipment, for which it will no longer have any use. For the reasons outlined above, the resultant stockpiles may well surface in areas of conflict in the developing world. Certainly, the sale of this equipment will be a more profitable exercise than its destruction, and may be necessary to help finance the NATO standardization.

Where the Bulgarian authorities have taken action to frustrate the illicit trade it has tended to be at the prompting of the US. For example, in 1993 *Forbes* magazine exposed the trafficking of arms from the port of Varna to Croatia. Acting on information provided by the US, in September 1992 the Bulgarian authorities intercepted the fourth in a series of shipments of Soviet-calibre heavy artillery and ammunition, this one worth US$7.5 m. The Maltese-flagged ship *Ofirtal* used false Bolivian end-user certificates, which proved sufficient to by-pass the Bulgarian authorities until the US intervention, despite the fact that the Bolivian General who had signed them was entirely fictitious and Bolivia had no Soviet-calibre weapons.[124]

By the mid-1990s, Bulgaria was a primary source for weapons where there was a need to by-pass embargoes, or where the destination was a warring region where other suppliers may have felt constrained by public opinion or their own national guidelines. Neither, as the examples cited above suggest, was there any compunction about arming both sides in such circumstances. For example, between 1995 and 1996, in the aftermath of its border war with Ecuador, Bulgaria exported 236 IGLA missiles to Peru, as replacements for those lost in the conflict with Ecuador (worryingly for the UN Register of Conventional Arms initiative, while Peru records these deliveries for the 1996 Register, Bulgaria submitted a nil export return[125]). At the same time, in 1995 Air Sofia was discovered attempting to deliver 100 tonnes of arms, apparently originating in Belarus, to Ecuador.[126] Air Sofia was also involved in shipping arms to Eritrea in July 1998, ferrying them from Burgas to the Eritrean capital Asmara, after the outbreak of war with Ethiopia.[127] In late November 1998 it was revealed that it had also sold T-55 tanks to Ethiopia.[128] Bulgarian arms also surfaced in Sudan, Rwanda, and southern Yemen. In addition, Human Rights Watch discovered evidence of a regular route between Ostend and Bulgaria, with freight aircraft regularly travelling from Ostend to pick up arms.

In another case, in 1997 US Customs agents in Miami arrested two Lithuanians, Alexandr Pogrebevskij and Alexander Darichev. The Customs officials, posing as members of a Colombian drug cartel, had been offered arms by the two, who produced a "briefcase filled with shiny brochures from a company in Bulgaria called Armimex", which produced a range of Soviet arms under licence.[129] The undercover agents agreed to buy a total of 40 Bulgarian-manufactured ground-to-air missiles (including Strela 2M, Strela 3M, and Igla 1Es), at a cost of US$3.2 m. The Lithuanians even suggested that once the missile deal had been concluded they would be able to supply tactical nuclear weapons.[130] They produced false end-user certificates from the Lithuanian Ministry of Defence, signed by a former minister of defence, emphasizing that the Bulgarian company could only legitimately sell the missiles to a government. The missiles were to be shipped from Bulgaria on the *Al Fares*, a vessel owned by a Cypriot, Angelo Zeini, to Puerto Rico, complete with paperwork indicating that this was the ship's final destination and that it was carrying fifteen fifty-foot containers of machinery and general cargo. The missiles would be concealed within the more general cargo so that the ship would pass an inspection at the Straits of Gibraltar. The Lithuanians were subsequently sentenced to four years in prison.

Since 1993 Bulgaria has been a source of arms for UNITA despite a UN embargo on arming UNITA and a 1995 UN call "upon the Government of Angola and UNITA to cease any acquisition of arms and war materiel, as agreed upon in the 'Acordos de Paz', and to devote their resources instead to priority humanitarian and social needs".[131] In addition to the sale of tanks and armoured combat vehicles to the government, Air Sofia has delivered light arms and ammunition to UNITA, for example, in 1996 via N'Djili airport in Kinshasa (AK-47s, 60 and 120mm mortars, grenades and launchers).[132] With the May 1997 replacement of Mobutu in Zaire, and the shift in UNITA's resupply operation, eyewitness testimony suggests that Bulgaria has remained a source of arms via Mozambique, while the Angolan government claimed that Bulgarian arms were still being delivered via Uganda, after the Angolan and Ugandan governments supported opposing sides in the conflict in the DRC (Angola, the Kabila government, Uganda the anti-Kabila rebels). In another indication of the close relationship with UNITA, Human Rights Watch discovered that a UNITA delegation visited Bulgaria at the beginning of 1999, supposedly on a "sight-seeing" tour.[133]

Russia

There have been numerous cases involving the illicit transfer of Russian arms in recent years, where "the collapse of the old order and discipline, the disintegration of the armed forces, and the sudden arrival of the spiviest end of western business, have produced an explosive cocktail."[134] The range of conventional arms which have been made available is impressive – running from second hand Kalashnikovs to MiG aircraft. In 1993, a Kalashnikov sold in eastern Europe for the equivalent of just £68. Inevitably, there has been little evidence of discernment regarding customers.

In this atmosphere, the conflict in Chechnya took on the overtones of a black comedy, as both sides fought each other with the same weapons, with the Chechens' weapons often being bought from the soldiers they were fighting. As one Chechen trader explained, the Russian army, "is an amazing army. The army is selling weapons which are killing its own men. But the soldiers are fully aware that the top leadership is making huge amounts of money from this war, so they are too." Captains and Majors appear to have sanctioned the sales by the Russian soldiers in return for a cut. "I have to say the Russian army doesn't like its own roubles, they prefer US dollars", the trader explained. "As long as the Russian army exists, we'll have weapons", said another.[135] In one case, in late 1996, Russian General Vladimir Semyonov, the third highest-ranking general in the Russian armed forces, was suspended over allegations that he sold arms to the Chechen forces he was leading the fight against.[136] When fighting resumed in 1999, Chechen soldiers shot down two Russian aircraft (an SU-24 and an SU-25) at the beginning of October. One was reportedly shot down by a US Stinger missile, raising the question of just where it was acquired? One option was clearly via the Taliban in Afghanistan, but another theory, indicative of the degree of illicit trading during the earlier war, was that the missile in question had been a Russian Igla missile – similar to the Stinger – sold to the Chechens by Russian soldiers between 1994 and 1996.[137]

Covert or concealed state-to-state deals involving Russia and Iraq have also emerged. How Iraq's fleet of MiG aircraft have remained in service during the almost ten-year arms embargo would be hard to explain without reference to the covert supply of spare parts. Similarly, Soviet anti-aircraft defences remain operational. According to one report, these servicing arrangements have been "handled via banks and front companies in Turkey, Jordan and the Balkans. One of the more favoured conduits is Bulgaria, where Russian dealers have set up a number of companies." As one Russian arms specialist was quoted as saying: "Yes, our people have been on business trips from Moscow to Baghdad, to repair and put in working order Iraqi hardware, including the latest equipment from Russia. And what do you expect? The

Russian government pays us nothing, so we have to go to Baghdad just to survive."[138]

However, it is not just the leakage of conventional arms and technologies from Russia which is of concern. A weakening of controls and safeguards in the post-Communist era has also heightened the risk of nuclear materials being smuggled out of the country. In recognition of this risk, since 1991 the US has spent more than US$3bn via the Co-operative Threat Reduction (CTR – Nunn-Lugar) programme, addressing the danger of nuclear proliferation through Russia. The Departments of Defense, State and Energy, have all been involved in initiatives intended to safeguard Russia's nuclear stockpiles and discourage Russian nuclear scientists from being drawn into the nuclear weapons programmes of threshold states. However, hundreds of tonnes of Russian nuclear material are considered to be vulnerable to theft, and thousands of Russian nuclear scientists are sufficiently underpaid and underemployed to be a cause of concern. In short:

> the physical and human infrastructure responsible for monitoring Russia's nuclear arsenal are in serious disrepair. Unable to pay their electric bills, nuclear weapons installations have actually been without power at times. The equipment that controls nuclear weapons malfunctions frequently. Crews are receiving less training, and serious housing and food shortages are causing great disaffection among the troops guarding the Russian arsenal.[139]

Although, as John Berryman points out,[140] the risk has not yet translated into a significant number of known cases of successful smuggling, various reports suggest this is as much a consequence of good luck as effective security. For example, in September 1998, "a U.S. team visiting the Kurchatov Institute in Moscow was shown a building containing 100 kilograms of highly enriched uranium – potentially enough for several nuclear bombs – that was totally unguarded, because the Institute could not afford the $200-a-month salary for a guard."[141] In addition, it has been reported that at some nuclear facilities, Ministry of Internal Affairs guards:

> have left their posts to forage for food. Others have been reluctant to patrol facility perimeters because they did not have winter uniforms to keep them warm on patrol. At some facilities, recently installed security equipment is not being used because there is no money to maintain it; at others, guards who had not been paid in months were expected to man unheated posts in sub-freezing conditions. At some facilities, entire security systems – alarms, surveillance cameras, portal monitors, etc. – have been shut down because the facilities' electricity was cut off for non-payment of bills. At other facilities, guards have intentionally turned

off alarm systems, or even cut their cables, because they were annoyed by frequent false alarms.[142]

To cite just two further cases from a wide range: in one it was claimed that two drunken workmen stole two atomic warheads from a factory east of the Urals in November 1993 for a bet. The warheads were later traced to a garage in a residential area.[143] In another case, in 1991 Greenpeace negotiated to purchase a nuclear warhead from a Russian officer, a "senior lieutenant in the army assigned to the special troops of the general staff responsible for nuclear security", based at Altengrabow, 30 miles south-west of Berlin, in order to highlight the danger of "loose nukes". The Russian was offered US$250,000 and help in escaping to Sweden. Planning was reportedly well-advanced when the officer disappeared.[144]

There is also evidence of attempted nuclear smuggling via Turkey. The Monterey Institute of International Studies has compiled a catalogue of 18 acts of attempted nuclear smuggling via Turkey between 1993 and 1999, at least some of which involved materials intended for either Libya or Iran.[145] While none of these incidents appear to have involved highly enriched uranium or plutonium, and most seem to involve amateurs with little understanding of what they had acquired,[146] it would be remarkable if this was the sum total of efforts to smuggle nuclear material, and hence that Turkey boasts a 100 per cent interdiction rate, or that there are not complementary routes which do not boast Turkey's interdiction success rate. Perhaps the professionals are simply more adept at smuggling.

Bosnia

In September 1991, three months after fighting broke out between the Bosnian government and Bosnian Serbs, a UN embargo was instituted on arms sales to the belligerents in the former Yugoslavia (UNSCR 713). This affected the Bosnians more than the Serbs, who had retained the vast bulk of the former Yugoslavia's armaments. Nevertheless, despite the embargo, arms continued to flood in to Bosnia by air, sea and road. As the Bosnian Ambassador to Washington, Sven Alkalaj, put it: "There's no problem acquiring arms. There are lots of arms sellers in the world who have access to any kind of weaponry you wish to buy." The existence of an embargo merely raised the price, making it "three or four times higher" than if openly available.[147]

In addition, geopolitical interests led to states involving themselves in or acquiescing in the serial breaches of the embargo. The Clinton Administration tacitly approved Iranian arms shipments to Bosnia. Arms or financing were also provided by a range of other states, including Saudi Arabia, Malaysia, Brunei, Turkey, and Pakistan. Croatia and Bosnia also received arms via

Argentina, while Germany allegedly facilitated the transfer of former East German MiG-21s to Croatia via Hungary.[148] In South Africa, allegations surfaced that the Vatican had funnelled US$40 m worth of bearer bonds to Croatia to facilitate weapons purchases.[149] The ease with which Serbian forces acquired Russian arms reflected support from Moscow. The scale of smuggling and range of actors involved rendered the embargo meaningless.

Particular attention came to focus on the supply of military equipment from Iran to the Bosnian government via Croatia. First exposed in May 1994, when an Iranian air force transport plane was observed at Zagreb airport unloading heavy crates marked "humanitarian aid" and "no smoking", this route supplied essentially small arms, but nevertheless "enabled the Bosnian government to fight the Serbs to a standstill and even, in some areas, to regain territory lost in the early years of the war."[150] It attracted attention because, although the Clinton Administration was notionally upholding the UN embargo, and although some 20,000 US troops were being deployed in the region, it was aware of and acquiesced in the Iranian arms airlifts. This stood in marked contrast with the actions of the Bush Administration, which had protested over an earlier Iranian re-supply flight in September 1992 carrying 4,000 assault rifles which was subsequently impounded by Croatia.[151] Not only did the Clinton decision raise the spectre of revenge attacks against Western forces in the area, it was also counter to the Administration's declared policy of isolating Iran internationally. It was "the height of insanity", said Lawrence Eagleburger. "We are inviting Bosnian Islamic connections with a terrorist state that wishes us as much damage as they can possibly inflict upon us."[152] In an election year, Republican-led investigations in Congress were inevitable, although attempts to label US acquiescence in these violations as a "Democrat Iran-Contra' were somewhat fanciful, there having been no US finance, aircraft or arms involved, as in the Reagan-era debacle. The operation, said to have been personally approved by President Clinton, included the shipment of anti-tank weapons, mortars, surface-to-air missiles, AK-47 rifles, and ammunition, and continued until January 1996. As well as aiding the Bosnians, the operation also aided Croatia which, in return for its role in facilitating the deliveries, imposed an "arms tax" of around 30% of the arms delivered. These were then deployed in the action to force Croatian Serbs out of Krajina in 1995.

The pipeline itself was set up through Zagreb following Croatia's April 1992 normalization of relations with Iran. In the wake of this a Muslim Croat, Osman Muftic, was sent to Tehran as Croatia's first ambassador. Muftic used his position to work out the logistics of supply along with the Bosnian ambassador and Hasan Cengic, a Bosnian Muslim arms dealer who later became Bosnia's deputy defence minister. The US ambassador to Croatia, Peter Galbraith, subsequently explained that in April 1994 Croatian President Tudjman had asked if the US would acquiesce in an arms pipeline from Iran via Croatia. Galbraith subsequently recalled that he, "knew the question was coming because I had been alerted by other Croatian officers. I cabled Washington back to make sure that I had the policy right and that I had got it to the letter." Galbraith then went back to Tudjman, "and the answer I gave him was 'No instructions'. I said: 'Pay attention to what I am not saying.' "[153] The route was activated shortly afterwards, with the number of flights averaging eight per month and ultimately amounting to an estimated 14,000 tonnes of equipment.[154]

Because the UN embargo was inadequately enforced – UN forces on the ground explained that they did not have a mandate to search shipments for smuggled weapons, while NATO and WEU ships in the Adriatic only searched a small fraction of the ships they challenged, and these challenges produced very few illegal cargoes[155] – once a government had agreed to such a supply and the US had acquiesced, the flow was unlikely to be interrupted. As one UN official explained: "What is suspicious is that planes can fly into Zagreb without undergoing any independent checks. It is done completely on the honour system. It depends completely on the honesty of the country where the plane was loaded to make sure that no guns are being shipped and then its up to the Croatian customs people to match what's on the manifest with what's in the cargo hold."[156]

However, the Iranian supply route was just one utilized by the Bosnian government, as became clear when the Vienna office of the Third World Relief Agency – from 1992, effectively a front for trafficking arms into Bosnia – was raided. Prior to the establishment of the Iranian link this agency collected funds from sympathetic states and non-state actors (Osama Bin Laden was reportedly a donor), set up offices in Sarajevo, Moscow, Istanbul, and Budapest, and procured arms for the Bosnian cause. In 1992, US$80 m flowed into its bank account at the First Austrian Bank, rising to US$231 m in 1993, and falling to US$39 m in 1994 and 1995 as the Iranian pipeline came on stream. It has been estimated that half this total was used to procure arms.[157] The Bosnians were supplied via flights of arms aboard Soviet transport aircraft travelling from Khartoum to Maribor in Slovenia. The arms are said to have come from stocks of Soviet weapons formerly held in East Germany.[158]

The recent history of the Balkan region means that it is awash with arms which are now finding their way on to the black market. Rioting and looting in Albania in 1997 involved the ransacking of government arms stores, and the theft of hundreds of thousands of AK-47s, many of which were smuggled over porus neighbouring borders. In the mountain town of Gramsh, for exaample, 110,000 AK-47s were looted from a factory. When one woman offered a visitor as many of the guns as he wanted at US$40 each, she was interrupted by a man shouting; "Hey, I can get them for you for $20 each."[159]

In the wake of the Kosovo war, the Kosovo Liberation Army's (KLA) weapons were to be collected under a the terms of a NATO agreement. However, elements within the KLA have been reluctant to comply – NATO forces have seized ten times the number of weapons that have been voluntarily surrendered. Largely stockpiled in Albania, and moved across borders that boast almost no controls, KLA arms – rifles, explosives, grenades, anti-personnel mines – are now being touted for sale from the bars of Pristina, with a Kalashnikov AK-47 reportedly selling for just £52, semi-automatic pistols for under £30. Moreover, these arms are being offered across Europe, with AK-47s and other KLA-origin small arms being offered for sale in London.[160]

Argentina

The question of state knowledge of and acquiescence in illicit arms deliveries is raised again in cases involving Argentina. 8,000 Argentinian FAL automatic rifles and 75 tonnes of ammunition, notionally intended for Venezuela, found their way to Ecuador during its 1995 border war with Peru, despite an embargo and the fact that Argentina was one of the four guarantors of an existing Peru-Ecuador peace agreement. President Menem, who had signed a decree authorizing the shipments, claimed that the arms were diverted illegally by private arms traffickers. However, a retired Ecuadorean general had inspected the arms in Buenos Aires prior to shipment, and the arms trader who arranged the deal claimed to have dealt directly with the head of the state arms company, Fabricaciones Militares. In his defence, Menem claimed that his predecessor, Raul Alfonsín, had also sold arms to warring states, particularly Iran. Under fire from congress, Defence Minister Oscar Camilión complained that: "If every time a crime is committed in the administration the minister responsible should resign, we would be left without ministers."[161] Nevertheless, Camilión resigned in July 1996.[162] Already, in 1995, Argentinian arms had surfaced in UN-embargoed Croatia. These had notionally been intended for Panama, although given that Panama doesn't have an army, its use for the 6,500 tonnes of weaponry should perhaps have been called into question.[163] Moreover, the arms were picked up by a Croatian ship. The Argentinian press quoted a former US State Department official, Daniel Nelson, as claiming that the US government was aware of the transfer but reportedly "turned a blind eye, wishing to help Croatia resist Serbian offensives."[164]

Libya

Libya, a permanent priority fixture across arms control regimes, and from 1992 to April 1999 subject to a UN arms embargo arising from Libya's alleged responsibility for the Pan Am 103/Lockerbie bombing,[165] continues to attempt to smuggle in military technology in defiance of those regimes. With an ageing conventional force capability, most of it purchased from the Soviet Union in the 1970s, Libya's procurement priorities came to lie in maintaining its conventional forces in the face of the UN embargo as well as in chemical weapons and ballistic missiles.[166] As one Western reporter observed in 1994 at a military parade to commemorate the 25th anniversary of the coup that brought Colonel Gaddafi to power: "Once upon a time, military attachés would have had their binoculars trained on this display of Libya's huge arsenal. But... the greater part of the 1,100 tanks on view were outdated T-62s and modified T-54/55s. They were in a shabby state and far from combat-ready. Only a handful of previous-generation MiG-23, MiG-25, Sukhoi-22 and Mirages were sufficiently airworthy to take part in the fly-past."[167]

Since then, various Libyan efforts to smuggle non-conventional technology have been exposed. Conventional arms technology has been shipped via both Italy and Malta.[168] With regard to Italy, for example, in late 1995 a Libyan procurement front operating from Turin was uncovered following the discovery of NATO serial numbers in the wreckage of Libyan aircraft shot down during the 1995 border conflict with Chad. Italian Customs investigators subsequently seized a ship in Genoa, notionally carrying coffee machines and truck parts to Libya, but also containing undeclared aircraft components. Two weeks later, at Cassella airport in Turin, a shipment of auto parts, soft drinks and electrical products was instead discovered to be made up of MiG components.[169] As a result, three British companies, five American companies, and four German companies were investigated. Both orders had been placed by Trade Libya Development, a company run by brothers Gabriele and Maurizio Villone. As one Italian investigator explained: "Villone was the linchpin in this complex network. He would buy plane parts and then tell Italian customs in Genoa that they were truck parts. The Americans sold to the British, the British to the Italians and the Italians to the Libyans."[170]

In another case, in January 2000, it was revealed that 32 crates of Scud missile components, labelled as automotive parts, were discovered on a British Airways flight at Gatwick airport bound for Malta en route to Tripoli.[171] Documents discovered during the seizure suggested that earlier disguised shipments had been delivered successfully. They were thought to be part of a process of gradually transferring North Korean missile technology to Libya via Taiwan, the UK and Malta. The seized shipment had been sent in the name of a Taiwanese knitwear company, Hontex. This was, in fact, the logo of products manufactured by the Taiwanese Nan Liong Enterprise in its mainland China affiliate, the Hong Liong Textile Co. The company denied any involvement, although the Taipei-based *United Evening News* quoted military sources as suggesting that, "the Chinese communists might have infiltrated Taiwanese investments in the mainland and used them as windows for export of missile technology and import of high technology."[172]

Although initial reports stated that the seizure had occurred in November 1999, it was subsequently revealed that the joint MI5-Customs operation actually took place in May 1999 – crucially, two months prior to the re-establishment of diplomatic links between Libya and Britain – and that Foreign Secretary Robin Cook, "brushed the disclosure aside at the time, seeing the restoration of relations with Libya as too important to be deflected by an illegal attempt to import missiles through Britain."[173]

Peter Bleach

Another case which illustrates well the increased involvement of amateurs in the illicit arms trade is that of Peter Bleach, a former British Army Intelligence Corps officer and one-time prison officer in Zimbabwe.[174]

Bleach set up a company called Aeroserve, installed himself as director, and decided to enter the arms trade from his Yorkshire farmhouse headquarters. In July 1995 he was approached by a Danish company, represented by New Zealander Kim Davy, and asked to supply a quote to deliver a consignment of US$170,000 worth of arms to a destination in southern Asia. Bleach says he realized that this proposition was "anything but a legitimate arms deal. It was clearly on behalf of some terrorist group", and so informed the Defence Export Services Organisation. He subsequently met with Special Branch officers and details of the proposed weapons drop were eventually passed on to the authorities in New Delhi in November 1995, some five weeks before it occurred. Bleach claimed that as a result of his information, he expected the arms flight to be intercepted as soon as it crossed into Indian air space. In November, Bleach ordered the arms through a UK company, Border Technology and Innovations Ltd (BTL), giving the end-destination as Dhaka, Bangladesh, with the aid of forged end-user certificates. An invoice supplied to Bleach by BTL suggests he had also tried to buy parachutes through them, a requirement which should perhaps have aroused their suspicions:

> Peter. . . Total price $170,000. . . We need EUC quickly to effect licences. Payment: $85,000 in advance, balance by Bankers draft. Commission: $10,000 is in this for you. Parachutes not available.[175]

In December 1995, a Russian-made Antonov AN-26 aircraft, leased from a company based in Hong Kong, and flown by a Latvian crew, carried the

Bulgarian-sourced arms[176] together with Bleach and Kim Davy into India, dropping them by parachute near the town of Purulia in West Bengal, where they were apparently destined for the radical Hindu Organisation, Ananda Marga (Path of Bliss), engaged in a long-standing dispute with the state government. The aircraft then flew on to Thailand, but on its return flight was ordered to land at Bombay. There, Davy absconded while Bleach was arrested. Far from being a New Zealander, Davy turned out to be one Neils Christian Nielson, a Dutch member of Ananda Marga with 46 known aliases, travelling on a forged passport, and wanted by Interpol in relation to numerous cases of smuggling, forgery, and money laundering.

Bleach was charged with "abetting the waging of war against India", and as such faced the death penalty. Throughout his four year trial he maintained that he was the victim of a sting operation which had gone wrong. For their part, the UK Ministry of Defence claim that Bleach was told by them to have nothing more to do with the scheme, although Bleach went on with his efforts to buy a plane from the Latvian state airline. Bleach contested the MoD claim, telling UK Special Branch: "It is not at all true that I was categorically instructed to back-off. Rightly or wrongly, I was left with the impression that your men were not particularly concerned whether or not a consignment of arms were delivered to a remote area of West Bengal." However, a former colleague suggested that Bleach, reportedly short of money at the time of the initial proposal, had "back[ed] both ends against the middle" in going ahead with the deal while informing the UK authorities.[177] In February 2000, Bleach, and the Latvian crew, were found guilty of "conspiring to wage war against India", but cleared of the capital offence. The judge said the episode was part of, "an international conspiracy to overthrow the democratically elected government of West Bengal", and that it was "the first time in the history of this country that such a crime has been committed."[178] It was also a graphic illustration of the way in which the illicit arms trade has seen the entry of a number of amateurs and the potential costs of failure. On 2nd February 2000, Bleach and the Latvians were jailed for life.

Conclusion

The post-Cold War era has seen two parallel developments in respect of the illicit arms trade. Firstly, heightened regional conflict ("New Wars") combined with an increased application of embargoes has fuelled the illicit arms trade. Secondly, to a significant extent, the end of the Cold War has depoliticised the illicit arms trade and so helped create the political space required to attempt to tackle the problem. However, the omens are not encouraging. What emerges from a study of the contemporary illicit arms trade is a picture of a diverse trade, operating at various levels, sometimes still with tacit governmental support. Acknowledging the complex inter-relationship between states and the illicit arms trade is essential, as doing so places the obstacles to effective control in their proper context. Although state involvement and acquiescence in the illicit arms trade are not constants, they ebb and flow with the geopolitical tides (currently they ebb, but a change of circumstance could see them flow again), clearly a trade in which states have the capacity to be significant players is harder to regulate than one in which the international community is united in its desire to stamp out what Aaron Karp has termed this "antipolicy".[179]

It must also be said that Western condemnation of and demands for supply-side control of the illicit trade sit uneasily alongside aspects of the West's own involvement in the licit arms trade. For example, in 1999 the British Labour Government, self-proclaimed pursuers of an ethical dimension in foreign policy, lifted an informal block on the supply of spare parts for Zimbabwe's Hawk fighter aircraft. The Hawks, along with 11,000 Zimbabwean troops, were directly involved in the war in the DRC, and the spare parts were required to keep a proportion of Zimbabwe's ten Hawk aircraft in action.[180] In addition, it emerged that Britain was not just prepared to arm Zimbabwean forces involved in the war, but was also training them. A British Military Assistance Training Team, supposedly preparing troops for regional peacekeeping, was in fact training troops being deployed in the war.[181] The line which distinguishes this licit trade from the illicit trade is not a particularly thick one.

There is also the question of companies engaging in licensed production so as to overcome national restrictions, a practice not a million miles removed from brokering arms. Take the example of Heckler and Koch, the former German-owned small arms company which became a subsidiary of British Aerospace. Heckler and Koch products such as the G3 rifle and MP5 submachine gun are produced under licence agreements across the world. For example, the MP5 is produced under licence in Pakistan, Greece, Iran, Turkey, and Mexico. The UK government has no control over the destinations to which these countries export the gun. Hence, it can be sold to locations for which the British government may well not issue an export licence. For example, from Turkey Makina ve Kimya Endustrisi Kurumu (MKEK) concluded a 1998 deal to supply the Indonesian police with 500 MP5s – a deal that is unlikely to have been granted an export licence in the UK.

Because these practices continue, there is a sense in which the existence of the illicit arms trade serves a useful function. By representing one extreme of the arms transfer spectrum, the existence of the trade helps legitimize practices which would themselves constitute the extreme of the spectrum if the illicit arms trade were successfully regulated. Western governments have no interest in facilitating this progression and shining a light on their involvement in the licit arms trade, which represents something of a moral quagmire. Luckily for them, all the indications are that effectively controlling the illicit trade will prove to be a task little short of Sisyphean.

Notes

1. Defined by the UK government as "acting as an agent in putting a deal together between supplier and customer or making the practical arrangements for the supply of the goods." Foreign Affairs Committee, *Sierra Leone* (2nd Report, Session 1998–99, HC116-I), p. xxxviii, note 327.
2. See, for example, Philip Noel-Baker, *The Private Manufacture of Armaments* (New York: Dover Publications, 1972 – original edition, London: 1936), and Fenner Brockway, *The Bloody Traffic* (London: Victor Gollancz, 1933).
3. See Audrey R. Kahin and George McT. Kahin, *Subversion as Foreign Policy: The Secret Eisenhower and Dulles Debacle in Indonesia* (New York: New Press, 1995).
4. George Thayer, *The War Business: The International Trade in Armaments* (London: Weidenfeld & Nicolson, 1969), Ch. III.
5. On the UK response see Mark Phythian, *The Politics of British Arms Sales Since 1964* (Manchester: MUP, 2000).
6. This stated that: "all states shall cease forthwith any provision to South Africa of arms and related *matériel* of all types, including the sale or transfer of weapons and ammunition, military vehicles and equipment, paramilitary police equipment, and spare parts for the aforementioned, and shall cease as well the provision of all types of equipment and supplies and grants of licensing arrangements for the manufacture and maintenance of the aforementioned." http://www.un.org/documents/sc/res/1977/77r418e.pdf
7. See Jane Hunter, *Israeli Foreign Policy: South Africa and Central America* (Boston: South End Press, 1987); Michael Brzoska, "Arming South Africa in the Shadow of the Embargo", *Defense Analysis* 1991, 7, 1: 21–38.
8. Seymour M. Hersh, *The Samson Option*, (London: Faber and Faber, 1991), p. 265.
9. On Bull's career, see Mark Phythian, *Arming Iraq* (Boston, Mass.: Northeastern University Press, 1997); William Lowther, *Arms and the Man: Dr Gerald Bull, Iraq and the Supergun* (Basingstoke: Macmillan, 1991); James Adams, *Bull's Eye: The Assassination and Life of Supergun Inventor Gerald Bull* (New York: Times Books, 1992); and Dale Grant, *Wilderness of Mirrors: The Life of Gerald Bull* (Scarborough, Ontario: Prentice-Hall Canada, 1991).
10. United States District Court for the Eastern District of Pennsylvania: United States v. James H. Guerin. Superceding Indictment.
11. Alan Friedman and Tom Flannery, "Bush Adviser Seeks Clemency for Former Ferranti Executive", *Financial Times*, 8.6.92.
12. William D. Hartung, *And Weapons for All* (New York: HarperPerennial, 1995), p. 193.
13. On ISC, South Africa and Cardoen, see also Alan Friedman, *Spider's Web: Bush, Saddam, Thatcher and the Decade of Deceit* (London: Faber & Faber, 1993).
14. John Stockwell, *In Search of Enemies: A CIA Story* (London: Futura, 1979), pp. 57–58. See the appendices for lists of US arms delivered to UNITA in this period.

46 MARK PHYTHIAN

15. Office of the White House, "Statement by the President on Conventional Arms Transfer Policy", 9.7.81.
16. Charles G. Cogan, "Partners in Time: The CIA and Afghanistan Since 1979", *World Policy Journal* 1993, 10, 2: 73–82, 76.
17. Cited in James M. Scott, *Deciding to Intervene: The Reagan Doctrine and American Foreign Policy* (Durham: Duke University Press, 1996), p. 48.
18. George P. Shultz, *Turmoil and Triumph: My Years as Secretary of State* (New York: Scribner's, 1993), p. 692.
19. On the impact of the Stingers, see Alan J. Kuperman, "The Stinger Missile and US Intervention in Afghanistan", *Political Science Quarterly* Summer 1999, 114, 2: 219–263.
20. Kuperman, "The Stinger Missile", p. 253.
21. Hartung, *And Weapons For All*, p. 3.
22. Kuperman, "The Stinger Missile", pp. 253–254.
23. Ibid, pp. 245–245; Daniel McGrory, "CIA Stung by its Stingers", *Sunday Telegraph*, 3.11.96.
24. Elaine Sciolino, "Qatar Rejects US Demand For Return of Illicit Stingers", *New York Times*, 28.6.88.
25. Chris Smith, "Letter from Dara", *New Statesman & Society*, 11.11.94., p. 11.
26. Chris Smith, "Light Weapons and Ethnic Conflict in South Asia", in Jeffrey Boutwell, Michael T. Klare and Laura W. Reed (eds.), *Lethal Commerce: The Global Trade in Small Arms and Light Weapons* (Cambridge, Mass: American Academy of Arts and Sciences, 1995), pp. 61–80, p. 64.
27. Ibid, p. 65.
28. Tara Kartha, "Controlling the Black and Gray Markets in Small Arms in South Asia", in Jeffrey Boutwell and Michael T. Klare (eds.), *Light Weapons and Civil Conflict: Controlling the Tools of Violence* (Lanham, Maryland: Rowman & Littlefield, 1999), pp. 49–61, p. 53.
29. Chris Cowley, *Guns, Lies and Spies* (London: Hamish Hamilton, 1992), pp. 109–110.
30. The following draws on Swedish Peace and Arbitration Society (SPAS), *International Connections of the Bofors Affair* (Stockholm: SPAS, December 1987).
31. Formed in 1975 as a forum for the discussion of safety, transport and related issues.
32. Cited in Kenneth R. Timmerman, "Europe's Arms Pipeline to Iran", *The Nation*, 18–25.7.87., p. 48.
33. Concurrently, Nobel was involved in controversy over Bofors' payment of bribes/commissions to Indian officials to secure a 8,400m kronor deal for howitzers. See, Henrik Westander, *Classified: The Political Cover-Up of the Bofors Scandal* (Bombay: Sterling Newspapers, 1992).
34. Timmerman: Europe's Arms Pipeline to Iran, p. 50.
35. Ibid, p. 48.
36. SPAS: *International Connections of the Bofors Affair*, p. 35.
37. *Wall Street Journal*, 10.9.87.
38. At the time one dollar = 6.349 kronor.
39. See Gaylord Shaw and William C. Rempel, "Billion-Dollar Iran Arms Search Spans US, Globe", *Los Angeles Times*, 4.8.85.
40. James Adams, *Trading in Death* (London: Hutchinson, 1990), p. 129.
41. *The Washington Post*, 10.2.91.
42. See, Lawrence E. Walsh, Independent Counsel, *Iran-Contra: The Final Report – Vol.1: Investigations and Prosecutions* (New York: Times Books, 1994), Ch.8.
43. Hartung, *And Weapons For All*, p. 183.

44. Reproduced in Tom Blanton (ed.), *The White House e-mail* (New York: New Press, 1995), p. 124.
45. Blanton (ed.), *The White House e-mail*, p. 125.
46. Senate Committee on Foreign Relations, Subcommittee on Terrorism, Narcotics and International Operations, *Drugs, Law Enforcement and Foreign Policy* (Washington, DC: GPO, 1989), Introduction.
47. Ibid, IV, "Drug Trafficking and the Covert War".
48. Described in the Report as "the head of the Costa Rican 'air force' and personal pilot to two Costa Rican presidents". Ibid.
49. Ibid.
50. Cited in Scott, *Deciding to Intervene*, p. 118.
51. Ibid, p. 134.
52. Ibid, p. 138. See also, Victoria Brittain, *Death of Dignity: Angola's Civil War* (London: Pluto Press, 1998), Ch. 3.
53. Schultz, *Turmoil and Triumph*, p. 1124.
54. See *Angola Peace Monitor* at www.anc.org.za/angola/ for a regular summary of allegations of arms smuggling to UNITA and UN and international efforts to enforce the embargo.
55. Alex Vines, *Angola Unravels: The Rise and Fall of the Lusaka Peace Process* (New York: Human Rights Watch, 1999), Ch. IX, "Arms Trade and Embargo Violations", at www.hrw.org/hrw/reports/1999/angola/
56. Ibid.
57. For its part, UNITA emphasizes Angolan government use of mercenaries. For example, in its "Latest News" bulletin of 28.10.99. it draws attention to "the supply of mercenaries from Israel, Russia, Ukraine, Portugal and Brazil and the exchange of military information with specialized agencies of some NATO countries" and reports that the, "military planes of Eduardo dos Santos' regime, piloted by Russians and Brazilians have been overflying the central highlands at very high altitudes to avoid our defences. They have been dropping lethal napalm, phosphorous, cluster chemicals and air-fuel- explosives bombs indiscriminately." See the UNITA website at www.kwacha.com
58. James Rupert, "Zaire Reportedly Selling Arms to Angolan Ex-Rebels", *Washington Post*, 21.3.97.
59. Vines, *Angola Unravels*, Ch. IX. Vines lists those air freight companies operating out of Kinshasa and flying to UNITA-held areas in 1995 as being: Trans-Service Airlift (TSA); Trans-Air Cargo (TAC); Guila Air; Express City Cargo; Skydeck; Fil Air; and Walt Air.
60. See, for example, Peta Thorneycroft, "SA Arms Going to UNITA", *Electronic Mail & Guardian*, 20.6.97., at www.mg.co.za/mg/news/97june2/20june-unita.html
61. Vines, *Angola Unravels*, Ch. IX.
62. John Mullin, "Honeymoon's Over for Mandelson", *Guardian*, 29.1.00.
63. For one account, see Adams, *Trading in Death*, Chs. 2–3.
64. Henry McDonald, "Smuggled US Guns for IRA Truce Rebels", *Observer*, 16.11.97.
65. Toby Harnden, "IRA Dissidents Seek Gaddafi Arms", *Daily Telegraph*, 4.5.98.
66. Maeve Sheehan, "Britain Sought to Aid Libya Despite Gadaffi's IRA Arms", *Sunday Times*, 26.9.99.
67. David Usborne, "Suspect Says He Was Buying Arms For IRA", *Independent*, 30.7.99.
68. See, Anthony Davis, "Tamil Tiger International", *Jane's Intelligence Review*, October 1996, pp. 469—73. See also, Rohan Gunaratna, "LTTE Fundraisers Still on the Offensive", *Jane's Intelligence Review* Dec. 1997: 567–570; Raymond Bonner, "Rebels in Sri Lanka Fight With Aid of Global Market in Light Arms", *New York Times*, 7.3.98.

69. www.cdi.org/issues/World_at_War/wwar00.html
70. Margareta Sollenberg, Peter Wallensteen and Andrés Jato, "Major Armed Conflicts", in *SIPRI Yearbook 1999: Armaments, Disarmament and International Security* (Oxford: OUP/SIPRI, 1999), pp. 15–25.
71. For example, Charles Hables Gray, *Post-Modern War: The New Politics of Conflicts* (London: Routledge, 1997); Mark Duffield, "Post-Modern Conflict: Warlords, Post-Adjustment States and Private Protection", *Civil Wars*, April 1998, 1, 1: 65–102.
72. Mary Kaldor, *New and Old Wars: Organized Violence in a Global Era* (Cambridge: Polity Press, 1999), p. 2.
73. Ibid.
74. *SIPRI Yearbook 1999*, p. 25.
75. See David Shearer, "Africa's Great War", *Survival* Summer 1999, 41, 2: 89–106.
76. US State Dept. Bureau of Intelligence and Research, Bureau of Public Affairs, "Arms and Conflict in Africa", July 1999.
77. *Hansard*, 26.7.99., cols.149–50w.
78. Anthony Lake, "Confronting Backlash States", *Foreign Affairs* March/April 1994, 73, 2: 45–55. These were North Korea, Iran, Iraq, Libya, and Cuba. Cuba is primarily included for domestic political reasons and barely features in Lake's discussion. For a similar exercise, see Raymond Tanter, *Rogue Regimes: Terrorism and Proliferation* (Basingstoke: Macmillan, 1998). To Lake's original list, Tanter adds Syria.
79. State Dept, "Arms and Conflict in Africa".
80. The network was first exposed in November 1996. See Sam Kiley, "British Company Supplied Arms to Hutu Militia", *Times*, 18.11.96.
81. Richard Duce, Daniel McGrory, Ian Murray and Jon Ashworth, "How the Mil-Tec Trail Led From Sussex to Sark", *Times*, 19.11.96.
82. Ibid. See also, Christopher Elliott and Richard Norton-Taylor, "Mystery of Arms Sales to Rwanda", *Guardian*, 19.11.96; Michael Gillard, David Connett and Jonathan Calvert, "How the West Fuelled Genocide", *The Observer*, 24.11.96.
83. Foreign and Commonwealth Office, "Report by Inter-Departmental Committee on Trafficking in Arms", 21.1.97.
84. Mark Honigsbaum and Anthony Barnett, "UK Firms Armed Hutu Killers", *Observer*, 7.3.99. See also, David Connett and Michael Gillard, "UK Dealers Escape Action on Arms Sales to Rwanda", *Observer*, 26.1.97.
85. Tim Butcher, "Firm's Chairman Quits Over "Arms to Africa' Claim, *Daily Telegraph*, 19.11.96.
86. FAC, *Sierra Leone*, para. 26.
87. *Hansard*, 11.7.97. col.625.
88. UNSC Resolution1132, 8.10.97., at http://www.un.org/Docs/scres/1997/9726713E.htm
89. See the evidence of Sir John Kerr to the FAC, *Sierra Leone*, Minutes of Evidence 17.11.98. Q.1771-82 (HC116-II).
90. FAC, *Sierra Leone*, para. 13.
91. FAC, Sierra Leone, evidence of Sir John Kerr, Q.1770.
92. For example, *Hansard*, 12.3.98. col.841.
93. FAC, *Sierra Leone*, para.21.
94. Sir Thomas Legg KCB, QC and Sir Robin Ibbs KBE, *Report of the Sierra Leone Arms Investigation*, ("Legg Report") (London: The Stationery Office, 27.7.98), para. 3.28.
95. www.sandline.com
96. Ibid.

97. There are numerous reports of this contact. See, for example, Fran Abrams and Andrew Buncombe, "The Anatomy of a Very Secret Coup", *Independent on Sunday*, 7.5.98; Nicholas Rufford, "Diamond Dogs of War", *Sunday Times*, 10.5.98. See also, Abdel-Fatau Musah, "A Country Under Siege: State Decay and Corporate Military Intervention in Sierra Leone", in Abdel-Fatau Musah and J. "Kayode Fayemi (eds.), *Mercenaries: An African Security Dilemma*, (London: Pluto Press, 2000), pp. 76–116.

98. Philip Sherwell, "The Peace Dividends", *Sunday Telegraph*, 17.5.98.

99. FAC, *Sierra Leone*, evidence of Sir John Kerr, Q.1778 & 1833.

100. FAC, *Sierra Leone*, para.27.

101. Legg Report, para. 5.18.

102. FAC, *Sierra Leone*, para 31.

103. *Hansard*, 21.1.97. col.537.

104. Mark Honigsbaum and Antony Barnett, "British Firms in African Arms Riddle", *Observer*, 31.1.99. It is unclear whether the company's directors were aware of the use to which the aircraft was being put. One of their aircraft had been chartered by a Congolese airline. "What they use the planes for is anybody's guess", one of Air Atlantic Cargo's directors told the newspaper.

105. Paul Lashmar, "British 'Arms' Cargo Seized by Customs", *Independent*, 11.2.99.

106. Mark Honigsbaum, Antony Barnett and Brian Johnson-Thomas, "British Pilot Flies Arms to Sudan", *Observer*, 14.3.99.

107. Ibid.

108. See Human Rights Watch, *Sudan: Global Trade, Local Impact: Arms Transfers to all Sides in the Civil War in Sudan*, August 1998, at http://www.hrw.org/reports98/sudan/. Ch.V, "Arms Transfers to the Government of Sudan".

109. Ibid, Ch.II, "The Civil War".

110. Al J. Venter, "Africa Greets Gun-Runners With Open Arms", *Jane's International Defense Review* 1998, 8: 63–66.

111. "Top Officers Involved in Arms Trafficking", *New African*, May 1998, at http://www.africalynx.com/icpubs/na/may98/naaa0504.htm

112. *Commission of Inquiry into Alleged Arms Transactions Between Armscor and One Eli Wazan and Other Related Matters*, First Report, Johannesburg, 15 June 1995, p. 23.

113. See John Pomfret, "E. Europe's 'Merchants of Death' Elude US Sting", *Washington Post*, 24.4.93.

114. Julian Borger, Ian Traynor and John Carvel, "Booty Parade for Sharp Shooters", *Guardian*, 27.11.93.

115. "Polish Police Catch East European Arms Smugglers", Reuters, 24.10.99.

116. "Arms Transfers Continue From NATO Member to Hostile States", *STRATFOR's Global Intelligence Update*, 14.5.99., at www.nyu.edu/globalbeat/nato/GIU051499.html; "Scandal with MiG-21 Sale to North Korea May Affect Kazakhstani Arms Market", *Arms Control Letters*, PIR, 8.10.99., at www.nyu.edu/globalbeat/nuclear/PIR1099.html.

117. George Bernard Shaw, *Major Barbara* (London: Penguin, 1988 ed. – originally 1905), p. 138.

118. Human Rights Watch, *Bulgaria: Money Talks – Arms Dealing with Human Rights Abusers*, April 1999, at www.hrw.org/reports/1999/bulgaria/

119. For a summary of the shortcomings of Bulgaria's arms export guidelines, see HRW, *Bulgaria: Money Talks*, Ch.III. For a summary of the regulations, see the SIPRI arms export controls project entry at http://projects.sipri.se/expcon/natexpcon/Bulgaria/bulgaria.htm

120. HRW, *Bulgaria: Money Talks*, Ch.IV.

121. John Pomfret, "E. Europe's 'Merchants of Death' Elude US Sting", *Washington Post*, 24.4.93.
122. HRW, *Bulgaria: Money Talks*, Ch.IV.
123. Ibid, Ch.VI.
124. Peter Fuhrman, "Trading in Death", *Forbes*, 10.5.93., pp. 96–100.
125. 1996 UN Register of Conventional Arms, via www.un.org-Depts-dda-CAB-register.htm Neither did Bulgaria declare the export in its 1995 or 1997 returns.
126. The shipment was detained in Cape Verde. Human Rights Watch, *Bulgaria: Money Talks*, Ch.III.
127. Raymond Bonner, "Despite Cutoff by US, Ethiopia and Eritrea Easily Buy Weapons", *New York Times*, 23.7.98.
128. Raymond Bonner, "New Weapon Sales to Africa Trouble Arms-Control Experts", *New York Times*, 6.12.98.
129. "Russian Roulette", *Frontline*, at http://www.pbs.org/wgbh/pages/frontline/shows/russia/
130. See the Indictment at http://www.pbs.org/wgbh/pages/fro. . .s/russia/scenario/ indictment.html
131. UNSC Resolution 976, February 1995, via www.un.org/Docs/scres/1995/
132. Rupert, "Zaire Reportedly Selling Arms to Angolan Ex-Rebels", *Washington Post*, 21.3.97.
133. Human Rights Watch, *Bulgaria: Money Talks*, Ch.VI.
134. Borger, Traynor and Carvel, *The Guardian*, 27.11.93.
135. Thomas De Waal, "Corrupt Russian Arms Deals Help Chechens Fight On", *Independent*, 17.2.95.
136. Carey Scott, "General 'Sold Rockets' to Chechens he was Fighting", *Sunday Times*, 8.12.96.
137. Patrick Cockburn, "Chechen Missiles Bring Down Two Russian Jets", *Independent*, 6.10.99. See also, Giles Whittell, "Chechens Buy Off Russians to End Bombings", *Times*, 17.1.00.
138. Con Coughlin, "Russian Weapons Experts Confirm Baghdad Connection", *Sunday Telegraph*, 21.2.99. See also, Con Coughlin, "Revealed: Russia's Secret Deal to Re-arm Saddam", *Sunday Telegraph*, 14.2.99. See also the detailed exposé of the origins and implications of Iraq's post-Gulf War attempts to covertly procure Russian missile technology: Vladimir Orlov and William C. Potter, "The Mystery of the Sunken Gyros", *The Bulletin of the Atomic Scientists* Nov/Dec 1998: 34–49.
139. Coalition for a Liveable World Education Fund, "The Nuclear Crisis Deepens", September 1999, at http://www.nyu.edu/globalbeat/nuclear/CLW0999.html
140. John Berryman, "Russia and the Illicit Arms Trade", in this volume.
141. Matthew Bunn, "Loose Nukes Fears: Anecdotes of the Current Crisis", *Global Beat Issue Brief* No. 45, 5.12.98. at http://www.nyu.edu/globalbeat/pubs/ib45.html
142. Ibid.
143. "Workmen Took Nuclear Arms", *Guardian*, 21.4.97.
144. Steve Boggan, "Greenpeace Tried to Buy Atom Bomb", *Independent*, 25.7.98. For other cases see, for example, Oleg Bukharin and William Potter, "'Potatoes Were Guarded Better", *The Bulletin of the Atomic Scientists* May/June 1995, 51, 3: 46–50; "Heading Off a Nuclear Nightmare: Illicit Trade in Nuclear Materials, Technology, and Know-How", *Carnegie Quarterly* Spring-Summer 1996, XLI, 2-3: 1–6; Paul N. Woessner, "Chronology of Nuclear Smuggling Incidents: July 1991 – May 1995", *Transnational Organized Crime* Summer 1995, 1, 2: 288–329; Emily S. Ewell, "NIS Nuclear Smuggling Since 1995: A Lull in Significant Cases?", *The Nonproliferation Review* Spring-Summer 1998, 5, 3: 119–125; Christopher Ulrich, "Transnational Organized Crime and Law Enforcement

Cooperation in the Baltic States", *Transnational Organized Crime* Summer 1997, 3, 2: 111–130; Andrew and Leslie Cockburn, *One Point Safe* (London: Little, Brown, 1997); Phil Williams and Paul N. Woessner, "The Real Threat of Nuclear Smuggling", *Scientific American*, January 1996, at http://www.sciam.com/0196issue/0196williams.html

145. "Factsheet on Reported Nuclear Trafficking Incidents Involving Turkey, 1993–1999", at: http://cns.miis.edu/research/wmdme/flow/turkey/factsht.htm

146. These characteristics also seem to apply to seizures in west and central Europe. See, for example, Rensselaer Lee, "Smuggling Update", *The Bulletin of the Atomic Scientists* May/June 1997, 53, 3: 11–14.

147. Quoted in Michael T. Klare, "The Guns of Bosnia", *The Nation*, 22.1.96., p. 23.

148. Tim Judah, "German Spies Accused of Arming Bosnian Muslims", *Sunday Telegraph*, 20.4.97.

149. Chris McGreal and Philip Willan, "Vatican Secretly Armed Croatia", *Guardian*, 19.11.99.

150. Klare, "The Guns of Bosnia", p. 24.

151. John Pomfret and David B. Ottaway, "Balkan Arms Smuggling: Wider Than US Acknowledged", *International Herald Tribune*, 13.5.96.

152. Tom Rhodes, "Clinton Approved Iran's Secret Arms Deals with Bosnia", *Times*, 6.4.96.

153. Ed Vulliamy, "Clinton's Irangate Spooks CIA", *Observer*, 2.6.96.

154. Tom Hunter, "The Embargo That Wasn't: Iran's Arms Shipments Into Bosnia", *Jane's Intelligence Review* December 1997: 538–540. See also, House of Representatives Committee on International Relations, *US Role in Iranian Arms Transfers to Bosnia and Croatia*, Business Meeting and Hearing, 8 & 30.5.96., 104th Congress, 2nd Session.

155. For example, Peter Fuhrman claimed that in the six months from November 1992, 9,083 ships were challenged, of which 125 were searched, and from which eight illegal cargoes were discovered. Fuhrman, "Trading in Death", *Forbes*, 10.5.93., p. 100.

156. Quoted by Robert Block, "US Turns Blind Eye to Iran Arms for Bosnia", *Independent*, 3.6.94.

157. John Pomfret, "An Arms Pipeline Uncovered", *Washington Post National Weekly Edition*, 30.9-6.10.96., pp. 6–7.

158. Ibid. In addition, "the organization was also forced to move large amounts of money to Croatia to bribe Croatian officials to allow the weapons to cross their country. The price of such passage skyrocketed in 1993 when Croat nationalists launched their own war for a separate state inside Bosnia. Money was also smuggled into Sarajevo on flights of the office of the UN High Commissioner for Refugees; Bosnian government officials used the money to buy weapons from both Serb and Croat middlemen who operated inside Bosnia. . ." p. 7.

159. Mike O'Connor, "Albanians, Struggling to Survive, Sell Stolen Rifles", *New York Times*, 24.4.97.

160. Kim Sengupta, Steve Brogan and Mary Braid, "In the Bars of Kosovo, the KLA is Holding the Great Weapons Bazaar", *Independent*, 16.8.99.

161. "Secret Arms Sales Scandal Escalates", *Latin American Weekly Report*, 16.5.96, p. 206. See also, "Plot Thickens in Ecuador Arms Row", *Latin American Weekly Report*, 23.5.96, p. 218.

162. "Camilión Quits Over Arms Scandal", *Latin American Weekly Report*, 1.8.96, p. 338.

163. "Arms and the Men", *The Economist*, 12.9.98., p. 62.

164. Phil Davison, "Illegal Arms Sales Test for Menem", *The Independent*, 27.10.98.

165. At the time of writing, Libya is still subject to an EU arms embargo.

166. For a detailed overview, see "Libya's Chemical weapons program" at http://cns.miis.edu/research/wmdme/flow/libya/. See also Joshua Sinai, "Libya's Pursuit

of Weapons of Mass Destruction", *The Nonproliferation Review* Spring-Summer 1997, 4,3.

167. Charles Richards, "Libya Parades its Obsolete Weapons of War", *Independent*, 2.9.94.
168. On suspected smuggling of Serbian arms via Malta, see Chris Hedges, "Serbia is Suspected of Arming Libya", *International Herald Tribune*, 8.11.96. There have also been cases of the direct shipment of dual-use goods allegedly destined for a military application. For example, see "British Companies 'Broke sanctions' to Equip Libya", *Sunday Times*, 3.11.96.
169. John Glover and John Mullin, "Italians Link Arms Ring to UK Murder of Libyan", *Guardian*, 2.12.95; "UK Plane Parts Break Libya Sanctions", *Sunday Times*, 21.4.96.
170. "UK Plane Parts Break Libya Sanctions", *Sunday Times*, 21.4.96.
171. Nicholas Rufford, "Libyans Smuggled Scuds Through UK", *Sunday Times*, 9.1.00.
172. "Taiwan Firm Denies Involvement In Illegal Arms Shipment For Libya", Agence France Presse, 10.1.00.
173. Richard Norton-Taylor, Ewen MacAskill and Ian Black, "Cook Dismissed Libyan Arms Find", *Guardian*, 11.1.00.
174. The following account draws on: "Flight of Fancy", *The Economist*, 6.1.96., p. 53; Tim McGirk, "Would-be Hero Poisoned By His Own Sting", *The Independent*, 11.9.96; John Gilbert and Jan McGirk, "An Amateur's Guide to the Arms Trade", *Independent on Sunday*, 1.12.96; Richard Norton-Taylor, "Gun-running Briton Faces Indian Death Sentence", *Guardian*, 21.8.97; Richard Norton-Taylor, "Army Told of Indian Arms Deal", *Guardian*, 12.9.97; David Graves, "Tory MP Denies Plot to Free Briton From Prison Cell in India", *Daily Telegraph*, 22.9.97; Stephen Grey, "Arms-Deal Briton May Hang", *Sunday Times*, 28.9.97; Peter Popham, "I Was Betrayed by MoD, Says Briton Facing Execution", *The Independent*, 9.7.98; Raymond Bonner, "Murky Life of an International Gun Dealer", *New York Times*, 14.7.98; "UK Alleged Gun Runner's Conspiracy Claims", BBC News Online, 23.7.98; Julian West, "I Know I'll Get Justice, Says Briton Who Could be Hanged", *Sunday Telegraph*, 23.1.00; Oxfam UK, *Out of Control: The Loopholes in UK Controls on the Arms Trade*, (London: Oxfam, 1999), pp. 6—7.
175. Oxfam UK, *Out of Control*, p. 7.
176. The consignment included: 300 Kalashnikov AK-47/56s; 10 RPG-6 rocket launchers; night vision equipment; 100 anti-tank grenades; 100 hand grenades; 25,000 rounds of 7.62 ammunition; 25 9 mm pistols; and 6,000 rounds of 9 mm ammunition.
177. Jon Stock, "Alterations' Claim Delays Arms Trial of Briton", *Daily Telegraph*, 18.1.00.
178. Jon Stock, "Briton Faces Long Jail Term for 'War Plot Against India' ", *Daily Telegraph*, 1.2.00.
179. Aaron Karp, "The Rise of Black and Grey Markets", *The Annals of the American Academy* Sept. 1994, 535: 175.
180. Ewen MacAskill, "Britain's Ethical Foreign policy: Keeping the Hawk Jets in Action", *Guardian*, 20.1.00.
181. Christina Lamb and Peter Almond, "Britain Trains Magabe's Army for Congo War", *Sunday Telegraph*, 23.1.00.

Crime, Law & Social Change **33**: 53–84, 2000.
© 2000 *Kluwer Academic Publishers. Printed in the Netherlands.*

The origins of Iran-Contra: Lessons from the Durrani Affair[1]

ALAN A. BLOCK
The Pennsylvania State University, 103 Weaver Bldg, University Park, PA 16802, USA

Abstract. This essay concentrates on the hitherto unknown origins of Iran-Contra. Through a series of interviews with participants and access to previously private papers, the essay establishes the role played by the U.S. and Israel in initiating arms deals with Iran before any hostage taking in Lebanon. Therefore, it corrects the proposition advanced by Special Prosecutor Walsh and others who linked the clandestine sale of weapons to Iran with the deteriorating situation in Lebanon.

> Besides, the overhead expenses of a trafficker in what is considered a fair way of business are enormous. There are always false birth, marriage and death certificates to be obtained and travelling expenses and bribes to pay quite apart from the cost of maintaining several identities. You have no idea of the cost of forged documents Mr. Latimer. . . . The point is that a trafficker needs plentyof capital. If he is known there are always plenty of people willing to provide it, but they expect fantastic dividends. It is better to have one's own capital.
>
> (Eric Ambler, *A Coffin For Dimitrios*, 1939)

Introduction

For many interested in the contemporary history of the Iran-Contra affair, its origins appear to be a settled issue. Debate has moved to other topics such as whether or not Iran-Contra represented a chronic or episodic dysfunction in the processes of U.S. foreign policy; whether or not it signaled a profound and permanent change in the style of U.S. National Intelligence covert operations; and whether or not it marked the introduction of "privatized" covert activities and what that might mean in light of certain Constitutional and other legal principles. Academically speaking, Iran-Contra is increasingly in the preserve of scholars such as Yale's Harold Hongju Koh who points out, for example, the NSC "had taken on significant operational responsibilities" by 1974 that ultimately led to a swapping of roles with the CIA. This swap completed "an inversion of institutional responsibility that first began during the Vietnam era."[2] He adds amusingly that "[c]ongress no more designed the NSC to execute national security policy than it designed the Council of Economic Advisers to print the nation's money."[3]

I am of the opinion, however, that the origins of U.S. weapons sales to Iran are far from settled. Despite the various public bodies that investigated the affair and published their accounts and much of the fine and authoritative work by careful writers such as Theodore Draper,[4] there still seem to be certain consequential issues and individuals virtually unexplored. A close look at them and their activities pushes the weapons transactions with Iran sufficiently back in time to challenge the standard interpretations.

Standard accounts

There is a standard view of when and why the U.S. decided to sell weapons to Iran. It was supposedly the path chosen to get Iran to lean on its Shiite surrogates in Lebanon who had kidnapped several Americans. The view is composed of two closely related scenarios which nonetheless merge into one generalized claim. The first was developed by President Reagan's Special Review Board chaired by Senator John Tower of Texas. Edmund Muskie and Brent Scowcroft were its other members. Officially established by the President on December 1, 1986, it was directed to produce a report examining "the proper role of the National Security Council staff in national security operations, including the arms transfers to Iran." The President gave the Board (called the Tower Commission), which had virtually no legal powers to investigate (it could not subpoena documents, compel testimony, grant immunity[5]) only a couple of months to complete its work. After approximately three months (it requested and received a few weeks extension), the Tower Commission produced its findings. I have supplemented them with material from the National Security Archive's chronology.

Both chronologies determined that the idea of clandestine sales of U.S. weapons to Iran originated in the summer of 1984 when international arms dealers including Adnan Khashoggi,[6] and most importantly Manucher Ghorbanifar a former Savak officer, desired to move the U.S. and Iran into an "arms relationship."[7] The question of precisely when Khashoggi and Ghorbanifar came together is unsettled, however. One version has Ghorbanifar, who lived in France (and still does), presenting his "bona fides" in a November 1984 meeting with American Intelligence operative and former CIA officer, Theodore Shackley, in Hamburg, West Germany. There Ghorbanifar claimed to represent the interests and desires of Iran's Prime Minister Hussein Mussavi. Confirmation of Ghorbanifar's influence for skeptics in American Intelligence was provided by the ex-head of Savak's counterespionage branch, former General Manucher Hashemi.[8]

The munitions men and their allies worked diligently on their plans and deals from the summer into the following year, although the Central Intelligence Agency did issue a warning to other government agencies, holding Ghorbanifar was a fabricator.[9] Ghorbanifar had a bit of an uphill fight to convince the Americans of both his sincerity and ability. He thus suggested several tests, for instance, trading captured (in Iraq) Soviet equipment for American TOW missiles, or arranging a cash ransom paid to Iran for the release of four Americans kidnapped in Lebanon including CIA Beirut station chief, William Buckley.[10]

At this point the evidence presented by the Tower Commission, and the National Security Archive, is somewhat vague on whether the weapons deal was approved by CIA director Bill Casey or still anxiously awaiting NSC authorization. One line suggests that through the winter and early spring of 1985, there was little movement in the Iran arms deal. But then, Lieutenant Colonel Oliver North, a U.S. Marine officer assigned to the National Security Council as Assistant Deputy Director for Political-Military Affairs, was given documents and other material stating "that Shackley had contact with an Iranian [Ghorbanifar] who said he thought he could ransom Buckley."[11] Subsequently the deal was put into motion.

Another line holds that Casey and a former legal client of his, Roy Furmark, helped initiate important meetings between all the principals – Ghorbanifar, Khashoggi, Yaacov Nimrodi (arms dealer and former Israeli Defense Attaché in Teheran), Amiran Nir (advisor to Israel's Prime Minister Shimon Peres on counter terrorism), Adolph Schwimmer (weapons merchant and a Special Advisor to Peres) – as early as January 1985.[12] The Israelis had a number of items on their agenda including, of course, making certain that Iran had enough munitions to continue, but not win, the war against Israel's foe, Iraq. Quite obviously, Israeli interests, as seen by Prime Minister Peres, Nimrodi, Nir, and Schwimmer, were best served by a prolongation of the Iran-Iraq war.

This second line which advocated an early CIA presence behind the entire affair, gained a stronger measure of credibility through the actions of Casey's man, Furmark who was also a business associate of Khashoggi's. In this line, Furmark appeared to have been responsible for bringing together Khashoggi and Ghorbanifar. According to Furmark's testimony before the Tower Commission, he met Ghorbanifar in January 1985 and then introduced him to Khashoggi a little later.[13] This, if it is accurate, puts Casey at the center of the conspiracy.

Nevertheless, whether inspired and directed (at arms length) by Casey of the CIA, or waiting in the wings for NSC approval which was soon enough on the way, the arms dealers' machinations came at a propitious moment for them. American National Security Council staffers had vainly, so far, looked for a way back into Iran, a method that would provide the U.S. with some leverage. Weapons were always the first and foremost consideration even though it was reported that an October 1984 study conducted at the highest national security levels on the issue of access to Iran through a resumption of weapons deals concluded that the U.S. had little to look forward to.[14] In fact, one year earlier, a National Security Council study called for "operations to limit arms" from third countries to Iran. This was part of a decided "tilt" toward Iraq likely stemming from its recent battle-field performance. The study noted "U.S. interests would not be served if Iraq were to collapse."[15]

Shortly after the study had percolated around, on January 23, 1984, the State Department placed Iran on its list of countries supporting international terrorism. Iraq, on the other hand, had been taken off the dreaded list in December 1982 and was almost immediately granted over $200 million in "credit guarantees to finance sales of U.S. farm products." Much later this would be understood as the start of a long-term massive illegal weapons deal paid for by U. S. taxpayers involving an Italian bank – Banca Nazionale del Lavoro – with a branch in Atlanta, Georgia.[16] This was the so-called BNL scandal which lightly brushed over Henry Kissinger and George Bush. In addition, the Administration encouraged certain Persian Gulf Arab countries to "increase financial support for Iraq," and in the early spring of 1984 sent Special Envoy Donald Rumsfeld to Baghdad to discuss improving bilateral relations with Iraq, paying special attention to a proposed pipeline deal which involved several quite shady characters who were exceedingly close to CIA Director Casey.[17]

Lawrence E. Walsh was appointed Independent Counsel on December 19, 1986, to investigate the Iran-Contra scandal. In his *Final Report* released in January 1994, Walsh held the origins of "The Iran operation involved efforts in 1985 and 1986 to obtain the release of Americans held hostage in the Middle East through the sale of U.S. weapons to Iran, despite an embargo on such sales."[18] Walsh added the Iran "initiative, was actually a series of events" that began in the summer of 1985 and lasted through the following year. Supplying Iran was a joint effort between Israel and the U.S. Israel sent U.S. manufactured weapons to Iran three times in 1985. The initial shipment took place August 20. Walsh noted the 1985 shipments led to the release in September of that year of a single American hostage in Lebanon.[19]

Walsh also commented on several other issues relating to arms sales to Iran including Israel's desire for U.S. help in gathering intelligence on Iran, and an offer from Iran to purchase artillery shells from Israel. These issues were broached during a May 1985 meeting between Prime Minister Shimon Peres and Michael Ledeen who was a part-time consultant to the National Security Counsel. Ironically, one of the messages Ledeen gave to Peres dealt with America's desire for Israeli help in securing intelligence about Iran. Peres told Ledeen that Israel would do nothing about the artillery shells without U.S. approval. Ledeen reported the discussion to National Security Adviser Robert McFarlane.

According to Walsh there was also a third concern that surfaced in a Special National Intelligence Estimate in May 1985. Requested by CIA Director Casey, the Estimate dealt with a potential Soviet influence in Iran which had to be countered with "new approaches" that could include eliminating "restrictions on weapons sales to Iran."[20] Casey tried to elevate the Estimate into a National Security Decision Directive. In June 1985 the NSC drafted the document for McFarlane's consideration. On June 17 he sent it to Casey who endorsed it and to the Secretaries of State and Defense (George P. Schultz and Casper W. Weinberger) who opposed it.[21]

While there were other issues and considerations, it is clear that both the President's Special Review Board (John Tower, Edmund Muskie, Brent Scowcroft) and Independent Counsel Walsh agree the weapons deals with Iran were done in the hope of securing the release of American hostages. Independent Counsel Walsh returned to this theme in his 1997 memoir *Firewall: The Iran-Contra Conspiracy and Cover-up*. "Beginning in March 1984," he noted, "members of Hezbollah, a fundamentalist Shiite group sympathetic to the government of the Ayatollah Khomeini, kidnapped seven Americans – including William Buckley, the CIA chief of station – in Beirut, Lebanon." What Walsh sought to establish when it came to President Reagan was that he had indeed authorized the sale of arms to Iran in order to free the hostages, thus making a mockery of his oft-repeated statement of "no concessions to terrorists," and violating both the Arms Export Control Act and the National Security Act.[22] In the second paragraph of *Firewall* Walsh succinctly states his case: "Reagan was within range of impeachment for his secret authorization of the sale of American weapons to Iran in exchange for American hostages... Moreover, breaking the cardinal rule of covert operatives, he had begun to believe his own cover: He had persuaded himself that he had not been trading arms for hostages; he had merely tried to establish a friendly relationship with Iranian moderates."

By happenstance

I came to this project quite by accident, the result of an interest in a former Assistant U.S. Attorney of some renown. This was E. Lawrence Barcella, Jr. who had been the lead prosecutor in the Orlando Letelier murder case in Washington, D.C., and subsequently served on the several prosecutions of

Edwin Wilson, Jr., the former CIA agent convicted of selling C4 explosives to Libya and plotting to murder several people including Barcella.[23] What piqued my interest was a news story that Barcella, while still an Assistant U. S. Attorney, had given a supposedly improper opinion on an arms deal that was part of Iran-Contra. Lyn Bixby of *The Hartford Courant*, had picked up this information from a deposition given during the appeals process of an arms case prosecuted in Connecticut.[24] The case was USA v. Arif Durrani, a resident alien from Pakistan, in the arms trade for many years. Durrani was convicted of violating the Arms Export Control Act by arranging to transport Hawk missile parts to Iran in 1986.

On Friday, August 9, 1991, Durrani's lawyer, William M. Bloss, deposed a former beauty queen, right-wing radio personality and arms dealer, Barbara F. Studley. Bloss asked her about a shipment of weapons from Poland to Honduras in 1985. Ms Studley was a difficult witness and when pressed by Bloss answered both crossly and somewhat off the point – "I had absolutely nothing to do with Iran. I don't know anything about the Iran-Contra Iran segments. This was a legitimate shipment approved in writing by the Justice Department before we shipped it. Absolutely legitimate."[25] Bloss asked who had approved the operation and Studley responded, "Larry Barcella signed it."[26]

I called Barcella to ask about this. He said that a government official had contacted him for a legal opinion on a weapons transaction. The official told him that "an asset of the United States, a person who brokered weapons," had been approached by someone and invited in on an arms deal. The official explained to Barcella the business involved foreign weapons shipped to foreign ports. The asset had asked the official to find out "if it was appropriate." Barcella told me that he had checked with those who oversaw ITARS, which turned out to mean International Trafficking Arms Regulations, and concluded it was not our business. It was neither inappropriate nor illegal. Pressed to reveal the government official's identity or at least position, he wouldn't say. In a telephone interview with Bixby in 1992, however, Barcella did acknowledge Studley's name was mentioned in his conversation with the unidentified official.[27]

I was not particularly impressed by Barcella's answers any more than I had been by his handling of the Letelier and Wilson cases. I wondered why a government official, presumably from the CIA or the National Security Council or some other Intelligence agency (officials in the Department of Agriculture do not run assets), would ask a sitting AUSA for a legal opinion. The CIA has a General Counsel's Office, and the others have something similar. Why go out of shop?

Lyn Bixby's relentless probing turned up several likely suspects as Barcella's visitor. One was Oliver North. Bixby wrote: "During congressional hearings in 1987, [retired Major General John] Singlaub, an associate of Ms Studley's, testified that he had talked with North about his desire to support the Nicaraguan contras and had cleared the items in his weapons shipment with North. The delivery went from Poland to Honduras, and Swiss banks were used for money transfers. In advance of the arms shipment, Singlaub said he also discussed the legality of the venture with North, who gave him some rules to follow after checking with 'someone in the Justice Department.' "[28]

The work that made Barcella famous had some very rough corners. The Letelier case ended up with the main culprits lightly punished.[29] According to the FBI case agent, Al Seddon, a deal was cut with Michael Townley, the mastermind of the assassination and dozens of other murders, who was extremely close to the Agency.[30] The Wilson cases had an even larger share of odd corners and strange occurrences. Additionally, in the early 1980s, command of the Wilson investigations was taken from Barcella by high officials in the Department of Justice. Explaining the change, Deputy Assistant Attorney General Mark M. Richard stated Barcella was not "well-liked" and thought not competent to handle the complex multi-jurisdictional task force involved in the Wilson case. Richard also remarked that Barcella's superiors in the U.S. Attorney's office in Washington felt he was not keeping them informed of crucial developments, and that the relationship between Barcella and the FBI was strained.[31]

The Durrani Affair

The only thing left to do was to speak to Durrani. We met in the summer of 1997 in Manhattan and then a week later in New Haven, Connecticut, at Bill Bloss's law office. Durrani said he was wrongfully convicted and that Barbara Studley and General Singlaub could have established his innocence had they chosen to tell the truth in their depositions. Durrani's innocence hinged on his assertion at trial that when he was arrested he had been working on a U.S.-Israeli sanctioned transaction. He was asked in the spring of 1986, he said, by representatives of the Israeli Ministry of Defense to locate 240 specific parts for the U.S. manufactured Hawk missile system that Iran had purchased back in the 1970s. He ended up working on this project with a Portuguese arms dealer, who held a Spanish passport, Manuel J. Pires. In years past, Pires had handled secret CIA arms transfers to Angola, and later to both Iran and Iraq.

Hawk missiles and spare parts

For an effective counter-weight to Iraq's air campaign, Iran needed both spares for their older Hawk batteries and new Hawk missiles as well. As far as the Iran-Contra investigators determined, in the summer of 1985, Pires was the middleman in a shipment of Hawk parts that came from U.S. stockpiles. They were shipped to Iran through Brussels and West Germany. In October of that year, National Security Advisor, Bud McFarlane, approved another shipment of Hawk parts. The following month a CIA proprietary delivered 18 new Hawk missiles to Tehran.

Hawk transactions never ran smoothly, however. Oliver North wrote that this happened because the U.S. and Israeli private operatives "were unfamiliar with the operational parameters of the HAWK."[32] The weapons they agreed to ship were absolutely "inadequate" to meet Iranian requirements. In addition, Iran's military situation was critical: "The Iranian descriptions of the state of their equipment, lack of competent management, inability to use much of the remaining U.S. materiel portends the real possibility of a military collapse (at least by the Army) in the near to mid-term." Thus, North noted, "there is considerable pressure on the interlocutors in Europe to produce quickly."[33]

In late November 1985, North asked retired Air Force General Richard Secord to work with the Israelis on the Hawk program. Later the Israelis delivered 80 Hawks to Lisbon, Portugal. These Hawks were loaded on "three chartered aircraft, owned by a proprietary," North wrote, which then took off for Iran.[34] In March, the Iranians declared they desperately needed 240 types of spare parts for their stock of older Hawks. They were particularly anxious to get Klystron electron tubes, without which their older Hawks were so much scrap. However, finding parts for these weapons was not easy. Standard military supplies no longer carried them. In the middle of April 1986, North wrote that he was unable "to locate all the parts that Iran" wanted. The list was in the hands of both the CIA and the National Security Council.

Durrani's niche

Shortly after the Iranian revolution, Durrani became close to a number of the most important Iranian Revolutionary Guards who controlled Iran's military forces. He was particularly cozy with Rahim Malekzadeh, an engineer educated in Germany, who was in charge of logistics and was reportedly the second most important figure in the Revolutionary Guards. At times Durrani acted as an advisor or weapons inspector for Malekzadeh. He also gave Malekzadeh the use of a corporate credit card and a Swiss bank account through which millions of dollars passed as the Iranians paid for some of their logistical needs. To say the least, he was trusted by the Iranians. "Interlocutor" Pires was especially chummy with the Israelis, particularly Abraham Shavit who was based in Belgium and was the manager of a Belgium company called ASCO.[35]

The Iranian "interlocutor" handling the Hawk spare parts problem at this time was the notorious George Hassan. Under the Shah, Hassan had been the Chief of Police in Tehran, a Savak officer, and a CIA operative. During the Iranian revolution Hassan was detained by members of the Revolutionary Guards but soon released after a hefty bribe. He very quickly headed for Turkey and from there went to Germany and then briefly Austria. He finally moved to Portugal establishing himself in Lisbon. Either despite his past or because of it, Hassan had become the key weapons broker for Iran.

It was Hassan who first approached Durrani about helping on the Hawk spare parts problem. They met briefly in Portugal where Durrani was inspecting an Israeli shipment of Hawk missiles as a favor for Malekzadeh. Durrani was noncommittal; he had other business interests to tend. Hassan then told Pires to try and coax Durrani into cooperating. Pires sent various emissaries to him. Finally, after about eight months Durrani agreed to meet with Pires. Early in 1986 they finally met in Portugal. Durrani said he would help locate the parts. He was told he would get the list when he returned to the U.S. At Washington's National Airport, Durrani was handed the list by a National Security Council staffer. He went to work.

Durrani found many of the parts at the Radio Research Instrument Company in Danbury, Connecticut. This firm bought surplus military parts as scrap, and then sold the parts as reconditioned equipment. In making the deal with Radio Research Durrani lied, telling the company the parts were to be exported to Jordan and that he would soon have all the necessary papers and permits. Radio Research became suspicious and notified the U.S. Customs Service which put Durrani under heavy surveillance, tapping his phone calls to Radio Research and videotaping his meetings. The first shipment was allowed to proceed in order for Customs to trace its various permutations on the way to Iran. On August 29, Durrani was joined by Pires at Kennedy Airport to see the shipment off and to take care of any last minute problems. The cargo headed for Brussels where it was met by a Pires-affiliated company called Comexas.[36] New invoices were produced that showed the final destination was the National Iranian Oil Corporation. The parts were then loaded on a plane heading to Iran.

Between August 29 and October 3, 1986, when Customs nabbed him at Radio Research after he had arranged a second shipment, Durrani travelled to London where he says he met North who was using the alias Mr. White. At the meeting Mr. White urged him to move with dispatch in getting the parts.[37]

Trial and tribulation

The lead prosecutor in the Durrani trial was Assistant U.S. Attorney, Holly
Fitzsimmons; the judge was Chief Judge T. Gilroy Daly who ran a very tight
court. Daly refused to allow into evidence any of the emerging Iran-Contra
material. The prosecution did present a witnesses from the CIA, Charles
Moyer, who testified that "all the HAWK parts shipped by the CIA in 1986
were procured by the Agency in the month of May, and were transferred to
Israel for transshipment to Iran in May and August."[38] That was it for the
CIA. A National Security Council witness testified there were no records of
Oliver North being in London when Durrani claimed to have met him. That
was it for the NSC. The rest of the case was concerned with the desiderata
of the Radio Research deals. Audio and video tapes were played for the jury.
And then, it was all summed by the prosecution – with the Agency out of the
Hawk parts business before Durrani's first shipment, the transaction had to
represent a private, unsanctioned, illegal, greedy, criminal act.[39] Other proof
can be found in a once "secret" Israeli chronology of the Iranian transactions.
Amiran Nir, "the Prime Minister's advisor on Combatting Terrorism," was
the primary Israeli contact during what they called "the second stage" of
Iranian deals. There were three transactions that took place in this stage. It
is the second deal that is significant for Durrani's assertion. According to
the Israelis, the second was "the supply of spare parts for HAWK missiles
by the U.S. to Iran through Israel." They reported that this took place over
the course of three months – May through August 1986, although they also
point out that the stages and transactions always overlapped with one another
and thus there was "no clear and unequivocal distinction" between them. The
jury agreed and on May 13, 1987, Durrani was sentenced by Judge Daly to
ten years in prison and fined $2,000,000.

There are many codas to the Durrani case, however. The first has to do
with Pires. Durrani's team wanted him to appear as a witness for the defense.
But before the trial Pires was visited in Lisbon by both Fitzsimmons and
Special Agent Stephen Arruda from Customs. Pires gave them some telexes
and faxes that passed between Durrani and himself and then added that he
had nothing to do with the U.S. government, nothing to do with the U.S.
clandestine arms trade to Iran. Pires agreed to appear as a witness for the
prosecution, but only if he could testify from either Portugal or Spain. He
then decided not to testify at all. The defense began to wonder why Pires was
not indicted either as a co-conspirator or accessory. Fitzsimmons' answer was
that he was not a U.S. citizen and thus could not be charged with knowing that
the sale of the Hawk parts was against U.S. law.[40] This despite the seemingly
elementary fact that the Comexas airfreight manager, T. Van de Meerssche
averred to both Fitzsimmons and Arruda that Pires "gave instructions for all

respective freight to the respective freight forwarders involved," and that "Our [Comexas] instructions for forwarding were given only" by Pires and/or his representatives in Belgium.[41] Pires was therefore in charge of changing the false freight-forwarding documents, etc. Clearly, these were the actions of a co-conspirator. Fitzsimmons' explanation became even more retrospectively strange in light of subsequent events.

Precisely 56 days after Durrani was convicted, Pires turned up as a surprise visitor at the Federal prison in Phoenix, Arizona. At the request of Holly Fitzsimmons, Warden Carlson "approved a *one-time* visit for Mr. Manuel Pires to visit inmate DURRANI, Arif, Reg. No. 09027-014."[42] According to Durrani, Pires came to threaten him; according to Holly Fitzsimmons she ran into Pires at the Phoenix airport but had nothing to do with his visit. She did say to writer and reporter Lawrence Lifschultz that "it was not a coincidence that Pires, Arruda and herself were in Phoenix at the same time," and then added in a moment of lucidity that to have arranged this visit would have denied Durrani his constitutional rights.[43] Later Pires admitted visiting Durrani, but he said he did it "officially... through the legal channel," but he denied having met with Fitzsimmons and/or Arruda.[44] The warden said the visit had been arranged by Durrani's attorney, the "lady attorney," which clearly would have been news to Bill Bloss and Ira Grudberg. In addition to confronting Durrani, Pires may have been in Arizona to meet with General Singlaub because they were both working on the little-noticed Renamo hostage crisis in Mozambique. In a recent interview, Louis Serapiano, Renamo's representative in the U.S., stated that he spoke to Pires who called him from the U.S. Custom's office in Newark, New Jersey in the summer of 1987. Any way one looks at it, the Arizona interlude was exceptionally peculiar.

Curious episodes

There are still more odd occurrences. The Customs officer who was really in charge of law enforcement's Durrani operation was John B. "Joe" King although his name was redacted from the Studley deposition mentioned above and only appears in one of the Durrani court documents and government papers. Although he was present at Durrani's arrest, he was never called as a witness. There was a concerted effort to keep King on the extreme outside of the Durrani case for two reasons. King, a former New York City policeman, was part of a highly-secret team, a special multi-agency task force sometimes described as an "anti-terrorist unit," established in the late 1970s to track weapons sales to South Africa and Iran. Among the companies set up by King (who had many code names) and his team was Fino Enterprises in New York, an arms brokering firm. The team was "allowed to kidnap suspects, make deals to drop charges against arms merchants and even sell arms to Iran," all supposedly for the purpose of controlling the illicit traffic.[45] Second, King and members of his team worked closely with Barbara Studley and her weapons operation. At least one "secret team" member was actually hired by her in September 1986. And he has stated that all of his activities were cleared by "U.S. Government officials."[46] To complete the circle, Larry Barcella is one of King's strongest supporters. Barcella told me that King worked with him on the Letelier case, that he has known him for more than 20 years, that he believes King is the "most imaginative and effective federal investigator" he's ever known, and that they worked the October Surprise investigation for Representative Lee Hamilton's congressional committee. Barcella added that he would not have worked on the investigation without King and so told Hamilton.[47]

Of course it is difficult to fathom why anyone would place much faith in Hamilton's judgement on the staffing of his October Surprise investigation given his early performance in the Iran-Contra scandal. In the summer of 1986, Hamilton was easily beguiled by North into believing that he had nothing to do with illegal aid to the Contras. Following Hamilton's meeting with North in the White House Situation Room in August 1986, NSC counsel Bob Pearson remarked that Hamilton "underlined his appreciation to Admiral [John M. Poindexter] and to Bud [McFarlane] for full cooperation offered by NSC." Hamilton did not think there was any merit in media reports of North's illicit activities and was prepared to recommend that Congress mind its own business.[48]

Examining the Durrani case places one inside the always confusing and often inept world of weapons dealers made up of brokers, deal makers, hustlers and grifters who mixed and mingled with spies from every intelligence service in the world. Services that were insular and crime ridden. Services in which just about any action could be and was justified. Services, as Arthur Schlesinger, Jr. once described the CIA, in which men were "professionally trained in deception, a wide choice of weapons, reckless purposes, global charter, maximum funds and minimum accountability."[49] To put it most mildly, this has always been a volatile mix. Secret weapons projects are never neat and tidy, always unkempt, prone to breakdown, riddled through with profit takers. One thing is certain, however. Selling weapons to Iran by official representatives of the U.S., with the approval of the Administration, no matter the ways in which involvement was hidden, started before the Palestinians and/or their supporters took a single U.S. hostage in Lebanon. As I will show, this is the history lesson buried in the details of the Durrani case and its aftermath which continues on leveraging secret documents and finding secret people.

The Iran side[50]

When it comes to the Iran side of Iran-Contra, neither the Tower Commission, nor the Independent Counsel, nor the congressional committees that investigated the ensuing scandals, got it right. The U.S. sale of weapons to Iran was assuredly begun prior to the hostage taking in Lebanon. There is some intimation of this in a Congressional Research Service paper written by Richard M. Preece in January 1984 and updated that August. Preece noted that by 1983 a considerable illicit traffic in U.S. arms to Iran had developed. "American companies were using South Korea and Israel as cut outs for both new weapons and spare parts sent to Iran."[51] This was certainly common knowledge in the region, for Preece wrote that Iraqi officials were disturbed by this traffic and angered that Washington had done nothing about it. In March 1984, he noted, the State Department gave Richard Fairbanks, Ambassador-at-large, the job of pressuring Israel and the "friendly Asian states" to cut it out.[52] But while there might have been some arms traffickers in Western Europe cutting their own deals, there is little doubt that many of the transactions in which American firms were using Israel and South Korea, and other nations, to mask their sales were known and approved by U.S. Intelligence and the Reagan Administration. In the main, this was not an illicit nor an illegal traffic.

Barbara Studley and GeoMiliTech

The first U.S. plan to provide Iran with U.S. weapons was prior to August 15, 1983, the date when an ostensibly private company was formed in Delaware, which actively sought either to sell or exchange weapons with Iran as well as to supply the Contras.[53] The firm, GeoMiliTech Consultants Corporation (GMT), was established by Barbara F. Studley, the former beauty queen from Miami who became a conservative radio talk show host for WNWS in South Florida. In 1984, she claimed to have had fifteen years as a "political lobbyist" including eleven working the Pentagon. Studley was GMT's President. According to its 1984 brochure, the company had corporate offices in Washington, D.C. and Tel Aviv, Israel. Before it moved to Washington, it was located in Miami Lakes, Florida. The 1984 brochure also claimed four Regional Offices and Affiliated Agencies established in Brussels, Frankfurt, Seoul, and Tel Aviv.

In addition to President Studley, GMT's corporate structure by then included an Executive Vice President, two Vice Presidents, a Secretary-Treasurer, and four consultants. The Executive Vice President was Ron S. Harel, a veteran of the Israeli Air Force who specialized in "tactical cargo and light and early warning aircraft." He was also the co-pilot of the C-130 that rescued Israeli hostages in the famous raid on Entebbe, Uganda. Since the late 1970s, Harel reportedly was a consultant to a number of "leading U. S. Defense Department contractors" particularly helpful in the field of international marketing. Harel was in charge of GMT's Tel Aviv office and also headed his own development firm called Maced Marketing Consultancy & Development located in Ramat-Gan, Israel. Harel was officially brought into the GMT fold on May 11, 1984, when GMT established "branch offices of the Corp., including but not limited to an office in Israel."[54] On the same date, GMT's corporate minutes reflect the decision to set up bank accounts in foreign countries including Israel. GMT's bank in Tel Aviv was the Israel Discount Bank Ltd.

Navy Captain Bruce E. Herbert was one of the Vice Presidents. Herbert was described as "a recognized authority on intra-theater airlift to support deployed combat forces." Herbert, a naval aviator, had retired from the Navy but was called back to active duty on several occasions including the Falkland Islands War where he worked on "Foreign Military Sales and Precision Guided Munitions." Herbert also had coordinated modernization plans for the Air Force, Army, and Navy while assigned to the Pentagon. Finally, he had been a staff member for a standing House Committee not, however, identified.

The other Vice President was Joel Arnon who had been an Assistant Director General in the Israeli Ministry of Foreign Relations. According to GMT's announcement, Arnon had around 30 years of experience in Israel's Diplomatic Service including work with the Israeli Mission to the United Nations. From 1976 to 1983, he was described as Israel's Consul General for the Southeastern U.S. At the time of his initial relationship with GMT, Arnon was also the Executive Vice President of GTL, Global Technologies, Ltd.

Global was a mirror company of GMT, controlled by Studley who laid out the "inter-working conditions between GMT and GTL" in a memo to both Harel and Arnon. While Harel was in charge of GMT's Tel Aviv office, located in a building called the Asia House at 4 Weizman Street, Arnon would be a GMT consultant. On July 1, 1984, Arnon was to "begin working for Global Technologies" from an office in Jerusalem. Harel would then become a consultant to GTL. Studley was insistent that "GTL and GMT remain separate corporations with separate identifications, addresses, phones, etc."

The rest of GMT's initial corporate structure was composed of four consultants: Major General George J. Keegan, Jr, USAF (retired); Major General John Kirk Singlaub, USA (retired); John E. Carbaugh, Jr.; and Louis F. Petrillo. Keegan was a former head of Air Force Intelligence who was a "leader in efforts to revise the faulty U.S. estimates about the Soviet quest for military superiority, shortfalls in judgement of Soviet spending for defense, violations of SALT agreements and massive deception of the Free World and the

USSR's efforts to exploit détente." Not surprisingly, Keegan retired in 1977, and then served in various capacities with conservative organizations such as the journal "Strategic Review," the Peace Through Strength Coalition, and as President of the Institute of Strategic Affairs.

Major General Singlaub had been Chief of Staff, U.N. Command, U.S. Forces in Korea, and the head of the U.S. Eighth Army in Seoul, Korea. During the Vietnam War, he was the "Commander of the Joint Unconventional Warfare Task Force." Before Vietnam, Singlaub was Deputy Chief of the CIA mission in Korea, and before that, China Desk Officer for the CIA. Left out of the brochure was Singlaub's creation of a new American chapter called the United States Council for World Freedom (USCWF) of the World Anti-Communist League at a meeting in Phoenix, Arizona, on November 21, 1981. The Vice-Chairman of the USCWF was Lieutenant Daniel O. Graham, formerly head of the Defense Intelligence Agency. To get the USCWF ball rolling, Taiwan lent it around $20,000.[55] By 1986, Singlaub had become the head of the World Anti-Communist League.[56]

Attorney John E. Carbaugh (who had a reputation for mental peculiarity) worked for eight years as Senator Jesse Helms Administrative Aide. He was thus a Professional Staff Member of the Senate Foreign Relations Committee and the Senate Armed Services Committee. With Ronald Reagan's election, Carbaugh served on the Transition Team for State, Defense, and the National Security Council. Studley noted that Carbaugh "brings to GMT a direct contact to the political and military structure of foreign governments, as well as a comprehensive insight into the inner workings of the United States government." She added that "[h]e is currently a consultant to major U.S. corporations involved in national security" and to the State and Defense Departments.[57] The GMT office in Washington, opened early in 1984, was adjacent to Carbaugh's law office.[58]

The final listed GMT consultant in its initial phase was banker Louis F. Petrillo. At that time he was Vice President and Director of International Services for Florida National Bank.

The Organized Crime element

Over the course of GMT's life, there would be other renowned military figures – Army Lt. General Robert L. Schweitzer who was once the Director of Strategy Policy and Plans, the Deputy Chief of Staff for Operations and Plans and enjoyed a post in the Reagan White House, comes to mind – springing up as consultants.[59]

But likely far more important was I. Irving Davidson who was never listed on any GMT paper at all. Davidson was a mobster's dream – "grease for the machinery," he once described himself – although his closest organized crime associate, the infamous Carlos Marcello, ended up behind bars. Writer John H. Davis thought Davidson was "the epitome of the Washington lobbyist, a schemer and promoter with a vast international network of powerful acquaintances" that included Persian Gulf potentates and the Sultan of Oman, tin-pot dictators from Central America and "Mafia bosses."[60] Davidson lobbied for the Teamsters Union and Jimmy Hoffa, Anastasio Somoza, "Papa Doc" Duvalier, and Rafael Trujillo, and he sold Israeli tanks to Nicaragua.[61] He knew everyone of importance in Washington and Israel; weapons were his metier.

On Saturday June 23, 1984, at a swanky Washington hotel, he spent some time with Barbara Studley, Ron Harel and General Keegan. The conversation covered a number of topics but finally got around to "technical sales representations."[62] A couple of months later, Studley once again met with Davidson. In between those meetings, Davidson spent time with several notorious organized crime figures including Abe Gordon, a Teamster official and top New York mobster.[63] Studley and Davidson kept in touch. They had a chat, for example, at GMT's office in October 1985. Perhaps Davidson's most interesting close friend, however, was Joseph Francis Nesline the leader of organized crime in Washington, D.C.

Nesline was born in Washington in 1913 and became a bootlegger during Prohibition. Following Repeal, Nesline who was a gambling manager opened illegal casinos in the Washington area. He also killed one of his rivals in the winter of 1951 during a dispute in a gambling club in the Northwest section of Washington. The homicide helped establish Nesline's reputation in the District.[64] From then on he was Washington's most menacing organized criminal. Nesline's closest associate was a New Jersey born gangster named Charles Tourine.[65] A formidable organized crime figure himself, Tourine was part of a gang of New Jersey racketeers led by Ruggiero Boiardo which was affiliated with the New York Genovese crime syndicate. Gambling was one of Tourine's specialties and he operated casinos in Havana in the pre-Castro days. Tourine, like Nesline, found opportunity everywhere. In 1976 he and several former federal and state officials from Alaska were charged with conspiring to establish organized prostitution and gambling for Alaska's pipeline workers.[66] Nesline and his associates also exerted a strong influence on the underworlds of Amsterdam[67] and Hamburg during the 1970s. The primary contact in Hamburg was Wilfried Schulz who owned restaurants in Hamburg's red-light district , and was a fight manager, a thief, pimp, gambler, and extortionist. Another Nesline connection in Hamburg was Davoud Dargahi born in Teheran in 1932. Dargahi had been living in Hamburg since 1957 and was associated with Schulz in organizing boxing matches and various criminal activities.[68] Moreover, Iranian authorities claimed Dargahi was involved in the smuggling of heroin to the U.S.[69] Nesline's criminal activities were primarily gambling, narcotics trafficking, pornography, prostitution, and the fight game.[70]

Obviously, Davidson had the talent and pluck to move in political power centers like the National Security Council, the Department of Defense, the GeoMiliTech crowd and in the world of Jimmy Hoffa, Carlos Marcello, and Joe Nesline. Davidson was, when all was said and done, both a tutor and facilitator for GMT.

All manner of secret deals

Although not officially in GMT's ranks until May 1984, Ron Harel worked with and for GMT from 1983 until the beginning of 1986. Indeed, according to Harel, his first meeting with Studley took place in Miami where the discussion centered on selling "M48-A5 tanks to Iran" using Israel and Korea as the cover.[71] Somewhere along the line there was a draft proposal concerning the tanks which stated the following:

> The Israel Ministry of Defense, Export Division, hereby acknowledges that GeoMiliTech Consultants Corporation (GMT) of 1919 Pennsylvania Ave., N.W., Washington, D.C. USA, has been granted the authority to present to the Government of Korea [the cutout for Iran] the following:
>
> 1. Technology of upgrading and modifying of M-47, M-48 tanks.
> 2. Systems and spare parts relating to M-47, M-48 tanks.
> 3. Technology of the Merkava tank.
> 4. Systems and spare parts relating to the Merkava tank.
>
> In addition, GMT, is hereby authorized to discuss the possibility of a joint venture with the government of Israel or their appointed foreign corporation.

Harel stated that Bruce Herbert, who ran GMT's Washington office when it first opened (either in January or February 1984), traveled to London to meet an Iranian middleman, E.J. Bajzert, in order to negotiate the deal. Bajzert was in contact with the London office of the National Iranian Oil Company (NIOC) on Victoria Street which handled the international network and housed a clandestine group of Revolutionary Guards running the show. The Iranians used NIOC accounts to pay for weapons and supplies.

Herbert's idea was to trade 200 tanks for Iran's fleet of U.S. built F-14 fighter aircraft.[72] The F14s had been bought by the Shah from the Grumman Aerospace Corporation during the 1970s. The tanks would be supplied by Israel, the cutout in the transaction.[73] To understand the background of this complicated plan, it is helpful to briefly review the Grumman-Iran deal. Back in 1974 Grumman sold 80 F-14s to Iran.[74] Grumman delivered 79, the last one in 1978. At Iran's request the 80th plane was kept in the U.S. for testing and further engineering.[75] The Shah paid $2.2 billion for the planes and the training and maintenance services that were crucial.[76] A scandal over the sale erupted in 1976 when it was announced that Grumman had paid "foreign agents" $6 million to make the deal despite the Shah's strong objections to this practice. On the heels of this disclosure, it was learned that Defense Secretary James R. Schlesinger upped Iran's "share of research and development costs involved in F-14 production," because he was angry with OPEC's 1973 rise in the price of oil. Finally, a State Department cable to the Pentagon's Foreign Military Sales Office that ordered price parity for the F-14, so that Iran was charged no more than the Navy paid, was "administratively misplaced" for almost a year.[77]

As the Iranian revolution gained steam in late 1978, one of the revolutionaries' targets was Grumman's headquarters in Isfahan which they firebombed. *Washington Post* reporter William Branigan wrote "that some of the U.S. weaponry supplied to Iran had been sabotaged,[78] although he did not indicate by whom. According to one source, Iran's F14 fleet had been targeted by U.S. Intelligence while another source alleges that Iranian military officers still loyal to the Shah destroyed the training and test manuals and, more importantly, the coded taped program (AWG9) that ran the fire control system which allowed the F-14 to identify six different targets at the same time and to fire both Sparrow and Phoenix missiles with deadly accuracy. The source added that some of the F-14s were still in their original crates and never were operational. Whether these were so or not, it is certain that U.S. military intelligence was profoundly concerned with the F-14s' formidable Phoenix missiles. Indeed, Grumman was attempting to get the missiles back through a Canadian company that was very close to the Canadian government. In the midst of these delicate negotiations, Grumman was charged by the Securities and Exchange Commission, in January 1979, for having paid somewhat more than $24 million "in secret commissions to sales agents" who had worked the F-14 sale to the Shah. It turned out the $6 million in illegal payments revealed in 1976 was only the first payment.[79] The Canadian ploy fell apart.

The F-14 saga is not quite over yet. In the waning days of 1981, after some serious setbacks in its war with Iraq, Iran sent a letter to Grumman's London office asking to buy spare parts for the F-14s. Iran's useable F-14s only numbered about nine and they were not flown in combat against Iraq. Instead, they were used as "control aircraft, with their advanced radar and electronics guiding other planes to their targets or warning the pilots of Iraqi aircraft attacks."[80] What kept the other 70 or so aircraft grounded was a combination of the missing program and the lack of spare parts, the latter of which were absolutely crucial. There was an added element to the F-14 issue by the time Herbert proposed the operation. The Navy had a new aircraft carrier but Grumman was not able to supply the required number of F14s.

This was the very complicated situation when GMT went into action. To get the ball rolling, Herbert, who it is said represented Naval Intelligence's interest in the matter, devised a code the better to hide the Iranian issue from prying eyes as correspondence was sent around the world. The overall Iranian deal was called The Chess Game. Juice meant explosives, while Mother stood for rocket launchers, and Children translated to missiles and rockets. Castle was Herbert's code name, Cleopatra was Studley's. Prince was Manuel J. Pires. Project Sea Lion was code for the proposed tank deal with Iran as were certain references to Taiwan and Korea. Albatross stood for the Grumman F14 transaction. Bishop was Iran.

Back and forth the talk went. Harel and Herbert had several meetings with Bajzert who finally informed them that Iran agreed to swap part of the F14 fleet for the tanks – all but 30 planes – and wanted spare parts for the remainder.[81] Either the Navy and/or Grumman and/or Herbert said no. It was over this issue that the deal finally floundered. Herbert left GMT sometime after July 1984. He says that Studley fired him when the deal fell through but other insiders suggest he left because the Navy's interest had waned. In either case, Studley informed Harel there was "[n]o way it can fly–our end will not supply spares for the remaining fleet."[82]

Before he left GMT, however, Herbert sent a status report of "all realizable Washington sales activities" of which he was aware. Because GMT was an Intelligence-based operation – a third channel as Bruce Herbert likes to characterize it – activities were strictly compartmentalized; only Studley and perhaps Singlaub and CIA Director Bill Casey knew everything. Herbert reported there were ten on-going activities including a Hawk aircraft one with Iran that had the potential to bring into GMT's coffers $5,875,000.[83]

GMT's role in the Hawk operation was to act as a middleman for Michael Austin the owner of Austin Aerospace. Studley informed Harel that Austin gave GMT a six month exclusive to handle the Hawk presenting it to "Taiwan, Korea, Israel, Morocco, Pakistan, Zaire, Peru, Ecuador, Yugoslavia, Guatemala, Philippines, and possibly South Africa. She added that "20 'HAWKS' can fit in a Boeing 747 in crates – can 'fly out of box'. Wings can be reassembled in minutes."[84]

That summer there were several other Iranian-based initiatives in the works, in addition to the Hawk proposition. One had to do with explosives, another with J79 and JF17 jet engines for F-4 aircraft that were to be supplied to Iran and a third concerned helicopters. On the latter issue Harel wrote to

Studley, on September 13, 1984, that he had "met with Teamco from Brussels and the Bell-Textron Helicopters President who reassured me that he would back us for our program in Iran and that we should come up with a proposal and plan to sell new Bell helicopters thru Teamco to Iran." He added that Westland helicopters "are seeking our assistance in selling helicopters to Iran (there is no conflict of interest with Bell since this is a bird of a different feather) and we shall work both."[85] (Actually, Westland's boss, Roger James, had allegedly already signed a contract with Iran for 36 helicopters and now "needed" GMT's "assistance in execution and performance.") Studley responded pointing out that one million dollars was hanging in the balance on both the explosives (fertilizer) and the jet engine arrangements. She was anxious, she told Harel, for any information.[86]

The complexity of GMT's activities was growing. For example, GMT had already entered into co-operative relations with both Teamco in Brussels, and Truventa A.G., a firm headquartered in Basel, Switzerland, owned by the Berger brothers who had exceptionally good connections with Iran. Likely their connections had been materially helped by their partner, George Hassan. The companies had signed contracts with Iran to supply spare parts and perform maintenance on Bell's helicopters.

Of all the firms in Europe selling weapons to Iran, Teamco might have been one of the most significant for it was supposedly a somewhat vaguely hidden large-scale Israeli Government operation. Of course Teamco and Truventa also provided another layer of camouflage for yet other companies working with Iran. For example, Stork facilities and Israel Aircraft Industries' (IAI) engine division were interested in contracts to overhaul the jet engines everyone thought were about to be bought by Iran. But Stork needed the "permission of its principals, Fabrique National," and IAI required "a European intermediate organization . . . to protect the source identification."[87]

The "full partnership" between GMT and Truventa covered all programs in Iran and Peru, the latter ones having to do with both the military and the police. Truventa was important for at least three reasons: the first was the Bergers' and Hassan's influence in Iran, the second was that it hid GMT's involvement. "For various known reasons," wrote Ron Harel, " both programs, Peru and Iran, shall be conducted through Truventa."[88] And third, GMT sold 22 jet engines to Truventa for around $40 million leaving GMT with a profit of $5,040,000.

In a few months there was another game on. This one featured reconstituted F-4s with additional spare engines. The transaction was in the hands of Austin Aerospace and GMT was a potential player. Austin was going to buy the F-4s from Egypt and sell them to Iran after running them (or the paper) through Turkey. In November, Austin Aerospace telexed Harel further details

about the F-4. Austin pointed out this offer would go to "3 other groups who-
ever comes in first that is who we are going to proceed with." Hidden behind
this chatter was the simple fact that Austin Aerospace was under the sway of
a cabal of former CIA and Defense Department swindlers who controlled the
transport of U.S. weapons to Egypt. Intriguingly, General Singlaub played
with the cabal when it came to Austin Aerospace. He was on its Board of
Directors.

There were 18 F-4s "overhauled as of last December 1983; there are spare
parts sufficient for 18 months operation." There were 20 spare engines. For
the entire transaction, the cost to the Iranians was over $300 million.[89] For
GMT to play, it had to come up with a serious and irrevocable letter of credit
which it did not do.[90]

One of the Iranian proposals that GMT capped was for the explosives
which appears to have been negotiated either in late 1983 or early 1984. On
February 14, 1984, Scandinavian Commodity, headed by Karl-Erik Schmitz
and located in Malmo, Sweden, sent a confirmation letter on this matter to
Ron Harel. The arrangement was for 2,000 metric tons of propellant for
155mm howitzers. It would be sent in plastic bags placed in cardboard boxes
on pallets in new containers painted white. The only printing on the containers
would be "SCANCOM"; there would not be any other marks or labels. The
price was $6.80 per kilo. The payment: "Net cash against presentation of
documents with Kredietbank, Luxembourg against irrevocable letter of credit
opened by Bank Melli (Iranian bank) London in buyers favour." The material
would be loaded on board a ship at a Dutch port and delivered to "southern
Iranian ports." Any problems "shall be constructed and decided in conformity
with the Iranian laws and also the place of jurisdiction will be in Iran."

Overall, GMT was pleased with the progress of the transaction although
there were some matters that had to be changed. Perhaps the most important
had to do with the Bank Melli and letters of credit (L/C). On the 25th of
July, GMT wrote to Schmitz the following: "Sub. Financial arrangements.
1) As discussed during our meeting in Vienna, neither IMI [Israel Military
Industries] nor Hirtenberger [one of IMI's chiefs] can receive Bank Melli's
direct L/C. It must be an L/C obtained by a European bank. If this issue
is solved then there are no problems whatsoever."[91] Over the course of a
few months, the deal had also grown a bit larger and even more complex.
There was now more material – 3,000 metric tons of T.N.T., fuses, and 81
and 120 mm mortar flare shells, and two types of 155 mm howitzer shells.[92]
Interestingly enough, some of the material in the transaction (not the T.N.T. or
155 mm shells, however) might have been produced at the U.S. Army arsenal
in Radford, Virginia, operated by Hercules.[93]

GeoMiliTech covered its tracks well when it came to its relationship with Scandinavian Commodity and Mr. Schmitz as can be seen when this particular Iranian exchange was exposed in 1987. A Reuters dispatch from Stockholm noted that Swedish Customs authorities were claiming "that Israel had sold millions of dollars worth of explosives, artillery ammunition and shell components to Iran through a Swedish middleman between 1984 and 1986." Israel heatedly denied the charge although the Swedes had seized documents that clearly implicated Israel Military Industries. (Reuters and the Swedes did not know, of course, that Israel's Ministry of Defense had a secret signed "understanding" with Major General Singlaub representing GMT[94] and that GMT itself had an agreement with the Ministry concerning the marketing of tanks mentioned earlier). One of the documents that showed IMI's involvement also detailed a series of subterfuges used in the operation. The actual orders for the explosives came from Sweden's largest arms company, Bofors, "with which Schmitz was closely associated." Other documents disclosed the shipments were supposedly bound from Western Europe to the Yugoslavian port of Bar.[95] There was no mention of GeoMiliTech which was well hidden behind Scandinavian Commodity, IMI, and Yugoslavia which came into the picture as the supplier of the most significant product in the deal – the 155 mm long range howitzer shells. The Yugoslav side was handled by Igor Schou Kjeldsen, affiliated with GMT and Scandinavian Commodity, who knew his way around Yugoslavia's Federal Directorate of Supply and Procurement, a part of the Federal Secretariat of National Defense. On July 18, 1984, the Federal Directorate in Belgrade sent Igor a copy of Scandinavian Commodity contract – No. V-2/MBL/DS-1.

The transaction was done; the items delivered to Iran; the profits deposited. Harel sent a telex saying all went smoothly; Studley responded–"Happy days."

"Better to have one's own capital"

Barbara Studley prepared the ground to hide money earned by GMT in 1984. The first step was to hook up with Jean B. de la Giroday who lived in Bethesda Maryland. His resume indicates a Ph.D. in international finance from Oxford University and many years experience with Eurodollar bond issues. It also shows seven years as the Managing Director of Banque Cantrade, Geneva, the founding of a Nigerian merchant bank dubbed the African Banking Company Ltd., and, the creation of the Turks and Caicos Banking Company Ltd (T&CBC).

While he may have indeed "structured and created" T&CBC, he was apparently never an owner of record. According to the T&CBS's 1983 brochure, it was established in Dec. 1980, and capitalized at US $500,000. "With significant business growth, the capital has been increased to US$2.65m," noted the brochure. There were two main shareholders: (1) "The Union Planters National Bank of Memphis, Tennessee, a leading regional bank with assets of over US $1.7 billion," and (2) "Motorships, Inc. of Monrovia, Liberia, wholly owned by Mr. Nils O. Seim," characterized by retired British banker David Whitby "as a secretive Norwegian shipping tycoon." Seim was Chairman of the Board of Directors of the Turks and Caicos Banking Company. One of its directors was William M. Matthews Jr., "chairman & CEO of Union Planters National Bank [UPNB]." Its other officers included Eustace A. Brooks, secretary (British American Life Insurance Company); general manager, Anton J.B. Faessler, "formerly of Zurich, Switzerland." Whitby recollected that "Faessler may have been ex-Banque Cantrade (merchant bank subsidiary of Union Bank of Switzerland.) At some point in the 1980s, Seim died and Bill Matthews left the Board of the Union Planters National Bank. When Matthews exited Union Planters, it sold out its investments in T&CNB as well as in a Paris financial company (Finacor) and a countertrade firm in Nigeria called Unitrade.

Studley's second step was the incorporation on December 10, 1984, of a Turks and Caicos company called Consulentia Ltd., whose sole director was Giroday.[96] Next she contacted Harel to tell him that he was the only one who could use Consulentia and the only one who would know about it, except, of course, for Giroday, Florida banker Petrillo, and Terence Donegan who was their attorney in the Turks and Caicos. She added that Harel was never to mention Consulentia over the phone or in a telex; never to call Donegan from Harel's office; and never to mention his name to Donegan if calling from another source. He was only to say "C.L. Corp." Consulentia, she literally underlined, must not be linked to his office, and, she further pointed out that there were *no records of the firm in the Washington office*.[97]

Consulentia raises other somewhat confusing but potentially dramatic issues in the burgeoning off-shore world Giroday constructed for Studley. Recollect that Giroday claimed in his c.v., that Banque Cantrade (Zurich) "asked" him to "*to create, structure and develop Banque Cantrade, Geneva. He did so and was the Geneva manager from 1970 through 1977.* What makes this extraordinary is the following: when Robert Vesco was busy looting Bernie Cornfeld's tottering mutual fund empire, Investors Overseas Services, he used the services of "Consulentia a sub of Banque Cantrade."[98] Vesco testified that in December 1970, he first approached George Phillipe, a "senior official at Bank Cantrade, a subsidiary of Union Bank" of Switzerland, "to determine if it had an interest in purchasing the Cornfeld shares."[99] Then, a few days before the closing on Cornfeld's stock in January 1971, it was reported that a shell corporation, Linkink Progressive Corporation S.A., was bought from Consulentia, the deal having been arranged by Phillipe.[100] Actually, Linkink was sold to the Vesco team by a Panamanian company, Red Pearl Bay, "whose principals have never been identified," although Phillipe was surely one of them.[101] The shifting from Consulentia to Red Pearl Bay was accomplished by Vesco and the Banque Cantrade gang to add another layer of almost impenetrable secrecy to their purchase of 6,000,000 Cornfeld-held IOS shares which had to be hidden from the purview of Union Bank's top officials. Linkink's usefulness quickly came to an end when it was bought by something called American Interland whose name was almost immediately changed to Hemispheres Financial.[102]

Consulentia needed a bank account. In the first week of February, 1985, Studley had Giroday instruct a lawyer in Zurich, Dr. Michel Haymann, to open an account for Consulentia at Bank Leu's branch in Zurich. The name of the account was "Lewistown-9020-40418-0." Haymann was to be the permanent and only custodian of the Lewistown records. On March 5th she wrote Haymann a "confidential" letter informing him that Ron Harel was to have total authority over the account. Furthermore, Harel's instructions had to be given in person at the bank and he had to present two proofs for verification of his identity: his Israeli passport number, 1373864, and the double account code. Harel was also allowed to phone in instructions from Israel but had to go through a very elaborate double call system replete with codes. Finally, she wrote "*[p]lease note that under no circumstances must my name ever be revealed to the bank as the beneficial owner of the account* [her emphasis]."

Consulentia and the Lewistown account were set up for several reasons. One was to hide money from others at GMT; another, as Ron Harel said, was both "to avoid taxes in the U.S." and scrutiny "because the transactions were not legal in the United States"[103] Money was moved back and forth between Consulentia and another GMT account named "Claude" at the Banque Nationale de Paris in Geneva, Switzerland, and likely others yet unknown as well. Handling "Claude" was Eddy Maisonneuve, BNP's *Sous Directeur*. On May 16, 1985, Studley cabled Maisonneuve to advise him "of confirmation received. . . transfer of $3.3 million to 'Claude.' "[104] A couple of weeks later, Harel sent a note to Paul Husser at Bank Leu, Zurich, in order to transfer funds from "Lewistown 9020-40418-0" into "Claude" at BNP.[105]

She was very good at concealing money and, it turned out, borrowing but not repaying large sums. In 1987, banker Petrillo started on his long slide to prison because of loans or money transfers to Studley who did not repay them. While the head of finance for GMT, Petrillo had moved from Florida National Bank to the Bayshore Bank of Florida, a small Miami-area institution. The year before, 1986, Petrillo had transferred $2 million from Bayshore to an overseas bank at the request of Studley. Unfortunately for Bayshore's depositors, this was about all of the bank's net worth.[106] Bayshore was crashing and hardly anyone besides the malefactors, it seems, knew where the money went, what it was used for, and whether it would ever be repaid.

It really was not much of a mystery. Petrillo gave Studley a $2 million line of credit when he was with Florida National. Studley used the money to pay GemoMiliTech's salaries and to purchase a house in Falls Church, Virginia. Studley hoped to make a profit and repay the loan. When Petrillo left Florida National he illegally changed the paperwork moving or converting Studley's "past due" account to Bayshore. He did it to gain some time while waiting for Studley to pay up. She did not, of course, although she did try but failed to sell around 20 percent of GMT's stock to raise the $2 million.

Bayshore stockholders filed a couple of lawsuits naming Petrillo, Geo-MiliTech, Studley, and General Singlaub as the irresponsible parties. They finally learned the $2 million was to cover two "bad checks" written by Studley, and that Petrillo gave her a $1.5 million cashier's check from Bayshore in order to hide a depleted $1.5 million line of credit he gave her when he was with Florida National Bank.[107] They got nothing from the lawsuits.

These financial flip flops took place as GeoMiliTech presented Bill Casey its ultimate plan – a coordinated series of weapons deals worth $80 million, many of them barter arrangements with Israel, all of them worked through a secret Swiss bank, the whole package guaranteed to evade the "consent or awareness of the Department of State or Congress."[108] The program was hand-delivered to Casey by Edward N. Luttwak, now a distinguished author and Senior Fellow in Preventive Diplomacy at the Center For Strategic & International Studies in Washington; then described as an employee of Geo-MiliTech. "He has served as a consultant to the Office of the Secretary of Defense, the National Security Council, and the U.S. Department of State. He is an associate of the Japan Finance Ministry's Institute of Fiscal and Monetary Policy. Dr. Luttwak is a frequent lecturer at universities and higher military colleges in the United States and abroad (recently in Argentina, Italy, France, Japan, and the United Kingdom). He was the 1988 Nimitz lecturer at the University of California, Berkeley, and 1989 Tanner lecturer at Yale University. He is author of eight books, including *The Endangered American Dream* (Simon & Schuster, 1993), *Strategy: The Logic of War and Peace* (Harvard University Press, 1985), and the constantly reprinted *Coup d'etat* (Harvard University Press, 1985), published in 14 languages. He serves on the editorial boards of *Geopolitique* (France), the *Journal of Strategic Studies*, and the *Washington Quarterly*. He received a Ph.D. from the Johns Hopkins University. He speaks French, Italian, and Spanish."

Petrillo went to prison for six months after pleading guilty to fraud. Studley and Singlaub, to the contrary, have carried on like old troopers. Most recently they have been peddling a "revolutionary missile guidance software system" developed by Rabbi Eliot Sherman, a U.S. citizen resident in Israel, and an unidentified associate. Working with them are Fob James, Jr., the Governor of Alabama, and Alabama's First Lady, Bobbie James, who are reportedly close friends of the Rabbi. In 1997, the Rabbi hosted the Alabama couple on a trip to Israel during which Bobbie James noted "Alabama's close ties with Israel have resulted in blessings like better student test scores. . . ."[109] This year the Governor arranged "an unusual meeting" in Washington, reported Brett Davis of the *Huntsville Times*, with both Washington military officials and Alabama's congressional delegation. Studley and Singlaub attended the meeting during which a request was made for more than $3 million from next year's defense budget to test Rabbi Sherman's guidance system.

Summary

Weapons are very big business although GeoMiliTech never seems to have hit the really big time either because the competition was too tough and equally well connected, or because its leadership was not all that competent. There were plenty of CIA "proprietaries" in the field, and many Israeli covert firms and operations that had been around for some time. Indeed, the Israelis had put in place Bahamian cover for weapons sales no later than 1972 when they formed the General Aviation Corporation Ltd. on July 11th of that year. The shareholders included a couple of New York attorneys, Yigal Dimant listed as an English merchant with a company called Lisbona Ltd., and several firms such as Intercontinental Aircraft Limited and Atlantic Pacific Aviation Corporation. Among the company directors in 1972 were Adolph Schwimmer and Moshe Nirim.[110]

Later on GeoMiliTech would have to compete with General Secord and his unseemly crowd who took a while to get started in the Iran-Contra game. They had to hold back because they had to extricate themselves from a potentially damaging investigation into crimes they committed as the transporters of U.S. weapons to Egypt following the Camp David Egypt/Israel peace treaty. Their transport company was named EATSCO. To save themselves they "greymailed" the White House by threatening to reveal bribes and kickbacks they had paid to extremely high Egyptian officials. This effectively killed the investigation but it did take some time. I must add that Larry Barcella helped in their resurrection and it was the EATSCO crowd that made up the cabal at Austin Aerospace.[111]

It also seems likely that the failure to make the original F-14 deal put somewhat of a damper on the operation though it is not possible to be sure. And that is because Studley and the gang were selling Hawk missile parts to Iran back in 1983–84. The spares were made in Oklahoma. They were also very likely brokering TOWs to Iran years before they became the stuff of conspiracy. Nevertheless, the other deals seemed modest in comparison to the F-14. There is also no telling what role the Iran-Contra scandal itself did to muddy the weapons field at such a profitably deadly time no matter what grandiose plan Luttwak handed Bill Casey.

GeoMiliTech looped together Studley's desire for enrichment with her right-wing passions as it likely did for Singlaub and perhaps others as well. For a while it was like a half-way house for spies, both official and self-selected, situated on a magical highway running between Tel Aviv and Washington, Lisbon and Tehran. GMT played with the big boys in Washington and Israel. Now it seems to have bottomed out with Fob James and Rabbi Sherman. Although GMT may end as comedy, it is nonetheless an essential part of the history of Iran-Contra.

Notes

1. Originally prepared for "Grand Crossings," a symposium honoring the life and work of Professor Alexander Saxton, UCLA and the Clark Library, September 25–26, 1998.
2. Harold Hongju Koh, *The National Security Constitution: Sharing Power After the Iran-Contra Affair* (New Haven: Yale University Press, 1990), pp. 56–57.
3. Ibid., p. 54.
4. Theodore Draper, *A Very Thin Line: The Iran-Contra Affairs* (New York: Touchstone, 1992).
5. President's Special Review Board, *The Tower Commission Report* (New York: Bantam Books and Times Books, 1987), p. 16.
6. For a while Khashoggi was something of a mystery man whose name was linked in the mid-1970s "in the U.S. to the overseas payoff scandals of Northrop and Lockheed," who was wanted for questioning by a federal Grand Jury and the Securities and Exchange Commission, and whose companies were held together by holding corporations "slithering between national tax jurisdictions." He survived the scandals of the 1970s and remained around the top of the arms world for another decade at least becoming intimately involved in the Iran arms deal. See my "The Khashoggi Papers," in *Contemporary Crises: Law, Crime and Social Policy* 1988, 13: 1.
7. The National Security Archive, *The Chronology: The Documented Day-by-Day Account of the Secret Military Assistance to Iran and the Contras* (Warner Books, 1987), p. 58.
8. Ibid., p. 72.
9. Ibid., p. 62.
10. Ibid., pp. 72–73.
11. Ibid., p. 77.
12. Ibid.
13. Ibid., p. 78.

14. Ibid., p. 69.
15. Richard M. Preece, Foreign Affairs and National Defense Division, Congressional Research Service, the Library of Congress, The Iran-Iraq War: Implications for U.S. Policy," Issue Brief Number IB84016, updated 08/03/84, date originated 01/23/84, p. 25.
16. See Peter Mantius, *Shell Game: A True Story of Banking, Spies, Lies, Politics – and the Arming of Saddam Hussein* (New York: St. Martin's Press, 1995).
17. See, James C. McKay, "Part Seven, Aqaba Pipeline Project," in Edwin Meese III (ed.), *Report of Independent Counsel* (Washington, D.C.: Government Printing Office, July 5 1988).
18. Lawrence E. Walsh, Independent Counsel, *Iran-Contra: the Final Report* (Times Books, 1994), p. xv.
19. Ibid., p. 10.
20. Ibid.
21. Ibid., p. 11.
22. Lawrence E. Walsh, *Firewall: The Iran-Contra Conspiracy and Cover-up* (New York: W. W. Norton, 1997), p. 9.
23. I was writing a paper dealing with the Wilson case, among other issues, that I called "Spies and Lies: The Serious Crime Community," for presentation at the annual meeting of the American Society of Criminology in San Diego, 1997.
24. Lyn Bixby, "Head of Iran Hostage Probe Linked to Arms Deal," *Hartford Courant*, May 29, 1992, p. A1.
25. United States District Court, District of Connecticut, United States of America, Plaintiff, vs. Arif Durrani, Defendant, "Deposition of Barbara Studley," Civil B-90-090, Crim. B-86-59, August 9, 1991, p. 51.
26. Ibid.
27. Bixby.
28. Ibid.
29. Taylor Branch and Eugene M. Propper, *Labyrinth* (New York: Viking Press, 1982), pp. 609–610.
30. Author's interview with former FBI agent Al Seddon, November 1997.
31. U.S., House of Representatives, Select Committee to Investigate Covert Arms Transactions with Iran, and U.S. Senate Select Committee on Secret Military Assistance to Iran and the Nicaraguan Opposition, "Deposition of Mark M. Richard," August 19, 1987.
32. Oliver North, Reply to note of 08/31/85 13:26, SECRET – Subject: "PRIVATE BLANK CHECK." This document is in Tom Blanton (ed.), *White House E-Mail: The Top Secret Computer Messages The Reagan/Bush White House Tried to Destroy* (New York: The New Press, A National Security Archive Documents Reader, 1995), Chapter 5.
33. Ibid.
34. Reply to note of 08/31/85 13:26 – SECRET –NOTE FROM: OLIVER NORTH, Subject: PRIVATE BLANK CHECK, Wrap Up as of 2030 EDT., in *White House E-Mail*, Chapter 11.
35. United States District Court, District of Connecticut, United States of America, Plaintiff versus Arif Durrani, Defendant, Civil B-90-090 (TFGD), Crim. B-86-59 (TFGD), "Sworn Statement of Ron Harel," March 21, 1992, in Montreal, Quebec, Canada, C.L. Klein, Official Court Reporter, p. 56. Hereafter noted as Roh Harel, "Sworn Statement."
36. T. Van De Meerssche, Manager airfreight/Comexas, to Honorable T.F.G. Daly, Chief Judge, U.S. District Court, Bridgeport, CT., "Subject: Proces Verbal B 827/86 vo 400 Dated Nov. 13th 1987, Fax Nbr 00/1/818/8892363, sent to Judge Daly on 29 December 1989 from Comexas N.V., Zaventem, Belgium.

37. Interestingly enough, in Joan Didion's review of Dinesh D'Sousa's *Ronald Reagan: How an Ordinary Man Became an Extraordinary Leader*, she writes "Yet D'Sousa's vignette casts Lt. Col. North, whose several code names included "Mr. Goode" and "Mr. White." *New York Review of Books*, December 18, 1997, p. 19.

38. Lawrence Lifschultz, Steven Galster, Rabia Ali, *Bordering On Treason? The Trial and Conviction of Arif Durrani* (East Haven, Connecticut: The Pamphleteer's Press, 1991), p. 40.

39. There is no doubt that the U.S. and Israel were in the business of supplying spare Hawk parts to the Iranians. Indeed, President Reagan "specifically authorized delivery of HAWK missile parts to Iran," on July 30, 1986. Early in August, the U.S. sent a dozen pallets of spare parts to Israel which then moved them to Iran. However, the shipment was still incomplete. There were approximately 170 parts still absent. Among the many proofs of the U.S. role in the Hawk spare parts shipments consider the following:
On November 11, 1986, Robert L. Earl, a Marine Lieutenant Colonel who had been on Vice President Bush's Task Force on Terrorism and subsequently moved to the NSC in the spring of 1986 to work in North's office as a Deputy Director of the Political-Military Affairs Directorate, compiled a list of the "the weight and cube of everything shipped" to Iran. "TOWS and *HAWK spare parts* [my emphasis] was 215,464 lbs and 18,782 cu.ft. The capacity of a C-5 is 291,000 lbs and 34,734 cu.ft. Ergo," he wrote, " room to spare" And he added, "All of the above remains SECRET, of course. CIA is reporting this info in greater detail to the SSCI [Senate Select Committee on Intelligence]." MSG FROM: NSRLE – CPUA TO: NSRKS – CPUA 11/25/86 11:14:55, To: NSRKS – CPUA, NOTE FROM: Robert L. Earl, SUBJECT: SUPPLIES cc: NSCPC – CPUA, in *White House E-Mail*, Chapter 6.

40. Lifschultz, p. 19.

41. T. Van De Meerssche. The 1989 fax memorializes the statement made by Van de Meerssche in 1987.

42. United States Government, Federal Correctional Institution, Phoenix, Arizona, Rick Stiff, Executive Assistant, MEMORANDUM, "Special Visit Authorization," July 8, 1987.

43. Lifschultz, p. 34.

44. Ibid.

45. King's statements about his team's *modus operandi* were told to reporter Ric Eyerdam of the *South Florida Business Journal*.

46. Michael E. Timpani to Arif Durrani, "Letter" 12 February 1993.

47. Author's interview with Barcella.

48. *White House E-Mail*, Chapter 7.

49. Arthur M. Schlesinger, Jr., *Robert Kennedy and His Times* (Boston: Houghton Mifflin Co., 1978), vol. 1, p. 477.

50. For non-specialists seeking to understand the recent history of Iran there are few studies in English more interesting than Manucher Farmanfarmaian and Roxanne Farmanfarmaian, *Blood and Oil: Memoirs of a Persian Prince* (New York: Random House, 1997), and on the era of the Shah and the revolution, Ryszard Kapuściński's *The Emperor: Downfall of an Autocrat* (New York: Vintage Books, 1984) and his *Shah of Shahs* (New York: Vintage Books, 1986); additional, William Shawcross, *The Shah's Last Ride: The Fate of an Ally* (New York: Touchstone, 1988). Robin Wright's *In the Name of God: The Khomeini Decade* (New York: Touchstone, 1989) is enlightening.

51. Preece, p. 25.

52. Ibid.

53. State of Delaware, Office of Secretary of State, "Certificate of Incorporation of Geo-MiliTech Consultants Corp.," August 15, 1983.

54. GeoMiliTech Consultants Corporation, "Certified Copy of the Minutes of the Board of Directors of GeoMiliTech Consultants Corps." a Delaware Corp., May 11, 1984.

55. Scot Anderson and Jon Lee Anderson, *Inside The League: The Shocking Expose of How Terrorists, Nazis, and Latin American Death Squads Have Infiltrated the World Anti-Communist League* (New York: Dodd, Mead & Company, 1986), pp. 150–152.

56. Ibid., p. 55.

57. One of Carbaugh's duties for GMT was to ask South Korea's "first Assistant Minister of Defense, General Park Choon Sik" about "providing 300,000 M-107 155mm empty shells and projectiles." Park responded that "these could only be for Iran and therefore he could not authorize such sales." John E. Carbaugh, Jr. to Barbara Studley, President, GeoMiliTech Inc., "Memorandum: A Report of the Activities in Korea," July 29, 1984.

58. Barbara Studley "letter to Mr. Ron Harel, MACED Marketing Consultancy & Development," January 6, 1984.

59. On Schweitzer see, Michael Getler, "2 Ed-Aides to Haig Ger Key Posts on National Security," *Washington Post*, January 22, 1981, p. A9; and "Pentagon Nominates Once-Criticized General," *New York Times*, April 30, 1983, p. 5; and, Susan F. Rasky, "North Urged Leniency for Honduran Linked to Assassination Plot," *New York Times*, February 23, 1987, p. 9.

60. John H. Davis, *Mafia Kingfish: Carlos Marcello and the Assassination of John F. Kennedy* (New York: McGraw-Hill, 1989), p. 425.

61. Ibid.

62. The information comes from I. Irving Davidson's personal calendar once in the possession of a detective from the Washington Metropolitan Police.

63. See U.S. Government, Federal Bureau of Investigation, Special Agent William A. Ver-icker to SAC, New York, "Subject: NY 3936-C, Criminal Informant, Re: John Dioguardi," NY 137-9495, September 16, 1963.

64. Washington, D.C., Metropolitan Police Department, "Statement of Facts in Case of Prisoner Joseph Francis Nesline," taken by Detective R.G. Kirby, D.C.P.D. 74798.

65. Federal Bureau of Narcotics, "Examination of Passport Office File of Charles Tourine, Sr.," December 6, 1961.

66. "Ex-U.S. Attorney and 8 Others Indicted in Alaska Prostitution," *New York Times*, August 9, 1976.

67. Direction de la Police Bureau Interpol, 47 Raamweg, La Haye to Interpol WASHING-TON, "Reference Your Letter No. 7522/LS of 5 April 1978 concerning Joseph Francis Nesline and others," Mensaje Postal Condensado, No. 7.323/3465 D/PR, May 8, 1978.

68. INTERPOL WIESBADEN, BUNDESKRIMINALAMT to Interpol Washington, "Investigation Reports submitted by the Landeskriminalamt Hamburg and Kiel, Re: Joseph Nesline," variously dated in 1977-78-79.

69. Interpol Teheran to Interpol Tokyo and copy to Interpol Washington-Rome, "Reference Radio-Message No: 386 of 6th June 78 regarding Dargahi Daviad dob. 5th Feb. 33 Iran," September 11, 1978.

70. This last point opens yet another series of connections – Nesline and Tourine worked with Nigerian fighter and former world middleweight champion Dick Tiger in a casino in Nigeria, and Nesline bought an interest in light-heavyweight champion Bob Foster from the fighter's manager Morris Salow a known bookmaker and loanshark. State of Connecticut, Department of State Police, Statewide Organized Crime Investigative Task

Force, "Historical Data Sheet Re: Morris Joseph Salow," sent to Department of Police, Montgomery County, Maryland, April 12, 1978.

71. Ron Harel, "Sworn Statement," p. 16.

72. Ibid., p. 21.

73. Ibid., p. 21.

74. Richard Halloran, "Iran Said to Use F-14's to Spot Targets," *New York Times*, June 7, 1984, p. A3.

75. Richard Halloran, "Iran Rebuffed By U.S. In Bid For Parts for Its F-14's," *New York Times*, December 13, 1981, p. 14.

76. Harold J. Logan, "Grumman Seeking Pilots for F-14 Training in Iran," *Washington Post*, April 11, 1977, p. A4.

77. Seymour M. Hersh, *New York Times*, September 11, 1976, p. 27.

78. William Branigin, "U.S. Firm's Offices In Iran Bombed: Exodus Continues," *Washington Post*, December 9, 1978, p. A1.

79. John F. Berry, "Iran Payoff Is Charged to Grumman," *Washington Post*, January 5, 1979, p. C8.

80. Halloran, December 13, 1981.

81. Roh Harel, "Sworn Statement," p. 23.

82. Barbara Studley to Ron Harel, "Re: Trip Report 13 September: Item 14," September 19, 1984.

83. Bruce E. Herbert, Vice President, "Memorandum for Barbara F. Studley, President, Subject: Status Report – Washington Office," July 24, 1984, p. 1.

84. Barbara Studley to Ron Harel, "Memorandum," September 26, 1984, p. 1.

85. Ron Harel to Barbara Studley, "Trip Report and General Status/Information," September 13, 1984, p. 2.

86. Studley to Harel, "Re: Trip Report."

87. Ron S. Harel, Executive Vice President to Mr. Werner Neumann, TRUVENTA A.G., Renweg 32, Basel, Switzerland, "Letter: The following is intended to summarize the various projects in which we are cooperating/*dots*", September 13, 1984, p. 4.

88. Ibid.

89. Michael Austin, Chairman Austin Aerospace, "Telex" Ron Harel, GMT, November 20, 1984.

90. A couple of months prior to Michael Austin's telex, another Iran weapons opportunity presented itself. Something called the European Consulting Service, registered in Panama, sent an inquiry to GMT for up to 5,000 TOW missiles, half with the improved warhead which had better armor piercing capabilities. Just to get into the game GMT had to come up with $500,00 and deposit it in a seller-designated bank. See, E.C.S. (European Consulting Service), Avenida Gusto Strosemena, Republic of Panama, "Quotation for TOW BGM 71A – Improved," September 5, 1984.

91. Ron Harel to Scandinavian Commodity, Telex, July 25, 1984.

92. Ron Harel, Maced Marketing Consultancy & Development to Barbara Studley, Geo-MiliTech Consultants Corp., Miami Lakes, Florida, "Letter," March 15, 1984.

93. The original telex was sent to Mr. Schmitz, the head of Scandinavian Commodity, by a representative of the Radford Arsenal, and a copy sent to Ron Harel, May 9, 1984.

94. Zvi Reuter, Director, State of Israel, Ministry of Defense, Foreign Defense Assistance & Defense Export, to M/G (R) Jack Singlaub, GMT, Washington, "Letter: I hereby prolong the option described in my letter No. 2581 of 20.3.85 until the 31st Dec., 1985," August 13, 1985.

95. Benny Morris, "Israel denies it is selling arms to Iran," *Jerusalem Post*, December 3, 1987, p. 1.

96. Meeting of the Subscriber to the Memorandum and Articles of Association, Terence Donegan QC, held on 10th December 1984, at the Fortress, Pond Street, Grand Turk, *Consulentia Limited*, number E2414.

97. Barbara Studley to Ron Harel, "Letter," December 13, 1984.

98. United States District Court, Southern District of New York, Securities and Exchange Commission, Plaintiff, – against – Robert L. Vesco, et al., Defendants, *Report of Investigation By Special Counsel*, David M Butowsky, Special Counsel, 72 Civ. 5001 (CES),. November 23, 1977, p. 291.

99. Ibid.

100. Ibid., p. 307.

101. Ibid., pp., 321, 324.

102. Ibid., pp. 322–323.

103. Ron Harel, "Sworn Statement," p. 7.

104. Barbara F. Studley to Mr. Eddy Maisonneuve, telex number: 904278 GMT Wash DC, May 16, 1985.

105. Ron Harel, GeoMiliTech Consultants Corporation, Asia House, Tel Aviv, Israel, to Mr. Paul Husser, Bank Leu, Pelikanplatz 15, Zurich, "Subj.: Acct. LEWISTOWN 9020-40418-0," May 31, 1985.

106. Anders Gyllenhaal and David Satterfield, "Shake-up at bank as U.S. investigates link to arms supplier," *Orange County Register*, June 11, 1987, p. A12.

107. Rick Eyerdam, "Loans That Sunk Bayshore Subject of New Investigation," *South Florida Business Journal*, October 14, 1991, p. 1.

108. Ibid.

109. Brett Davis, "Iran-Contra figures help James lobby for system," *Huntsville Times*, August 15, 1998, p. A1.

110. General Aviation Corporation Ltd, Bahamas Central Files #18,906/72. This file is part of a collection of Bahamian documents secured by IRS operatives, resident in The Bahamas, who were part of a secret undercover operation dubbed Tradewinds. See my *Masters of Paradise: Organized Crime and the Internal Revenue Service in The Bahamas* (New Brunswick, New Jersey: Transaction Books, 1998).

111. One of the EATSCO principals was former CIA officer Tom Clines. According to a memorandum prepared for the CIA's Inspector General on February 10, 1982, following an interview with Tom Clines by two members of the Inspector General's Office, Barcella "sent a letter to Salem and Clines' other Egyptian colleagues stating that Clines was cooperative on the Wilson/Libya matter. This was to enable Clines to placate his Egyptian colleagues who were disturbed by Clines' media attention. Clines believes that Barcella sent a copy of this letter to CIA's OGC [Office of General Counsel]. (COMMENT: OGC has provided OIG [Office of Inspector General] with a copy of this letter which is filed in the Wilson/Terpil/Clines soft file.)"

Crime, Law & Social Change **33**: 85–104, 2000.
© 2000 *Kluwer Academic Publishers. Printed in the Netherlands.*

Russia and the illicit arms trade

JOHN BERRYMAN
*School of Languages, Humanities and Social Sciences, University of Wolverhampton,
Stafford Street, Wolverhampton, WV1 1SB, UK*

Abstract. Since the disintegration of the Soviet military industrial complex, the prospect of conventional arms and nuclear, chemical and biological weapons of mass destruction and their ingredients finding their way from Russia into other hands has become a matter of concern for both the Russian Federation and the international community. This article explores the scale, forms and consequences of illicit transfers of conventional arms and weapons of mass destruction and their ingredients from the Russian Federation into the international community. Russian military and security forces seem to have been the main sources of a wide range of illicit conventional arms, whether as a consequence of the participation of Russian armed forces in regional conflicts or as a consequence of the sale of equipment by corrupt officers, the covert commercial export by Russian arms manufacturers being largely confined to small arms and light weapons. The illegal diversion of nuclear, chemical and biological materials from the Russian Federation seems to have been less than was at one time feared but Western cooperation with the Russian Federation to reinforce existing nonproliferation regimes remains a high priority.

The legacy: The Soviet military-industrial complex

The disintegration of the USSR in 1991 shattered the Soviet military-industrial complex (*Voenno-promyshlennyi kompleks*, VPK), the world's largest producer of conventional arms and for two decades one of the world's leading arms exporters.

The scale of the VPK may be briefly characterised. It has been estimated that in the late 1980s of a total workforce of 100 million, Soviet defence enterprises employed between 7 million to 11 million workers. With a separate Soviet military establishment of 5 million and between 3 to 4 million employed in the civilian sector of the military, a total of 20 million, or 60 to 80 million including dependants, were employed in the Soviet defence complex as a whole, defence expenditure consuming between 35 percent and 50 percent of Soviet gross domestic product. Following the Soviet collapse, the Russian Federation (RF) inherited some 80 percent of the Soviet Union's defence industry and around 6 to 9 million people in 33 Russian regions are estimated to be involved in military production in some 3 to 5 thousand factories.[1]

Thanks to the earlier decade of reforms between 1955 and 1965 considerable diversification had taken place within the VPK and apart from military

equipment its defence factories produced a wide range of domestic appli-
ances and even half of all motorcycles manufactured in the Soviet Union.
Further defence conversion was implemented ineffectually by administrative
command under Gorbachev and since 1992 conversion and diversification
have been constrained by the harsh new economic circumstances. Thanks
to the poor quality of Russian consumer products, competition from foreign
products and budgetary constraints, demand for Russian civilian products and
state defence orders has fallen annually by 60 percent between 1992 and
1995. Although the decline has been arrested somewhat since 1995, the Russian defence sector remains in a precarious state where most of its enterprises
have idle manufacturing capacity of at least 40 percent.[2] Indeed, international
financial institutions estimate that measured by Western standards around a
half of all Russian military enterprises are effectively bankrupt.[3]

With the collapse of the VPK and the consequent search by defence enterprises and research establishments for new sources of revenue, the prospect
of conventional arms and nuclear, chemical and biological weapons of mass
destruction (WMD) and their ingredients finding their way from Russia into
other hands has become an issue of concern for both the Russian Federation
and the international community. Efforts to secure the non-proliferation of
conventional arms and WMD have become dominant items within the agenda
of arms control in the post-Cold War era. However, despite the implementation of the United Nations" Register of Conventional Arms in 1992 and
the Wassenaar Arrangement on Export Controls for Conventional and Dual-
Use Goods and Technologies in 1996, such multilateral mechanisms do not
address the problem of "black" and "grey" market arms transfers.[4] Although
difficult to quantify, the growing salience of the black market in the post-
Cold War arms trade is not disputed. By some estimates constituting between
40 percent and 50 percent of the world-wide trade in small arms and light
weapons, illicit trafficking most commonly enables pariah states to circumvent international arms embargoes and provides the light weapons used in
the low-intensity intra-state conflicts which have largely displaced inter-state
wars in the post-Cold War period.[5]

Thanks to the huge social and economic dislocation generated by the political disintegration of the USSR, favourable conditions for such illicit arms
transfers have emerged within Russia and the other successor states of the
Former Soviet Union (FSU). Since it is impossible to monitor or measure ac-
curately the clandestine arms transfers out of or into the RF, widely different
estimates of the scale of the problem are available. By comparison with the
1993 estimates by the Russian Ministry of the Interior that black market sales
of Russian weapons were at least twice those of open sales, Western analysts
variously claim that illicit arms transfers account for between 15 percent and

20 percent of Russia's total arms trade, or suggest simply that large quantities of Russian arms, the scale of which cannot be measured, are illicitly entering the international market.[6]

This article explores the scale, forms and consequences of such illicit transfers of conventional arms and WMD and their ingredients from the RF into the wider international community. In view of the absence, by definition, of reliable and comparative data on such trade and the anecdotal nature of much of the information which is available in the public domain, the usual caveat should be noted. The analysis offered is, perforce, based on less than reliable information.

The illicit transfer of conventional arms

What impulses have underpinned Russia's illicit conventional arms transfers? What has been the size of these transfers? Which have been the main agents involved, what have been the chief destinations of illicit arms and what have been the consequences of such transfers?

Russian armed forces and illicit conventional arms transfers

Army Colonel-General Andrei I. Nikolayev, former Director of the Russian Federal Border Service, has estimated that the Russian military inherited some 20 million to 25 million small arms from the Soviet Armed Forces.[7] In the chaotic process which marked the reorganisation and redeployment of truncated Russian armed forces in the aftermath of the termination of the Warsaw Pact and disintegration of the Soviet Union, Russian military and security organisations were, not surprisingly, the primary initial sources of illicit supplies of conventional arms. Indeed, thanks to the weakening of central control over the institutions of state and society in the Gorbachev years, including the armed forces and the physical security arrangements for Russian ordnance depots, the involvement of military personnel in the unauthorised sale of weapons and ammunition had already become commonplace by the late 1980s. This activity may have been particularly pronounced within the ranks of those disillusioned servicemen returning from Afghanistan.[8]

Following the political upheavals in Eastern Europe in 1989, opportunities for illegal arms sales opened up during the phased withdrawals of the Groups of Soviet Forces deployed in the former German Democratic Republic, Central and Eastern Europe, the Baltic States and Kaliningrad between 1990 and 1994. During this period demoralised troops took advantage of the weakened regulatory and administrative arrangements to dispose of surplus military equipment to provide for their own basic needs. Although there is no evidence of any significant loss of control by Moscow over the handling of the withdrawal process, given the enormous quantities of men and equipment being moved even relatively small illicit transfers in percentage terms involved significant quantities of weapons.[9]

The most notorious case was the reported leakage of 81 million tons of military equipment from the Western Group of Forces (WGF) during the withdrawal from Germany. Some of the equipment, it was claimed, was sold to German criminals and neo-Nazi groups.[10] In the late summer of 1994 the investigations by the Russian Parliament elicited the admission by the Defence Minister Pavel Grachev that the WGF had indeed been involved in theft, smuggling and illegal deals. Following allegations that he had been involved in or had done little to prevent such activity, the nomination of the former Commander-in-Chief of the WGF, Colonel- General Matvey Burlakov, for the position of Deputy Defence Minister was suspended in October 1994. In the same month Dmitrii Kholodov, an investigative journalist for *Moskovskii Komsomelets* exploring these reports of corruption, was killed by a bomb placed in a briefcase that supposedly contained incriminating documentation. Burlakov was accused of playing a role in the assassination and he was dismissed by President Yeltsin in November.[11]

Notwithstanding the publicity surrounding this case, it should not be overlooked that within a short period of three years and eight months 22 divisions, 49 brigades and 42 independent regiments, a total of 546,200 troops, were withdrawn from Germany to Russia in an orderly fashion – a huge military undertaking which affected fundamentally the balance of power in Europe. At a special ceremony in Moscow in August 1994 to mark the final withdrawal of Soviet troops from Germany, Defence Minister Grachev pointed out that had Russia conducted the process according to the standards set for Western troop reductions it would have taken fifteen years.[12] Together with the parallel withdrawal of other Groups of Soviet Forces from Central and Eastern Europe and the Baltic States, this strategic draw-back represented "one of the most extensive and least appreciated force withdrawals in modern times".[13]

By contrast, the break-up of the Soviet Union and the emergence of fifteen successor states with weakened or negligible border controls within the framework of the Commonwealth of Independent States (CIS) created conditions which were positively conducive to the covert transfers of conventional arms from former Soviet armed forces. While Ukraine, Belarus and Kazakhstan took immediate control of the former Soviet military forces on their territory (with the exception of strategic forces), it was not until the spring of 1992 that Russia assumed direct control of former Soviet military forces in the Baltic States, Armenia, Azerbaijan, Georgia, part of Moldova, and some of the Central Asian states. Moscow consequently found itself assuming a primary responsibility for conflict management in these territories of the "Near Abroad", as well as confronting questions concerning the legal status of its forces located within what were now foreign states. Concerned for the security of these forward deployments, the Russian military seem to have played a more active part in shaping policy in the "Near Abroad" than the Ministry of Foreign Affairs.[14]

The most significant cases of covert transfers of conventional arms from Russian armed forces occurred within the three Transcaucasian states of Armenia, Azerbaijan and Georgia. All three states were affected by a chain of violent conflicts which put at risk the large quantities military equipment held by the eleven Russian ground force divisions deployed in these territories. All three states sought to establish national armed forces in large part on the basis of the codification of the seizure or dissolution of units of the former Soviet armed forces.[15] In the case of Armenia, it was the conflict with Azerbaijan over the status of Nagorno-Karabakh that provided the impetus for the formation of paramilitary units as early as the spring of 1989.[16] It was reported that between January and July 1990 some 6,700 weapons, including 1,200 automatic weapons, were acquired by these militia groups in Armenia and by the autumn of 1991 experts within the Soviet General Staff were predicting the eruption of armed conflicts in the Caucasus in the event of the dissolution of the USSR and arguing for the urgent withdrawal of military equipment from the region.[17]

Following the break-up of the Soviet Union, Moscow's policies towards all three states embraced the full range of approaches from direct involvement to covert operations to passive connivance in the activities of insurgent groups and the Russian military.[18] In the case of Armenia and Azerbaijan it appears that Russian military commanders in the field sold or "loaned" arms and ammunition first to Armenian forces fighting in Karabakh and later to Azerbaijani forces when Armenian forces seemed likely to prevail. The military equipment ranged from *Kalashnikovs* to tanks, armoured combat vehicles (ACVs), heavy artillery and *Grad* multiple rocket launchers. In the chaotic situation which prevailed it was unclear what level of control the authorities in Moscow had over these transfers of weapons by local commanders or the involvement of troops from the 147th and 366th Motor Rifle Divisions (MRDs) in different stages of the fighting.[19] Huge quantities of military equipment were also looted by militia forces from poorly protected Russian military depots. More than 1,100 railway wagons of artillery shells, rockets and ammunition were seized by Azerbaijani fighters from a Russian arms warehouse in the city of Agdam in February 1992.[20]

In the case of Armenia, detailed accounts provided by Aman Tuleyev, former Minister for CIS Affairs, General Igor Rodionov, former Defence

Minister, and retired General Lev Rokhlin, Chairman of the Duma Defence Committee and Chairman of the oppositional Movement for the Support of the Army, the Defence Industry and Military Sciences, in March 1997, claimed that between 1992 and late 1996 the Trans-Caucasian Group of Forces (TCGF), established in August 1992 to replace the Soviet Transcaucasus Military District (MD) as a structure appropriate for Russian troops operating on the territory of other sovereign states, covertly transferred to Armenia without payment around US $1 billion worth of military equipment. The equipment was said to include 84 T-72 tanks, 50 ACVs, howitzers, heavy artillery, anti-tank guided missiles and up to 32 *Scud* tactical missiles, as well as light weapons and ammunition including 26 mortars, 306 sub-machine guns, 7,910 assault rifles and 1,847 pistols.[21] Once more it is unclear whether the initiative reflected policy in Moscow or was undertaken by local commanders without authorisation. Although the Office of the Military Procurator took up the case, it was shelved the following year. Meanwhile in the summer of 1998 General Rokhlin, the initiator of the scandal, was shot dead in his dacha near Moscow.[22]

In Georgia the scale of enforced "nationalisation" of Soviet arms and equipment by local paramilitary forces was such that in March 1992 Vice-President Rutskoi called for the complete evacuation of Russian troops from the region.[23] Thanks in part to the strong statement of opposition by the then Commander of the Transcaucasus MD, Colonel-General V. Patrikeyev, withdrawal was rejected but the TCGF was subsequently reduced from 100,000 to 30,000 men between 1992–93.[24] As in Armenia and Azerbaijan, local Russian commanders and the military authorities in Moscow seem to have reached decisions to supply weapons or commit forces in Georgia on an *ad hoc* basis. Although Russian troops equipped Georgian forces, there is evidence that rebel forces in Abkhazia also benefited from significant supplies of Russian military equipment, including heavy weapons, channelled through the Russian military bases at Gudauta and Bombora. It is reported that the commanders of the Russian units based in Gudauta transferred to Abkhazian militias armoured cars, thousands of machine guns, more than 500 grenades, half a million rounds of ammunition and all vehicles belonging to the 643rd Anti-Air Defence Unit. In total it is estimated some thirteen railway wagons of Russian military equipment were supplied to Abkhaz forces.[25] Additionally, there is even evidence that some Russian pilots flew missions in SU-25s and SU-27s, bombing Georgian positions.[26] As a consequence of Russian support for Abkhazia, President Shevardnadze recognised that there was little alternative but to co-operate with Russia and in October 1993 Georgia joined the CIS, Russia securing four military bases in Georgian territory.

Following Russia's mediation in the negotiation of a cease-fire by the leaders of Armenia, Azerbaijan and Nagorno-Karabakh, and the stabilisation of the conflict in Georgia with the *de facto* establishment of the breakaway regions of Abkhazia and South Ossetia, by late 1994 all three armed conflicts (South Ossetia, Abkhazia and Karabakh) had effectively been put on ice and Russia had reduced its military presence in the region. All 60,000 Russian troops were withdrawn from Azerbaijan and apart from Russian peace-keeping contingents only Russian border troops plus two army divisions were left in Georgia while only one Russian division, the 127th MRD, was left in Armenia.[27] However, the region remained a centre for criminality and corruption and a corridor for smuggling across the North Caucasus border of the RF. Apart from arms and narcotics trafficking between Azerbaijan and Daghestan and Chechnya, and between South Ossetia and North Ossetia, the Russian-controlled airport at Vaziani in Georgia acted as something of a "free-port" for the covert shipment of individuals or cargoes to or from Russia.[28] Moreover in the brief resumption of fighting between Georgian and Abkhazian forces in May 1998 Shevardnadze once more accused Russian troops of having "loaned" tanks and armoured vehicles to the Abkhaz forces.[29]

Although limited stabilisation was secured in the Transcaucasus by 1994, in the North Caucasus Russia's failure to manage the efforts of Chechnya to establish its independence resulted in the disastrous campaign by Russian armed forces in Chechnya between 1994 and 1996. Thanks to the semi-independent status of Chechnya since 1996 the military airport at Grozny, off limits to Russian passport and customs control, remained a centre for illicit arms and drug trafficking.[30] Armed Chechen incursions into Daghestan and the destruction of apartment buildings in three Russian cities, killing almost 300 civilians, triggered the despatch of more than 100,000 Russian troops into Chechnya in September 1999. Remarkably, although Moscow has systematically pursued its second military campaign in the territory, at the Istanbul summit of the OSCE in November 1999 agreement was reached on a reduction in Russia's military presence in Georgia, Chechnya's neighbour. It was agreed that Russia will reduce the number of ACVs deployed in Georgia from 481 to 241 and will withdraw from two of its military bases at Gudauta and Vaziani by 1 July 2001, leaving only the two Russian bases at Batumi and Akhalkalaki. Since the bases to be vacated are located in the breakaway republic of Abkhazia, Abkhazian forces will move into the vacated bases.[31] It is therefore clear that in the longer term Moscow still entertains hopes of combining a progressive disengagement and withdrawal of Russian forces from the Transcaucasus with the maintenance of Russia as the guarantor of stability in the North Caucasus and the Caucasus region as a whole.[32]

Apart from the three Transcaucasian states, significant illicit transfers of arms from Russian military forces have been reported in two other states of the FSU which have been afflicted by violent conflicts – Tajikistan and Moldova (in Transdniestr). In both cases Russian troops rapidly found themselves parties to the conflicts.[33] In Tajikistan elements of the 201st MRD based in the Kulyab and Kurgan-Tyube Oblasts were involved in the illicit supply of arms, including four tanks and six ACVs, to the pro-communist Popular Front in the opening stage of the Tajik civil war, thereby preparing the ground for the official Russian support for Rakhmonov after November 1992 and the effective termination of such illicit transfers.[34] In April 1999 a Russian-Tajikistan Treaty established basing rights for the 201st MRD in Tajikistan for the next ten years.[35]

In Moldova, Soviet civil defence and paramilitary organisations started to supply weapons to the armed volunteer forces of the Russophone Dniestrian opposition to the Moldovan Popular Front probably as early as 1990. In an interview in 1995 Colonel Mikhail Bergman, Tiraspol garrison commander of the Soviet 14th Army, admitted that his forces were involved in secretly supplying weapons to the Dniestrian Republic Guard and that by the spring of 1992 14th Army troops were even engaged in combat alongside these forces. Concerned that the conflict might draw in Romania and Ukraine, the Soviet 14th Army was formally transferred to Russian control in April 1992 and the decision was taken in Moscow to use the 14th Army to separate the Moldovan and Dniestrian forces, paving the way for the cease-fire accord of July 1992.[36] It has subsequently been alleged that Russia's military forces in Moldova, drawing on an estimated 345,000 tonnes of Russian weapons stored in arms depots in the territory, have been supplying arms to criminals based in Moscow and Kiev and have been channelling military equipment through intermediaries in Romania, Turkey, Ukraine, Chechnya and Abkhazia to such destinations as the former Yugoslavia or even Latin America.[37] However, since the agreement reached in October 1994 on the phased withdrawal of Russian forces, the number of 14th Army troops deployed in Moldova has fallen from more than 9,000 to 2,500 and the status of the 14th Army has been downgraded to an operational group.[38] At the Istanbul summit of the OSCE in November 1999 Russia agreed to withdraw its remaining 2,500 troops from Moldova by the end of 2002.[39]

Within the borders of the RF the North Caucasus MD, Kaliningrad and the Far Eastern MD have been the main centres for the illicit transfer of arms from Russian armed forces. In the case of the North Caucasus MD, following a series of raids on Russian Interior Ministry depots and military installations in the territory of Chechnya, in which considerable quantities of small arms were stolen, the Russian MRD was withdrawn from Grozny in

June 1992 leaving behind a huge arsenal of military equipment. In January 1995 the Russian Ministry of Defence prepared an inventory for the Security Council of the military equipment abandoned which included two *Luna* (FROG) tactical missile launchers (with no missiles), 250 combat/training aircraft, 42 tanks, 60 ACVs, 153 artillery pieces and mortars and 590 anti-tank weapons. No clear explanation has emerged of this controversial decision which effectively equipped President Dudayev's forces.[40] Widespread pilfering of military equipment in other parts of the North Caucasus MD has also been endemic, including the "disappearance without a trace" in 1992 of over 1,000 railway wagons, each containing 20 tons of artillery shells.[41]

Kaliningrad has also been identified as a source of substantial covert transfers of small arms and light weapons. A fortified *oblast* of the RF, physically separated from the rest of Russia by Lithuanian and Belarusian territories, after 1989 Kaliningrad became something of a parking lot for troops, combat equipment and aircraft withdrawn from Central and Eastern Europe and the Baltic States and force levels reached 103,000 troops by 1993. With such a high concentration of military equipment inadequately guarded by demoralised poorly paid troops, Kaliningrad soon developed a reputation as one of the biggest black market arms bazaars in Russia.[42]

The rapid reduction in Russian ground forces within the exclave to around 24,000 by 1995, accompanied by a corresponding reduction in most categories of military equipment except tanks and ACVs, helped ease Baltic sensitivities.[43] Nonetheless, Kaliningrad has remained a centre for the smuggling of a wide range of illegal arms across Northern Europe, highlighting the extent of the links which have developed between the military establishment and the local criminal networks.[44] With the entry of Poland and Lithuania into the European Union (EU) in prospect from 2003, the challenge will be to establish borders between Kaliningrad and its EU neighbours which will prevent smuggling but will encourage tourism, cultural contacts, trade and cross-border cooperation.[45] Indeed, it has been argued that the process of integrating Russia into a new security order in Europe will stand or fall on how Brussels and Moscow manage the question of Kaliningrad.[46]

Apart from the North Caucasus MD and Kaliningrad, Russian military forces in the Far Eastern MD have also been involved in the black market sale of weapons to ameliorate their miserable living conditions. In addition, in 1994 official investigations exposed a questionable initiative by some former Soviet naval commanders to sell for scrap to a South Korean company two aircraft-carrying cruisers, the *Minsk* and *Novorossiysk* that formerly belonged to the Soviet Pacific Fleet.[47]

In sum, as the RF Ministry of the Interior has concluded, Russian military and security forces seem to have been the "main and stable source" of the illicit transfers of conventional arms, whether it be as a consequence of the participation of Russian armed forces in regional conflicts or as a consequence of the sale of equipment by corrupt officers, often working closely with criminal organisations. Moreover, thanks to the criminalisation of the armed forces in an average year it is estimated that approximately 30,000 weapons go missing.[48]

Russian arms manufacturers and illicit conventional arms transfers

Apart from the covert transfer of conventional arms by Russian military and security units, what has been the scale of illicit conventional arms transfers from Russian arms manufacturers?

During the Cold War the export of conventional arms from the Soviet Union was used primarily as an instrument to improve the military capabilities of target states, secure their close political alignment, gain regional basing facilities and rebuff efforts by the United States to advance its influence. While commercial considerations were not absent, ideological and political considerations were dominant and up to one-fifth of all weapons produced were exported either free of charge, with substantial discounts, or on the basis of long-term, low-interest loans, many of them still unpaid. Typically, in 1990 arms transfers from the Soviet Union totalled more than $16 billion, out of which cash receipts totalled only $900 million.[49]

In the post-Cold War era, by contrast, it is commercial calculations which now shape Russia's conventional arms transfers. However, thanks to the easing of tensions with the termination of the Cold War it has been Russia's misfortune to enter the export market for arms at a point when, discounting brief surges generated by international conflicts, global arms sales have been shrinking. Whereas the total world-wide trade in conventional weapons in 1987 was worth an estimated $88.5 billion (in constant 1997 US dollars) by 1997 it amounted to $46.3 billion.[50] Moreover, thanks to the widespread perception that much of its military equipment is technologically backward and uncompetitive, Russia's share in the global arms trade has steadily declined, her place being largely filled by the United States and Germany.[51] In short, in the ten years since 1987 the annual value of Soviet/Russian arms exports has fallen from $31 billion to around $2.5 billion, Russia's share of the global market dropping from 35 percent to 5 percent. Nonetheless, in 1997 1760 factories with a work-force of around 2.7 million were estimated to be still directly involved in military production.[52]

In the absence of any significant longer term funding or policy to restructure Russia's defence industry and stimulate defence conversion, Russia's defence plants have consequently been driven to rely ever more heavily on the revenues derived from the exports of weapons and military hardware. By 1997–8 export revenues accounted for 62 percent of all the funding channelled into the Russian defence sector and defence exports constituted one half of all the products manufactured by Russia's otherwise uncompetitive machine-building industries.[53] Hence, although sales of oil and gas provide three fourths of Russia's export revenues, arms sales constitute Russia's primary manufactured export. In November 1999 Russian Prime Minister Vladimir Putin emphasised that revenues derived from energy sales could not be relied upon and urged that Russia should make the development of its military-industrial complex a priority.[54] In this situation, thanks to the pervasive levels of corruption and the desperate need of many defence plants for revenue, the regulatory controls exercised over the final destination of arms transfers by *Rosvooruzheniye*, the main state organisation responsible for the oversight of arms sales, have not been rigorous.[55] Moreover the illegal production of small arms and light weapons located wholly outside any regulatory frameworks has flourished, often utilising idle and poorly controlled state-owned manufacturing facilities.[56]

What has been the scale and character of the export of illicit conventional weapons by Russian arms manufacturers? Since the black market sales of Russia's small arms and light weapons are neither monitored nor controlled, no precise figures are available as to the overall size of the trade. However, within Europe the black market availability of Russian small arms and light weapons of virtually every type in such places as Cyprus and Zagreb has been readily apparent. *The Economist* estimated that in 1993 around $2 billions worth of arms and ammunition, much of it Chinese or Czech, was delivered to Bosnia through black-market channels, while Serbia covertly obtained black market weapons from Russia and other states of the FSU.[57] The dangers of covert transfers of arms, drugs and refugees from the unstable new nations of the FSU into Europe consequently bulk large within the "soft security" agenda of post-Cold War European security.[58]

As noted above, the covert transfers of conventional military equipment from Russian military forces has included tactical missiles, combat aircraft, tanks, ACVs, heavy artillery and multiple rocket launchers, as well as small arms and light and medium weapons. By contrast, the covert commercial export of conventional weapons by arms manufacturers has been largely confined to small arms and light weapons. Since high technology conventional weapons systems such as combat aircraft, missiles or air defence systems require stable support and servicing systems for spare parts and maintenance, there is little evidence of the illegal commercial export of such systems.[59]

The roots of the commercial black market in Russian weapons lie in the 1980s. The development of commercial exports of conventional arms under Gorbachev, coupled with the lack of accounting and weakening of regulatory controls, gave rise to increased corruption and helped foster the development of a black market in weapons. Commercial ties developed by arms manufacturers with trading companies overseas in Cyprus and elsewhere were used as transit routes for the covert shipment of light weapons, especially from plants in Tula, which manufacture portable anti-tank missiles and rockets, and Izhevsk, which manufacture lightweight automatic weapons including *Kalashnikovs*.[60]

Other transit routes for the illegal funnelling of arms out of (and into) the RF are said to run through the Baltic states of Estonia and Latvia. During visits to the border town of Pskov, both Prime Minister Chernomyrdin in July 1993 and President Yeltsin in November 1994 denounced this illegal trade, together with the unrestrained export from Russia of strategic raw materials such as non-ferrous metals, huge quantities of which are shipped from Estonian and Latvian ports. Calls were made for stricter controls along the Estonian-Russian and Latvian-Russian borders.[61] Moreover Russia's proposals in November 1997 for a Pact of Regional Security and Stability urged that full use be made of the Council of Baltic Sea States (CBSS) group of personal representatives of the heads of government set up in 1996 to combat transnational organised crime.[62] Although the proposals elicited no immediate positive response, since both Russia and the Baltic States share an interest in limiting such illicit activities some sort of collective action by the CBSS may be taken in the future.

In view of the long and complex transit routes used by black marketeers in weapons through and from Russia and the other states of the FSU and the EU and Associated States in Central and Eastern Europe, efforts have been undertaken to strengthen concerted collective action by the EU and Associated states to limit this traffic. In May 1997 the EU Programme for Preventing and Combating Illicit Trafficking in Conventional Arms came into force, and in 1998 the EU Code of Conduct on Arms Exports and the EU Joint Action on Small Arms were adopted. Currently there is consideration of the need to strengthen end-use controls within the EU enlargement process to prevent the diversion of arms shipments while Non-Governmental Organisations (NGOs) are developing the International Action Network on Small Arms (IANSA).[63]

In the longer term the establishment of a democratic society and orderly governance in Russia, together with the restructuring of its overmilitarised economy, will be vital if there is to be any prospect of reducing this traffic. Ultimately, as Michael Klare has argued, multilateral arms control and nonproliferation regimes will be needed to regulate the trade in small arms and light weapons in much the same way as the world community has established regimes for the control of ballistic missiles.[64]

The illicit transfer of WMD and their ingredients

Thanks to the chaotic upheaval generated by the disintegration of the Soviet Union, the stockpiles, manufacturing potential and technologies of the
nuclear, chemical and biological (NBC) weapons of the Soviet arsenal of
WMD became a central focus for regional and world proliferation concerns.
The nuclear arsenal of the FSU numbered approximately 27,000 operational
nuclear weapons, of which 12,000 were strategic and 15,000 were tactical.[65]
With a stockpile of 40,000 metric tons of chemical agents contained within
bombs, artillery shells, missile warheads and other munitions, Russia held the
largest chemical weapons (CW) arsenal in the world. Finally, it was learned
in 1992 that in violation of the Biological Weapons Convention it had signed
in 1972 the USSR had conducted a Biological Weapons (BW) programme
"at least an order of magnitude larger than those of the USA and the UK".[66]
In these circumstances, as William Perry, former US Secretary of Defence,
and Ashton Carter, former Assistant Secretary of Defence, emphasise: "Fear
of 'loose nukes' in a fractious, revolutionary Russia was a chief U.S. security
concern'.[67] Widespread fears of the risk of former Soviet nuclear weapons,
weapons-grade fissile materials or chemical and biological weapons (CBW)
leaking out of Russia and finding their way into the hands of rogue states or
terrorist groups fuelled numerous Western studies of the problem.[68]

How far have such fears been vindicated? What has been the scale of
the covert transfer of WMD and their ingredients out of or into the RF? In
the first place, fears of nuclear proliferation among the newly independent
states of the FSU have been resolved and the RF is the sole Soviet nuclear
successor state. Tactical nuclear weapons, previously deployed in all Soviet
republics except Tajikistan and Kyrgyzstan, were all returned to Russia by
1992. Thanks to Western multilateral pressures and inducements all strategic
nuclear warheads were transferred from Kazakhstan, Ukraine and Belarus to
Russia by November 1996.[69]

Second, the highly publicised exposures in the West of the theft and smuggling of nuclear weaponry or radioactive weapons- grade fissile materials
look to have been exaggerated. In three cases in 1992-3 small quantities
of nuclear materials were stolen by individuals from civilian institutions or
from naval fuel storage sites without specific buyers and were apprehended.
In three other cases in 1994 highly enriched uranium (HEU) intercepted in
Europe allegedly had a Soviet origin but there is no firm evidence that the
HEU was illegally transferred from Russia. In one case it remains unclear
whether the disappearance of 145 grams of HEU from the research reactor
of Tomsk Polytechnic University was the result of theft or a miscalculation
of the inventory. The only case of the illegal transfer of nuclear material
from Russia was the interception at Munich Airport in August 1994 of 363

grams of weapons-grade plutonium-239 and 560 grams of uranium mixed-oxide (MOX) fuel stolen from the Obninsk research reactor. Although all the details of the incident are still not clear, the interception was exposed as a sting operation organised by German special services. In these circumstances the Russian Ministry of Nuclear Energy had some grounds for their argument that the operation was designed to discredit Russia as a reliable successor state to the USSR , unable to provide the necessary security for its nuclear facilities and control its nuclear exports, thereby undermining the efforts of Russian state companies to enter the legal world uranium market.[70]

What conclusions, therefore, can be drawn from these incidents? Although the illegal diversion of nuclear materials from the RF has taken place, albeit in quantities too small to be of direct use as a weapon, the existence of an international black market for such material, other than the artificial one created by the German special services, remains doubtful.[71] As one study concludes: "Nuclear smuggling remains a low-profile but potentially dangerous threat to international security. Smuggling incidents to date have been minor (most materials offered for sale qualify as radioactive junk, useless for making nuclear weapons)'.[72]

In the view of Western analysts, however, despite the success of the US Co-operative Threat Reduction (CTR) programme in providing \$2.4 billion of US Department of Defense funding for programmes to reduce and control WMD in Russia and the other successor states of the FSU, including the dismantling of 4,800 nuclear weapons, conditions conducive to the prospect of further leakage of WMD and their ingredients from the RF have persisted and even intensified. The slow progress made to date in the reduction of Russian CBW stockpiles, ever growing inventories of weapons-usable fissile materials, underdeveloped safeguards, inadequate export controls and a continuing rise in corruption and criminality, are cited in support of this judgement.[73] By contrast, in the view of Russian analysts the absence of any confirmed cases of illicit diversions and trafficking since 1994 suggests that the security of Russia's nuclear installations and stockpiles has improved. With the support of CTR assistance the Russian authorities have improved the material protection, control and accounting (MPC&A) of their nuclear stockpiles, export controls have been tightened and in the new Criminal Code of 1997 severe penalties have been introduced for the diversion or possession of radioactive materials.[74] Notwithstanding these differences of judgements, it seems clear that for the moment smuggling networks in the hands of organised crime to facilitate nuclear trafficking have not yet materialised.[75]

Third, while there is widespread fear of the illicit diversion of CBW, there has not yet been a confirmed report of such a transaction. The only exceptions include the sale of analytical samples of biological agents, like the enriched nuclear materials, too small to be of direct use as weapons.[76] However, there have been unconfirmed reports that Russian technicians are assisting Iran's development of CBWs, including the construction of a chemical plant which could be used for the production of poison gas.[77]

Fourth, it appears that the proliferation of nuclear weapons expertise from the RF has not taken place on the scale feared. Quite apart from the positive role played by the International Science and Technology Centre in Moscow in providing limited funds to employ under-employed and ill-paid nuclear and missile scientists on civilian research projects, the Russian authorities have tightened procedures for the issuing of foreign passports to between two and four thousand scientists with nuclear weapons expertise. In one case, at Moscow's Sheremetevo Airport, Russian special services intercepted a group of nuclear scientists about to leave for North Korea.[78]

Finally, Russian analysts have argued that, with the exception of two cases of confirmed illegal transactions of Russian missile technology to Iraq in 1995, the other reported cases of illicit missile technology transfer do not, represent clear cut breaches of the Missile Technology Control Regime (MTCR). Apart from those proposed transactions which were aborted, such as the possible transfer of SS-18 ICBM technology to China, it is argued that the delivery of *Scuds* to Armenia in 1994–96 did not breach the MTCR since Russia specifically exempted cooperation with other CIS countries when in 1993 it agreed to adhere to the MTCR guidelines (Russia did not become an MTCR member until August 1995).[79]

In conclusion, despite the considerable concern in the international community over the possible leakage of WMD and their ingredients from the RF into unsafe hands, to date these fears have not, in the main, been confirmed.[80] Nonetheless, Western cooperation with the RF to reinforce existing non-proliferation regimes and improve the MPC&A of NBC stockpiles must remain high priorities within the international security agenda.[81]

Notes

1. R.F. Staar, *The New Military in Russia: Ten Myths That Shape the Image* (Annapolis, Maryland: Naval Institute Press, 1996), p. 87; A. Shoumikhin, "View from Russia: The Weapons Stockpile", *Comparative Strategy* 1995, 14: 211–212.
2. M.I. Gerasev and V.M. Surikov, "The Crisis in the Russian Defense Industry: Implications for Arms Exports", in A.J. Pierre and D.V. Trenin (eds.), *Russia in the World Arms Trade* (Washington, D.C.: Carnegie Endowment for International Peace, 1997), pp. 9–19.
3. D. Holloway and M. McFaul, "Demilitarization and Defense Conversion", in G.W. Lapidus (ed.), *The New Russia: Troubled Transformation* (Boulder, Colorado: Westview, 1995), p. 211.
4. For more extended explorations of the distinctions between "black market" and "grey market" arms transfers see A. Karp, "The Rise of Black and Gray Markets", *The Annals of*

the American Academy of Political and Social Science. Special Issue on The Arms Trade: Problems and Prospects in the Post-Cold War World, vol. 535 (September 1994), pp. 175–89; R.T. Naylor, "The Structure and Operation of the Modern Arms Black Market", in J. Boutwell, M.T. Klare and L.W. Reed (eds.), *Lethal Commerce: The Global Trade in Small Arms and Light Weapons* (Cambridge, Mass: Committee on International Security Studies, American Academy of Arts and Sciences, 1995), pp. 44–57; I. Anthony, "Illicit arms transfers", in I. Anthony (ed.), *Russia and the Arms Trade* (Oxford: SIPRI/Oxford University Press, 1998), pp. 219–220.

5. M.T. Klare, "The arms trade in the 1990s: changing patterns, rising dangers", *Third World Quarterly* 1996, 17(5): 859; A. Karp, "The Arms Trade Revolution: The Major Impact of Small Arms", *Washington Quarterly* 1994, 17(4): 72–73; A. Karp, "Small Arms: The New Major Weapons", in Boutwell, pp. 17–30.

6. Staar, p. 96; K. Gonchar and P. Lock, "Small Arms and Light Weapons: Russia and the Former Soviet Union", in Boutwell, p. 122; A. Hull and D. Markov, "Trends in the arms market. Part Two", *Jane's Intelligence Review* May 1997, 9(5): 236.

7. Interview in article by Sergei Roy, *Moscow News*, 20–26 October 1999 40: 4.

8. G.H. Turbiville, Jr., *Mafia in Uniform: The "Criminalization" of the Russian Armed Forces* (Fort Leavenworth, Kansas: Foreign Military Studies Office, 1995), pp. 6–8; J. Serio, "Organised Crime in the Soviet Union and Beyond", *Low Intensity Conflict and Law Enforcement* Autumn 1992, 1(2): 147.

9. Anthony, p. 231.

10. RFE/RL Daily Reports, 4 January 1994.

11. Turbiville, Mafia in Uniform, pp. 21–23, 27–28; S. White, *Russia's New Politics: The Management of a Postcommunist Society* (Cambridge: Cambridge University Press, 1999), p. 168; C. Wallander, *Mortal Friends, Best Enemies: German-Russian Cooperation after the Cold War* (Ithaca: Cornell University Press, 1999), p. 78.

12. Wallander, pp. 71, 81: A.E. Stent, *Russia and Germany Reborn: Unification, the Soviet Collapse, and the New Europe* (Princeton: Princeton University Press, 1999), pp. 163–164.

13. B.S. Lambeth, "Russia's Wounded Military", *Foreign Affairs* March-April 1995, 74(2): 94.

14. J.W.R. Lepingwell, "The Russian Military in the 1990s: Disintegration or Renewal?", in D.W. Blum (ed.), *Russia's Future: Consolidation or Disintegration?* (Boulder, Colorado: Westview, 1994), p. 111; J.W.R. Lepingwell, "The Russian Military and Security Policy in the "Near Abroad", *Survival* Autumn 1994, 36(3): 72.

15. R.L. Garthoff, "Russian Military Doctrine and Deployments", in B. Parrott (ed.), *State Building and Military Power in Russia and the New States of Eurasia* (Armonk: M.E. Sharpe, 1995), pp. 48–52; R. Allison, *Military Forces in the Soviet Successor States*, Adelphi Paper 280 (London: Brassey's for the IISS, 1993), pp. 65–67; A. Zverev, "Ethnic Conflicts in the Caucasus 1988–1994", in B. Coppieters (ed.), *Contested Borders in the Caucasus* (Brussels: VUB University Press, 1996), pp. 35–37.

16. E. Fuller, "Paramilitary Forces Dominate Fighting in Transcaucasus", *RFE/RL Research Report* 18 June 1993, 2(25): 74.

17. G.H. Turbiville, Jr., "New Issues of Soviet National Security: Emerging 'Transnational Security Threats' and Future Soviet Defense Forces", in S.J. Blank and J.W. Kipp (eds.), *The Soviet Military and the Future* (Westport, Conn: Greenwood Press, 1992), p. 247; P. Baev, *Russia's Policies in the Caucasus* (London: Royal Institute of International Affairs, 1997), p. 23.

18. T. Goltz, "Letter from Eurasia: the Hidden Russian Hand", *Foreign Policy* Autumn, 1993, 92: 92–116.

19. Fuller, pp. 77–80; T. Dragadze, "The conflict in Transcaucasia and the importance of inventory", *Jane's Intelligence Review* February, 1994, 6(2): 71–73; E. Herzig, *The New Caucasus: Armenia, Azerbaijan and Georgia* (London: Royal Institute of International Affairs, 1999), pp. 16–18; R. Menon, "After Empire: Russia and the Southern 'Near Abroad'," in M. Mandelbaum (ed.), *The New Russian Foreign Policy* (New York: Council on Foreign Relations, 1998), pp. 128–129.

20. A. Popov, "Ethnic wars in the Transcaucasus", in M. Kaldor and B. Vashee (eds.), *Restructuring the Global Military Sector. Volume 1: New Wars* (London: Pinter for UNU World Institute for Development Economics Research, 1997), p. 196.

21. Anthony, pp. 224–225; Herzig, pp. 55, 67; Menon, pp. 132–33; *Jane's Defence Weekly*, 19 March 1997, p. 16.

22. A. Pikayev, "Russia and the Missile Technology Control Regime", in G.K. Bertsch and W.C. Potter (eds.), *Dangerous Weapons, Desperate States: Russia, Belarus, Kazakstan, and Ukraine* (London: Routledge, 1999), pp. 204–205.

23. D. Lynch, *The Conflict in Abkhazia: Dilemmas in Russian "Peacekeeping" Policy*, Discussion Paper 77, (London: Royal Institute of International Affairs, 1998), p. 22.

24. Allison, *Military Forces*, p. 79.

25. Fuller, p. 81; Lynch, pp. 26–27, 53 fn 29; Herzig, p. 77; Popov, pp. 196–197; D. Trenin, "Russian peacemaking in Georgia", in H.C. Ehrhart, A. Kreikemeyer and A. Zagorski (eds.), *Crisis Management in the CIS: Whither Russia?* (Baden-Baden: Nomos Verlagsgesellschaft, 1995), pp. 136–139. See also the provocative analysis by a former Colonel in Soviet Military Intelligence (GRU) S. Lunev, "Russian Military Policy in the Transcaucasus", *PRISM*, The Jamestown Foundation, vol. II, no. 8, part 4 (19 April 1996) (email).

26. Goltz, pp. 106–108.

27. Garthoff, pp. 60–61; A. Arbatov, "Russian Security Interests and Dilemmas: An Agenda for the Future", in A. Arbatov, A. Chayes, A.H. Chayes, and L. Olson (eds.), *Managing Conflict in the Former Soviet Union: Russian and American Perspectives* (Cambridge, Mass: MIT Press, 1997), p. 453; P. Baev, "Conflict Management in the Former Soviet South: The Dead-End of Russian Interventions", *European Security* Winter 1997, 6(4): 115.

28. Herzig, p. 90; Baev, *Russia's Policies in the Caucasus*, p. 20; Turbiville, *Mafia in Uniform*, p. 27; M. Galeotti, "Russia's Criminal Army," *Jane's Intelligence Review* June 1999, 11(6): 10.

29. L. Jonson, *Keeping the Peace in the CIS: The Evolution of Russian Policy*, Discussion Paper 81 (London: Royal Institute of International Affairs, 1999), p. 58 fn 16.

30. D. Trenin, *Russia's Use of Military Forces in Intra-State Conflicts in the CIS*, Berichte des Bundesinstituts fur Internationale und Ostwissenschaftliche Studien, No. 32 (Cologne: BIOst, 1996), pp. 10–11.

31. M.R. Gordon, "Georgia Boosted by Deal to Slash Russian Forces", *The Moscow Times*, no. 1845, Thursday 25 November 1999, p. 4; "Abkhazian military will occupy bases after Russian pull-out in 2001", *The Moscow Tribune*, 26 November 1999: 5.

32. V. Baranovsky, "Conclusion", in V. Baranovsky (ed.), *Russia and Europe: The Emerging Security Agenda* (Oxford: Oxford University Press for SIPRI, 1997), pp. 550–551. See also D. Danilov, "Russia's Search for an International Mandate in Transcaucasia", in Coppetiers, pp. 137–151. It should be noted that Georgia's President Shevardnadze was

the only CIS leader who unequivocally and openly supported the Russian war against Chechnya in 1994–96. See Baev, "Conflict Management", p. 124.

33. P.K. Baev, *The Russian Army in a Time of Troubles* (London: Sage for PRIO, 1996), p. 105.

34. K. Martin, "Tajikistan: Civil War without End?", *RFE/RL Research Report* 20 April 1993, 2(33): 21–22; M. Mesbahi, "Russian foreign policy and security in Central Asia and the Caucasus", *Central Asian Survey* 1993, 12(2): 200–201; I.B. Neumann and S. Solodovnik, "The Case of Tajikistan", in L. Jonson and C. Archer (eds.), *Peacemaking and the Role of Russia in Eurasia* (Boulder, Colorado: Westview, 1996), p. 89; L. Jonson, *The Tajik War: A Challenge to Russian Policy*, Discussion Paper 74 (London: Royal Institute of International Affairs, 1998), pp. 8–9.

35. Jonson, *Keeping the Peace*, p. 46.

36. S.J. Kaufman, "Elites, Masses, and Moscow in Moldova's Civil War", *International Security* Fall 1996, 21(2): 130–131; C. King, "Eurasia Letter: Moldova with a Russian Face", *Foreign Policy* Winter 1994–95, 97: 111–112.

37. *Moscow News*, no. 27 (14–20 July 1995), pp. 1, 4.

38. Jonson, *Keeping the Peace*, p. 44.

39. Gordon, p. 4.

40. Staar, pp. 16–17; Anthony, pp. 228–230; Baev, *Russia's Policies in the Caucasus*, p. 52; Turbiville, *Mafia in Uniform*, pp. 16–17.

41. I. Khripunov, "The Politics and Economics of Russia's Conventional Arms Transfers", in Bertsch and Potter, p. 148.

42. *The Guardian* 21 May 1992.

43. J. Berryman, "Russian Security Policy and Northern Europe" in W.E. Ferry and R.E. Kanet (eds.), *Post-Communist States in the World Community: Selected Papers from the Fifth World Congress of Central and East European Studies, Warsaw*, 1995 (Basingstoke: Macmillan, 1998), pp. 113–114.

44. M. Galeotti, *The Kremlin's Agenda: The new Russia and its armed forces* (Coulsdon: Jane's Intelligence Review, 1995), pp. 48, 52–53;

45. T. Forsberg, "Settled and Remaining Border Issues around the Baltic Sea", in L. Hedegaard and B. Lindstrom (eds.), *The NEBI Yearbook 1998: Northern European and Baltic Sea Integration* (Berlin: Springer-Verlag, 1998), p. 445; M. Nicholson, *Towards a Russia of the Regions*, Adelphi Paper 330 (Oxford: Oxford University Press for the IISS, 1999), pp. 60–62, 71–72.

46. G. Herd, "Competing for Kaliningrad", *The World Today* December 1999, 55(12): 7–8.

47. Shoumikhin, p. 216; Turbiville, *Mafia in Uniform*, p. 15.

48. Galeotti, "Russia's Criminal Army", p. 10; D. Clarke, "Military Main Source of Criminal Weapons", *OMRI Daily Digest* 5 April 1995, 68(1).

49. K. Sorokin, "Russia's 'New Look' Arms Sales Strategy", *Arms Control Today* October 1993: 7–8; Khripunov, p. 132.

50. M.T. Klare, "The Kalashnikov Age", *The Bulletin of Atomic Scientists* January/February 1999: 21.

51. D.V. Trenin and A.J. Pierre, "Arms Trade Rivalry in the Future of Russian-American Relations" in Pierre and Trenin, p. 117.

52. *The Military Balance 1998/99* (Oxford: Oxford University Press for the IISS, 1998), p. 107.

53. Khripunov, pp. 135–136.

54. *RFE/RL Newsline*, 7 December 1999, 3(236), Part 1.

55. R. Allison, "The Russian Armed Forces: structures, roles and policies", in Baranovsky, p. 194.

56. Gonchar and Lock, pp. 117–118.

57. "The second-oldest profession", *The Economist*, 12 February 1994, pp. 19–21; M.T. Klare, "An avalanche of guns: light weapons trafficking and armed conflicts in the post-Cold War era", in Kaldor and Vashee, pp. 59–60; M.T. Klare, "The Subterranean Arms Trade: Black-Market Sales, Covert Operations and Ethnic Warfare", in A. Pierre (ed.), *Cascade of Arms: Managing Conventional Weapons Proliferation* (Cambridge, Mass: The World Peace Foundation, 1997), pp. 43, 50–51.

58. A. Arbatov et al., "Introduction", in Baranovsky, p. 13.

59. C. Bluth, "Arms Control and Proliferation" in R. Allison and C. Bluth (eds.), *Security Dilemmas in Russia and Eurasia* (London: Royal Institute of International Affairs, 1998), pp. 314, 318.

60. Anthony, pp. 226–267.

61. L. Jonson, "Russian policy in Northern Europe", in Baranovsky, p. 313.

62. S. Medvedev, "Geopolitics and Beyond: The New Russian Policy Towards the Baltic States", in M. Jopp and S. Arnswald (eds.), *The European Union and the Baltic States: Visions, Interests and Strategies for the Baltic Sea Region* (Helsinki: The Finnish institute of international Affairs, 1998), pp. 255–256.

63. O. Greene, *Tackling Illicit Trafficking in Conventional Arms: Strengthening Collective Efforts by EU and Associate Countries*, (London: Saferworld, 1999); P. Eavis, "Awash With Light Weapons", *The World Today* April, 1999, 55(4): 19–21.

64. Klare, "An avalanche of guns", p. 72.

65. R.S. Norris, "The Soviet Nuclear Archipelago", *Arms Control Today* January/February 1992: 24.

66. G.H. Turbiville, Jr., *Weapons Proliferation and Organized Crime: The Russian Military and Security Force Dimensions*, INSS Occasional Paper no. 10, (Colorado: USAF Institute for National Security Studies, US Air Force Academy, 1996), pp. 32–33; I. Khripunov and D. Averre, "Russia's CBW closet poses ongoing threat", *Jane's Intelligence Review* May 1999, 11(5): 20–23; J. Perera, "Russia finally faces up to its CW legacy", *Jane's Intelligence Review* April 1999, 11(4): 23–27.

67. A.B. Carter and W.C. Perry, *Preventive Defense: A New Security Strategy for America* (Washington, D.C.: Brooking Institution Press, 1999), pp. 39, 70.

68. See for example O. Bukharin, "Nuclear Safeguards and Security in the Former Soviet Union", *Survival*, Winter 1994–95, 36(4): 53–72 and G.T. Allison, O.R. Cote, Jr., R.A. Falkenrath and S.E. Miller, *Avoiding Nuclear Anarchy: Containing the Threat of Loose Russian Nuclear Weapons and Fissile Material*, CSIA Studies in International Security No. 12, (Cambridge, Mass: The MIT Press, 1996).

69. Wallander, pp. 110–115.

70. Allison et al., pp. 23–28; W.C. Potter, "Before the Deluge? Assessing the Threat of Nuclear Leakage from the Post-Soviet States", *Arms Control Today* October 1995: 9–13; A.A. Pikayev, E.N. Nikitina and V. Kotov, "Harmful Legacies and Dangerous Weaknesses", in A.A. Arbatov, K. Kaiser and R. Levgold (eds.), *Russia and the West: The 21st Century Security Environment* (Armonk, New York: M.E. Sharpe, 1999), pp. 223–225; V.A. Orlov, "Export Controls and Nuclear Smuggling in Russia", in Bertsch and Potter, pp. 166–168.

71. G. Cameron, "Nuclear terrorism: a real threat?", *Jane's Intelligence Review* September 1996, 8(9): 422–425.

72. R.W. Lee, "Recent Trends in Nuclear Smuggling", in P. Williams (ed.), *Russian Organized Crime: The New Threat?* (London: Frank Cass, 1997), p. 117; R.W. Lee, *Smug-*

   gling Armaseddon: The Nuclear Black Market in the Former Soviet Union and Europe,
   (Basingstoke: Macmillan, 1998), pp. 19–20.
73. Potter, pp. 12–16: Bluth, pp. 307–308; Carter and Perry, pp. 77–82; K.M. Zisk, *Weapons, Culture and Shelf-Interest: Soviet Defense Managers in the New Russia*, (New York: Columbia University Press, 1997), pp. 19–20.
74. Pikayev, "Harmful Legacies", pp. 215, 225.
75. Orlov, pp. 174–175, 178–180; D. Averre, "Proliferation, Export Controls and Russian National Security", *Contemporary Security Policy* August 1996, 17(2): 193–194.
76. Pikayev, "Harmful Legacies", pp. 226–267; Khripunov and Averre, p. 23. On Western fears see A. Rimmington, "Fragmentation and Proliferation? The Fate of the Soviet Union's Offensive Biological Weapons Programme", *Contemporary Security Policy* April 1999, 20(1): 86–110.
77. G. Golan, *Russia and Iran: A Strategic Partnership?*, Discussion Paper 75 (London: The Royal Institute of International Affairs, 1998), p. 39.
78. Averre, pp. 194–197; Bluth, p. 306.
79. Pikayev, "Russia and the MTCR", pp. 201–212; Pikayev, "Harmful Legacies", p. 226.
80. For a cogent summary of the Western concerns see S. Blank, "Russia as a Rogne Proliferator", *Orbis* Winter 2000, 44(1): 91–107.
81. J.C. Baker, *Non-proliferation Incentives for Russia and Ukraine*, Adelphi Paper 309 (Oxford: Oxford University Press for the IISS, 1997).

Crime, Law & Social Change **33**: 105–129, 2000.

French arms, war and genocide in Rwanda

MEL MCNULTY
Department of Modern Languages, Faculty of Humanities, Nottingham Trent University,
Clifton Lane, Nottingham, NG11 8NS, UK

Abstract. France is now the world's second largest arms exporter, and the largest supplier of weapons to the developing world. The record of France's involvement in Rwanda from 1990 to 1994 has motivated the NGO lobby within France to subject French government policy – towards the developing world in general, and on arms supplies in particular – to unprecedented scrutiny. Accordingly, the level and volume of criticism of French involvement in Rwanda resulted in the first ever parliamentary commission to scrutinise French military activity overseas, although this and other official inquiries stopped short of identifying arms supplies as instrumental in exacerbating the Rwandan crisis.[1] A consideration of French arms supplies to Rwanda can offer a template by which to measure the nature and degree of France's support for the Habyarimana regime which planned, and the Sindikubwabo interim government which oversaw, the 1994 genocide in that country. Moreover, French arms supplies after France's own and the UN's arms embargo demonstrate how a process of unchecked militarisation may involve the supplier as well as the supplied in illegality.

Introduction

The Rwandan genocide of 1994 marked a watershed for French civil society, notably those Non-Governmental Organisations (NGOs) and individuals who had been to the forefront in advocating humanitarianism as a defining component of their country's foreign and development policy. France, uniquely in Europe, prides itself on having a global humanitarian mission, and evidence that this "homeland of human rights" was implicated in genocide through its military support until 1994 for the extremist regime in Rwanda shocked many who had applauded the declared pro-democracy, pro-humanitarian stance of President Mitterrand since 1981. Indeed, Mitterrand had been the first to appoint a Minister for Humanitarian Action in the person of *Médecins sans frontières* co-founder Bernard Kouchner, France's most prominent advocate of the right or duty of humanitarian intervention.[2]

The unprecedented creation in 1997 of a parliamentary commission to investigate France's role in Rwanda, presided by socialist deputy, former defence minister and chairman of the National Assembly's defence committee Paul Quilès, was seen as a direct result of the pressure generated by civil society, notably NGOs, some journalists and a number of academics, who had raised serious questions about the degree and extent of French support for the Habyarimana regime which planned and the Sindikubwabo interim government which oversaw the 1994 genocide. Yet the overwhelmingly military nature of this support, through training and major arms transfers from France to Rwanda, was not exceptional in the overall context of French military involvement in Africa over four decades and five presidencies since decolonisation. Yet many new NGOs, seeking to identify the cause and effect of French policy in the developing world in general and Africa in particular, emerged in France as a direct result of these events, notably *Agir ici*, *Survie*, *l'Observatoire permanent de la Coopération française* and *l'Observatoire des transferts d'armements*. The latter's newsletter noted, when the Quilès Commission's report was published in December 1998, that: "The implication of France in this tragedy, already denounced by NGOs, is thus confirmed. The Parliamentary Commission was forced to yield to this pressure from civil society, while attempting to diminish France's responsibility. The details on arms sales nonetheless speak volumes".[3]

The Quilès Commission[4] and other reports published to date – by the Belgian Senate[5] and the UN Security Council[6] – may represent an attempt to draw a line under the débâcle of the international response to the Rwandan genocide. However, all of these officially-sanctioned reports have failed to address the issue of the source of weapons supplies, although control of such supplies was identified in the UN report as key to preventing and defusing conflicts in Africa.

Crucially, it may be seen from the Rwandan case study that illegality in arms transfers flows from originally "legal" arms supplies, and that states overwhelmingly are the suppliers of new weaponry to civil conflicts. Boutwell and Klare have identified this "legal export from the major supplier states" as one of three factors along with domestic manufacture and black-market sales which have resulted in the circulation of "literally hundreds of millions" of small arms and light weapons throughout the world.[7]

War and genocide in Rwanda

It is now accepted by all except its perpetrators and their supporters that the Rwandan genocide of 1994, which resulted in the deaths of at least 800,000 people in three months, was one of the largest-scale crimes of the twentieth century. However, unlike the century's other genocides or mass politically-motivated killings – of Armenians, Jews and Cambodians – it is commonly assumed that the Rwandan genocide was spontaneous and conducted by a frenzied population armed with machetes, an impression created by much media coverage which typically fed stereotypes and reinforced Western prejudices that "Africa is a place of darkness, where furious savages clobber each other on the head to assuage their dark ancestral bloodlusts".[8] Two of

France's best known observers of African affairs, Stephen Smith and Antoine Glaser, wrote in 1994 that: "[T]he hands which cut to pieces men, women and children were Rwandan. They were not puppets' hands. They weren't even hands equipped with our help. Because, horror upon horror for their victims, the killers used machetes and not the firearms which we had delivered to them in abundance".[9]

In contrast, Stephen Goose and Frank Smyth of the Human Rights Watch Arms Project emphasised the significance of firearms to the Rwandan genocide: "The proliferation of weapons in Rwanda expanded the conflict ... Much of the killing was carried out with machetes, but automatic rifles and hand grenades were also commonly used. Their wide availability helped Hutu extremists carry out their slaughter on a horrendous scale. (...) Rwandan authorities distributed large numbers of firearms to militia members and other supporters months before the genocide began".[10] Michael T. Klare notes, in light of the Rwandan war and genocide and its spillover into the former Zaire, that: "While it is true, of course, that many factors contributed to these outcomes, it is also evident that, at each stage in this process, the acquisition of relatively small quantities of light weapons – never exceeding a few million dollars' worth at a given time – played a decisive role in sustaining and escalating the violence".[11] And a letter to the *Observer* a year after the genocide pointed out that: "Although the vilest images from last year are of massacre by machete, it is important to remember that Rwanda's government was backed in its tyranny by a formidable armoury provided by the West".[12]

Kathi Austin, researcher for Human Rights Watch Arms Project's reports on arms transfers to Rwanda, points out that: "Between 1992 and 1994, Rwanda was [sub-Saharan Africa's] third-largest importer of weapons (behind Angola and Nigeria), with cumulative military imports totaling $100 million"; and she concludes that: "Much of the killing was carried out with traditional weapons and farming implements, including machetes, knives and hoes; however, the security forces often finished off the survivors seeking refuge in churches, stadiums, or school buildings with automatic rifles and grenades. Sadly, a UN arms embargo was not imposed on Rwanda until a month and a half after the genocide had commenced".[13] It is also important to note that many of these traditional weapons and farming implements were specially imported for the purpose of killing; orders for such implements during the period of preparation for the genocide greatly exceeded Rwanda's agricultural needs.

The Rwandan genocide of 1994 was in fact highly organised[14] – Rwanda's *génocidaires* killed at five times the rate of the Nazis – and must also be viewed in context of the transformation of Rwanda in under four years from a sectarian but stable "hard state" to a "weapons state" and thence to a genocidal state; it has been argued that this would not have been possible without externally-sponsored militarisation.[15]

Motives and mechanics of French arms transfers

The headwaters of the flow of weapons to conflict in the African Great Lakes are to be found in those Western countries with the world's largest arms industries, notably the US, France, UK and Belgium. France's part of this one-way flow of weaponry, military equipment and expertise is labelled "co-operation" (which of course implies a two-way process); and this Franco-African military cooperation is given legal personality through bilateral treaties although equally influenced by traditions, personal interests, networks, covert operations and "bad habits".[16] Guy Martin notes that:

> Although camouflaged under the mantle of *coopération*, France's African policy is, in fact, primarily motivated by a narrow conception of its national interests, and blatantly disregards African concerns and interests. As former President Valéry Giscard d'Estaing once bluntly declared, "I am dealing with African affairs, namely with France's interests in Africa".[17]

French military support for favoured African regimes is based on a pyramid of militarism, built in the first instance on the defence treaties and military assistance accords which obtain between France and nearly half (23) of Africa's 51 states. France is the only ex-colonial power which retains this number of military agreements and such a complex system of military cooperation with so many states. This baseline of exceptionality, dating from the very inception of the African states concerned, has provided a firm foundation for the other aspects of French militarism in Africa. France is the only country to station its own troops in Africa – constituting what has been called "a permanent intervention"[18] – despite an OAU resolution as early as 1978 condemning the existence of foreign military bases on the continent.[19] France is also the principal supplier of weaponry and military equipment to Africa and, since 1996, the leading arms merchant to the developing world as a whole and, after the US, the world's largest arms exporter.[20] It is also the principal creator and instructor of African armies. This creation of military protégés on the French model is seen as a key aspect of Franco-African cooperation; Guy Martin also points out that:

> French leaders tend to link the concepts of security and development by arguing that their help in creating strong national armies has contributed to the stability and hence to the economic benefit of all concerned.

In fact, the French government's objective in creating African national armies at the time of independence was to build up units that could work closely with French units and effectively serve as branches of the French army overseas.[21]

The Rwandan state and the inherent conflict which led to war in 1990 functioned entirely outside of the Cold War framework which determined the context and distorted the nature of wars elsewhere on the continent until that date. Rwanda was of strategic importance to no extra-African power during or after the Cold War except, for its own unique reasons, for France. As early as 1975, Franco-Rwandan military cooperation was formalised in a military technical assistance accord. The Franco-Rwandan accord would be the twenty-second such document, and entailed an initially modest annual transfer of arms and military equipment from France to Rwanda worth about FF4m (£0.5m) per year. With regard to the deployment of French troops in the country, the accord states: "The government of the French Republic places at the disposal of the government of the Rwandese republic the French military personnel whose services are required for the organisation and instruction of the Rwandese national police".

Faced in October 1990 with an armed insurgency by his own exiled co-nationals organised as the Rwandan Patriotic Front (RPF), then Rwandan President Habyarimana swiftly contacted his principal foreign backers, President Mitterrand and his son Jean-Christophe (then head of the advisory "Africa Unit" attached to the French presidency), and claimed Rwanda had been attacked by an expansionist Ugandan President Museveni. This appeal struck the right chord in Paris, where defence of France's African sphere of influence was (until recently) a key pillar of foreign policy; and it produced the desired effect, a military intervention, and rapid, exponential militarisation. Three hundred French troops (Foreign Legionnaire paratroopers of the *1er* and *2e Régiment étranger parachutiste* (REP) and Marines of the *Régiment parachtiste d'infanterie de Marine* (RPIMa)) arrived in Rwanda on October 4, 1990. They brought with them 60-mm, 81-mm and 120-mm mortars and 105-mm light artillery guns.[22] In an interview with a former Foreign Legion officer who participated in this operation, codenamed *Noroît*, Stephen Bradshaw asked about the significance of these weapons on the development and outcome of the war:

Bradshaw: How important was the artillery in preventing the RPF advance?
Officer: Obviously very important because the RPF didn't have very much heavy artillery and the Rwandan government had that advantage over the RPF and there was no way that the RPF could go through the lines of heavy artillery.

Bradshaw: If the French hadn't been there what would have actually happened?

Officer: Well the Rwandan army would have been totally incapable of defending the country, and since they scarcely knew how to use the weapons and they knew very little about military tactics, the war would have been lost. There would have been a very, very small battle and in a day it would have been over, if the French hadn't been there.[23]

French troops were deployed in Kigali, initially to evacuate French citizens, but remained for three years. During this time, French personnel were directly responsible, through arming and training, for the exponential growth of the Rwandan Government Army (*Forces Armées Rwandaises* – FAR), which swelled from 5,200-strong in 1990 to 35,000 in 1993. Eventually, a Frenchman, Lt.-Col. Gilles Chollet, was made special military advisor to President Habyarimana and given overall command of operations. However, when it became apparent that France's first direct military intervention there necessitated the long-term support of Habyarimana's weak and disorganised army, the 1975 Franco-Rwandan military technical assistance accord was amended on 26 August 1992 to include the "Rwandese armed forces" as eligible for French assistance. It is noteworthy that French justificatory discourse changed at this time; the intervention, by then approaching its second anniversary with official troop levels near 700, was no longer intended merely to protect French nationals, but, according to French ambassador Martres, "to prevent destabilisation of Rwanda".[24] Uniquely, both sections of the Franco-Rwandan accord were classified, and did not appear alongside similar accords published in the *Journal officiel*.[25] The accord is only now in the public domain following its publication in the report of the Quilès Commission in December 1998.[26]

The extraordinary development of the FAR, comparable in scale, expense and inefficiency to the eventually fruitless American backing of the South Vietnamese Army, has been extensively documented. A UN-commissioned report published by the Danish foreign ministry on the international response to the Rwandan war concluded that: "The influx of weapons from foreign sources to the Rwandese government as well as to the RPF contributed significantly to the civil war. . . as well as to the massacres in 1994."[27]

Acknowledged French arms transfers to the FAR during the Rwandan civil war from 1990 to April 1994 included some heavy weaponry: three Gazelle helicopters with spare parts, as well as spare parts for French-manufactured Panhard automatic machine guns. Indeed, the use of this French-supplied matériel as helicopter gun-ships by the FAR and – allegedly – by their French allies, also radically altered the nature of the war in its early stages, confining the numerically-superior RPF to a small arc of territory in the mountainous north of the country (in Byumba préfecture).[28]

Former French Captain of Gendarmerie (and later military advisor to the Rwandan president) Paul Barril gives an enthusiastic description of the role of France's special military services in Rwanda, notably the use – redolent of *Apocalypse Now* – of French-piloted helicopter gunships to destroy RPF supply lines early in the campaign:

> France's official special services blocked in '90 the attack by the RPF terrorists and Uganda, a DGSE [*Direction générale de la Sécurité extérieure*, French military intelligence] job. A remarkable job which was a source of great pride in this first phase of the war. There were heroes on the French side who will never be known, extraordinary stories of guys who took crazy initiatives, who went out and blasted all around them with just a few helicopters and a few guns. There is material for a book on the heroism of the Secret Services in Rwanda, against Uganda and the RPF. . . which explains their hatred for France.[29]

Barril's account is corroborated by those on the receiving end;[30] Tito Rutaramera, a leading RPF tactician, explained that the use by the FAR of French helicopters forced the RPF to abandon their conventional advance on Kigali from their northern stronghold around Byumba, and to adopt the tactics of the *guerre mobile*.[31]

Given this evolution of the combat from conventional war to *guerre mobile* by the time of the second RPF offensive in 1991, French arms transfers thereafter consisted overwhelmingly of small calibre light weapons and ammunition, including assault rifles, anti-tank rocket launchers and hundreds of thousands of rounds of ammunition of all calibres; official policy throughout the war was to ensure that "the Rwandan Armed Forces were kept regularly supplied with munitions during the different serious offensives launched by the RPF".[32] This was demonstrated most effectively at the time of the RPF's successful capture and subsequent retreat from Ruhengeri in Febuary 1993; the Quilès Commission quotes the report of Col. Philippe Tracqui, commander of the French troops of *Opération Noroît* in early 1993, as follows: "Friday 12 February 1993: landing of a DC8 with 50 12.7mm machine guns plus 100,000 rounds for the FAR. Wednesday 17 February 1993: landing of a Boeing 747 with discreet unloading by the FAR of 105mm shells and 68mm rockets (Alat)".[33] The Commission notes that: "The deliveries of arms and munitions, along with the operational assistance mission led a few days later by Lt.-Col. Didier Tauzin, will allow the FAR within a fortnight to recover spectacularly the situation against the RPF".[34]

The Quilès Commission refuses to draw any conclusions from the record of French arms shipments to Rwanda; in response to multiple accusations of French complicity with the perpetrators of genocide through continued military support, the Commission's report starts with a disclaimer: "The Mission does not believe that it has uncovered the whole truth on this subject and particularly it does not claim, in respect of arms transfers, to have elucidated all the cases evoked in various articles and publications about parallel markets and deliveries carried out at the time of the massacres, in April 1994, or after the embargo announced by the United Nations on 17 May 1994".[35]

However, the Commission obtained unprecedented declassification of documents which otherwise would have been subject to *secret défense* for at least a further 30 years. Usefully, these were attached in annexes, which for the first time allow us to trace a pattern of French arms transfers to a country at war, and draw our own conclusions about the effect these transfers may have had on the evolution of the military and political situation there. Recent reports have underlined the need for "greater transparency efforts to illuminate just how small arms and light weapons [made] their way to the killing grounds of the 1990s".[36] The urgency of such transparency was demonstrated most dramatically in Rwanda where, as Michael Klare notes: "When societies are deeply divided along ethnic, religious, or sectarian lines and the existing government is unwilling or unable to protect minorities and maintain domestic order, the introduction and use of even small quantities of small arms and light weapons can have profoundly destabilizing effects".[37]

Technically, exports of light arms from France must be authorised by the Prime Minister in consultation with Interministerial Commission for the Study of Exports of War Materials (*Commission interministérielle pour l'étude des exportations des matériels de guerre* – CIEEMG), based on a set of confidential criteria.[38] This Commission includes representatives of the Ministries of Foreign Affairs, Defence, Economy and Finance. It examines all applications for arms exports and must give its consent before the deliveries can take place. The Commission's deliberations are confidential and subject to official secrecy.

However, in Rwanda there were also regular direct, complimentary transfers (*cessions*) from the Military Cooperation Mission (*Mission militaire de coopération*) within the Cooperation Ministry (*Ministère de la Coopération*).[39] According to documents declassified for the Quilès Commission, nine out of nineteen arms transfers by the Military Cooperation Mission were not subject to War Matériel Export Authorisation (*Autorisation d'exportation de matériels de guerre* – AEMG) controls. Moreover, the Quilès Commission notes that: "31 direct transfers of arms and munitions to Rwanda were carried out in disregard of correct procedure",[40] as well as regular deliveries of state-of-the-art communications systems. According to the *Observatoire des transferts des armements*: "This indicates clearly that these non-'authorised' bequests took place under the sole authority of the army".[41] Quilès suggests, regarding the French army's "reconstruction" of the FAR, that: "In this context of reorganisation, it is scarcely surprising that certain French military decision-makers could have felt that they were building an army, for which it was necessary moreover to ensure that it would be regularly supplied with munitions".[42] Acknowledged direct transfers of arms and ammunition during the 1990 to 1994 period were worth approximately 42 million French francs (c. £4m).[43]

Overall, according to official, declassified documents reproduced in annexes to the report of the Quilès Commission, total arms sales by France to Rwanda during the period 1990 to 1994 were composed of 62 contracts examined by the CIEEMG, 84 passed by AEMG and 19 free transfers. There is no indication whether the 146 arms "purchases" were actually paid for by the Rwandan government, or whether the majority of these transfers were in fact complimentary and paid for by Defence or Cooperation Ministry budgets. Other than these declassifed documents, no official account of the total amount of arms supplied by France to Rwanda between 1990 and 1994 is available, but African Rights concludes that such supplies amounted to "at least $6m worth in 1991–92 [alone], including mortars, light artillery, armoured cars and helicopters... France also supplied spare parts and technical assistance to maintain the vehicles of the FAR".[44] The authoritative account of the establishment of the International Criminal Tribunal for Rwanda by Morris and Scharf cites a further expenditure of $6 million, stating that: "The Rwandan authorities distributed six million dollars worth of firearms provided by France to militia members and other supporters of President Habyarimana from 1992 to early 1994."[45]

The Arusha Accords, signed by the warring parties in 1993, included stipulations that foreign forces should be withdrawn from Rwanda, and that arms supplies to the belligerents should cease. However, the Rwandan government's arms suppliers found means of circumventing these restrictions, as direct shipments were not the only means of rapid militarisation used by Rwanda and its supporters. South Africa (pre-Mandela), the only major arms manufacturer on the continent, was well-placed to sell material to Habyarimana, and arms acquisition was greatly facilitated by French financial aid to support the Rwandan war effort, which grew from a peacetime FF4m to FF55m per annum in 1993, a nearly fourteen-fold increase, placing wartime Rwanda sixth of the 26 African states which received such aid from France.[46] Human Rights Watch's 1993 annual report also noted that:

France has consistently supported President Habyarimana over the years and continued this policy during 1993 despite evidence of human rights abuses by his regime. Just after the beginning of the war in 1990, France sent a contingent of troops "to protect French citizens and other expatriates" in Rwanda. After the RPF violated the cease-fire in February, France sent an additional 300 soldiers some of whom actively supported Rwandan troops in the combat zones. Some of the French troops were withdrawn after the March cease-fire, but others remained in Rwanda, in violation of accords which called for the departure of all foreign troops. France supplied Rwanda with arms and with political and propaganda support within the European Community.[47]

Light weapons were also supplied by France through third parties (notably Egypt). Klare notes that, as illustrated in Human Rights Watch Arms Project's 1994 report, "The multiplicity of suppliers... facilitates the acquisition of arms by potential belligerents, particularly those that might be shunned by the traditional suppliers for political or human rights reasons. Prior to the massacres of 1994, for instance, the government of Rwanda was able to purchase large quantities of small arms from producers in Egypt and South Africa".[48] However Goose and Smith, authors of Human Rights Watch's report on arms supplies to Rwanda, note that Rwanda's principal supplier, France, was still involved in the Egyptian deal:

> A $6 million contract between Egypt and Rwanda in March 1992, with Rwanda's payment guaranteed by a French bank [the state-owned Crédit Lyonnais], included 60-mm and 82-mm mortars, 16,000 mortar shells, 122-m D-30 howitzers, 3,000 artillery shells, rocket-propelled grenades, plastic explosives, antipersonnel land mines, and more than three million rounds of small arms ammunition.[49]

Kathi Austin confirms these conclusions. In summary of her findings re non-French and third party transfers to the Rwandan *ancien régime*, she notes that: "President Juvenal Habyarimana also acquired rifles, machine guns and ammunition from South Africa in contravention of an international ban on South African arms exports. In addition, the Egyptian government provided Habyarimana with long-range artillery pieces, artillery shells, explosives, grenades, land mines and Egyptian-made Kalashnikov rifles in exchange for cash and tea; this $6 million transaction was financed with a loan provided by the French government bank, the Crédit Lyonnais".[50]

Nonetheless, the president of the state-owned bank Jean Peyrelevade has since denied that there had been any credit guarantee for this transaction, and the Quilès Commission's report stated that no definitive conclusion could be drawn from the supporting document supplied by Human Rights Watch.[51]

Mobutu's Zaire was an essential conduit for arms shipments which could not be sent directly to Rwanda for reasons of security or political sensitivity throughout this period. At France's request, the late Marshal-President's Presidential Guard had been in the frontline in repelling the first RPF offensive; and Zaire remained an indispensable supply route for weapons up to, including and subsequent to the Rwandan state's recourse to genocide. (Indeed, the significance of Mobutu's Zaire as a source of regional instability, comparable to that of apartheid South Africa, partly explains the subsequent imperative for post-genocide Rwanda and other threatened states to cooperate in its destruction in 1997.[52])

Arms transfers to Rwanda during the genocide and post-embargo

The UN-commissioned report published by the Danish foreign ministry on the international response to the Rwandan war concluded that: "The influx of weapons from foreign sources to the Rwandese government as well as to the RPF contributed significantly to the civil war... as well as to the massacres in 1994."[53] Goose and Smith concur that "Governments that supplied weapons and otherwise supported those forces [responsible for the genocide] bear some responsibility for needless civilian deaths."[54]

And on 20 August 1995, BBC Panorama's study of French involvement in Rwanda, "The Bloody Tricolour" included testimony from Belgian UNAMIR (United Nations Assistance Mission in Rwanda) Colonel Luc Marchal (Commander of UN Forces Kigali Sector 1993–94) who stated, in an interview with Stephen Bradshaw, that the French army had delivered munitions to the FAR when the genocide had already been underway for two days. Colonel Marchal described the arrival of French military aircraft on 8 April 1994 at Kigali airport:

> Marchal: The first lift was composed of three planes. Two of those three planes were carrying personnel and one was carrying ammunition.
> Bradshaw: Ammunition for the French soldiers?
> Marchal: No, for the Rwandese army.
> Bradshaw: How do you know this ammunition was for the Rwandese army?
> Marchal: Because they [the cases of munitions] just remained a few minutes in the airfield. Immediately after they were loaded in vehicles and they [were] moved to the Kanombe camp [FAR HQ in Kigali].

There is no confirmation of this shipment in the report of the Quilès Commission. However, of the principal accusations of French complicity in the genocide, the following were addressed by the Commission: French diplomatic and military personnel in Rwanda were partisans of the "Hutu Power" faction in the Rwandan government, and considered the RPF as an enemy; French military support for the FAR in its war against the RPF "bordered on direct engagement" (est "allée jusqu'au limites de l'engagement direct'); there was a secret dimension to Franco-Rwandan military cooperation; French support for the Habyarimana regime was never questioned despite the numerous human rights abuses which preceded the genocide; France had foreseen the risks of genocide from as early as 1990 and was aware of the implication of the most senior figures of the Rwandan regime in its preparation; a high-level meeting took place in May 1994 between the FAR and the head of the Mission militaire de Coopération at the Ministère de la Coopération in Paris even while the same FAR was overseeing the genocide in Rwanda; France maintained diplomatic relations until July 1994 with the interim government which carried out the genocide; and the "Safe Humanitarian Zone' created during Opération Turquoise facilitated the escape of the génocidaires.[55]

The May 1994 meeting in Paris is detailed in documents recovered by journalist Colette Braeckman of Brussels daily Le Soir. In a letter and report addressed to the Rwandan Defence Minister and FAR Chief of Staff (both based in Gitarama, south-central Rwanda, where the interim government had moved after fleeing Kigali in the face of the RPF advance), Lieutenant Colonel Ephrem Rwabalinda, adviser to the Chief of Staff, describes his visit to the Military Cooperation Mission in Paris from 9 to 13 May.[56] Lt. Col. Rwabalinda was received by head of mission General Huchon on Monday 9 May 1994. They met for two hours, and Rwabalinda spelled out the FAR's "urgent needs: munitions for the 105mm artillery battery (at least 2000 rounds); completion of the munitions for individual weapons, if necessary by passing indirectly via neighbouring countries friendly to Rwanda; clothing; transmission equipment."

The report details General Huchon's opinion that the French army was "tied hands and feet" by public opinion which would not permit a further direct French intervention to assist the FAR, and that there was an urgent need to limit damage to Rwanda's reputation abroad and turn around international opinion so that French aid could recommence. In the meantime, the Military Cooperation Mission would send "a secure telecommunications system to allow General Huchon and General Bizimungu of the FAR to communicate without being overheard"; and 17 transmitters and receivers to allow communication between military units in Kigali. This equipment was ready to be shipped at Ostende. General Huchon also urged the creation of a zone under secure FAR control, where deliveries could take place safely.[57]

However, in contrast to Braeckman, much of the francophone press supported official accounts that military supplies had ceased on April 8; Stephen

Smith of *Libération* stated in August 1995 that: "All the military sources whom I have been able to contact in the course of the last few months have denied categorically that there were French arms deliveries to Rwanda, even during the whole year of 1994".[58]

French arms transfers to Rwanda also continued after the 17 May 1994 UN arms embargo, to which France initially was opposed. The 1995 report of the *Observatoire permanent de la Coopération française* (formed as a response to French policy in Africa in general and Rwanda in particular) noted that: "At the UN Security Council on May 17, France [in the person of its permanent representative Jean-Bernard Mérimée] made common cause with the ambassador of the Rwandese interim government, who was trying to oppose the voting of an embargo on arms destined for Rwanda – on the pretext that this embargo would only penalise 'government' forces. France was opposed to it because the flow of arms deliveries was continuing, with the support of most of the [French] military personnel, who were hostile to the embargo".[59]

The Resolution – S/RES/918 (1994) – was finally adopted on 17 May 1994 by 14 votes to 1, the dissident voice being the Rwandan interim government which opposed the inclusion of the following, Section B of the draft resolution:

> Determining that the situation in Rwanda constitutes a threat to peace and security in the region,
> Acting under Chapter VII of the Charter of the United Nations,
> 13. Decides that all States shall prevent the sale or supply to Rwanda by their nationals or from their territories or using their flag vessels or aircraft or arms and related matériel of all types, including weapons and ammunition, military vehicles and equipment, paramilitary police equipment and spare parts (. . .)
> 15. Calls upon all States, including States not Members of the United Nations, and international organizations to act strictly in accordance with the provisions of the present resolution, notwithstanding the existence of any rights or obligations conferred or imposed by any international agreement or any contract entered into or any licence or permit granted prior to the date of the adoption of the present resolution.

Of accounts of breaches of this embargo by UN member states, Human Rights Watch's May 1995 report is the most categorical:

> Arms flows to the FAR were not suspended immediately by France after the imposition of the arms embargo on May 17, 1994. Rather, they were diverted to Goma airport in Zaire. . . Some of the first arms shipments to arrive in Goma after May 17 were supplied to the FAR by the French

government. Human Rights Watch learned from airport personnel and local businessmen that five shipments arrived in May and June containing artillery, machine guns, assault rifles and ammunition provided by the French government. These weapons were taken across the border into Rwanda by members of the Zairian military and delivered to the FAR in Gisenyi. The French consul in Goma at the time, Jean-Claude Urbano, has justified the five shipments as a fulfilment of contracts negotiated with the government of Rwanda prior to the arms embargo. In the view of Human Rights Watch, these shipments constituted a clear violation of the UN-imposed embargo, and are all the more to be condemned because the recipients were carrying out a campaign of genocide at the time.[60]

Kathi Austin also notes that: "In contravention of the UN arms embargo, weapons poured into eastern Zaire for the ex-FAR from governments or traffickers based in Belgium, China, France, South Africa and the Seychelles." But France's role was again exceptional; the Human Rights Watch Arms Project 1995 report "Rearming with Impunity" noted that: "France used private contractors to provide light weapons to ex-FAR units based in refugee camps in eastern Zaire and provided financial assistance to the Mobutu regime in 1996 for third-party arms transfers".[61]

Journalists corroborate accounts of arms deliveries to Goma in unmarked Boeing 707s[62]; *Libération* noted an official denial, and unofficial admission, that such a delivery was possible: "All sources on the spot – including well-placed French ex-pats – have expressed their 'certainty' that these arms deliveries were 'paid for by France'."[63] And the defence attaché at "a French embassy in the region" (most probably in Burundi), while rejecting the suggestion that there had been an official French delivery of arms, added: "But an under-the-counter assistance, by parallel circuits, is always possible. You know, I could tell you a story or two about shady arms traffic deals in Paris..."[64]

And key among the *Joint Evaluation of Emergency Assistance to Rwanda* Committee's findings, under the heading " Illegal Arms Trade Fuelled the Violence", was the following:

Outside arms suppliers contributed to and exacerbated the conflict in Rwanda in violation of the spirit if not the text of the Arusha Accords, preceding cease-fire agreements and the UN arms embargo. After the genocide, continued rearming of former government military and militia, as reported to have been occurring in Zaire, increased the threat of repetition of the cycle of massive violence. The recently established International Commission of Inquiry, charged with investigating these reports, will hopefully lead to a cessation of such arms shipments.[65]

The Quilès Commission report acknowledges the accuations of post-embargo arms shipments, while questioning their sustainability. There is also an element of whitewash concerning France's deliveries of arms and military equipment after France's own ban and the UN embargo:

> The press stated that France had violated its own embargo of April 8 and the UN's of May 17. The French state-controlled weapons and military equipment company SOFREMAS was accused of having broken the embargo by proceeding with deliveries via Goma in Zaire. Similarly, the Luchaire company, which is 100% owned by Giat Industries, was also accused of having made similar deliveries.
>
> In its May 1995 report, Human Rights Watch claims to have learned from airport staff and from a local businessman that five convoys had arrived at Goma in May and June 1994 containing weapons and munitions from France for the FAR.
>
> On these different points, the Mission has not been able to this day to gather substantive proof, despite requests it made to obtain, notably from Human Rights Watch, copies of documents or memos relating to SOFREMAS and found in Zaire in an abandoned bus near Goma.[66]

However, the French authorities have also proved slow to respond to requests; in November 1998, the UN International Commission of Inquiry reported that: "On 13 August 1998, the Chairman wrote to the French Ministry for Foreign Affairs to inquire if the Government of France was aware of the findings of the Attorney-General of Switzerland concerning the Banque nationale de Paris and the South African arms broker, Willem Ehlers, as described in the Commission's report (S/1998/63, paras. 16–27). The Commission has not yet received a response from the Government".[67]

Goose and Smith conclude that: "The leakiness of existing and past arms embargoes on individual nations is ample evidence of the difficulties involved. A major reason those embargoes have been difficult to enforce is that without any mechanism to control transfers, states can easily buy arms through second- and third-party transfers, without the knowledge of the original producer. (. . .) Clearly, private arms dealers would seek ways to illegally circumvent any control mechanism. 'Yet the biggest regular suppliers of weapons to the covert arms trade are not freelancing private arms dealers, but governments themselves,' reports *The Economist*. 'The main motive is cash.' "[68]

There is also evidence that arms transfers from France to the Former Government of Rwanda (FGOR) in exile continued at least until the collapse of the former Zaire in May 1997. *Joint Evaluation of Emergency Assistance to Rwanda* noted in March 1996 that: "Overt rearming and reorganization of the former leadership, military and militia in or beside internationally-supported camps in Zaire have posed a threat of war in the region for well over a year".[69] And William Cyrus Reed concludes his assessment of the FGOR by stating that:

> In short, the French ensured that the FGOR possessed a large, well-equipped military and that it could escape to Zaire, with its command structure and key troops largely in place. If troops were disarmed at the border, they quickly rearmed on the other side (. . .) [T]he FGOR gained access to the resources it needed to sustain itself by using its former sovereign status to loot the country of human and physical resources. Utilizing well-established alliances with France and Zaire, the FGOR then exported these resources across the border to Zaire. Here, the FGOR built upon the hospitality of its pariah host by activating long-established international contacts to re-establish its military and to recreate its de facto authority over its now exiled population (. . .) Within the military, ranks had been re-established, the former militias had been integrated into the regular forces, and because of the FGOR's control over the refugee camps, young recruits were constantly being added to the ranks. Now combined, the former military and the militias brought the total number of soldiers under the FGOR to 50,000.[70]

However, it is important to note that France was by no means alone in supplying weapons to the FGOR. In November 1996, it emerged that UK company Mil-Tec brokered the sale of arms from Albania and Israel to the former Rwandan government both before and during the 1994 genocide. In January 1997 it was reported that that the British government had "failed to implement all the requirements of a United Nations arms embargo on Rwanda, thus allowing a British company to supply weapons to extremist Hutu militia".[71] The then British Foreign Secretary Malcolm Rifkind responded by claiming that the company concerned, Mil-Tec Corporation Ltd., was based in the Isle of Man and hence not subject to the UN embargo. Eavis and Benson note that: "Despite the scandal that ensued and an interdepartmental report that called for brokering to be tackled, the issue remains unaddressed in both the United Kingdom and the majority of EU states".[72]

Conclusion

Sales and particularly transfers, i.e. donations of arms to one party in a conflict, constitute a direct intervention in that conflict's development, and often contribute directly to its prolongation; Boutwell and Klare emphasise "the dynamics by which the increased availability of low-cost small arms and light weapons contributes to the likelihood, intensity and duration of armed conflict within states".[73]

In Rwanda, rapid, externally-sponsored militarisation of an already authoritarian state (built on sectarianism, discrimination and enforced exiling or elimination of its opponents) acted as a catalyst for the hardening of the regime, and the state-sponsored emergence of extremist militias and assassination squads. External military support for the regime, in the form of arms supplies and sales, training, and direct military intervention, was perceived as open-ended and unconditional. This perception reinforced extremists to the extent that there was no room for the state to move from a military to a political counter-insurgency strategy; any form of compromise (such as that represented by the 1993 Arusha accords) was deemed betrayal by the state's military and the unaccountable militias it had created. Accordingly, assassination of any potential agents of compromise, and the subsequent implementation of a long-planned genocide, were perceived by newly dominant warlords as appropriate and effective responses to their enemies' political and military successes. Such a response was intended to eliminate all the state's opponents of any ethnicity who could constitute a support base for opposition, by applying an extreme counter-insurgency strategy: genocide, by inverting the Maoist principle, was an attempt to remove the water from the fish.

Initially, the Rwandan case was not unique. Most analysts would agree that the recurring causes of intrastate conflict on the African continent may be summarised as one or a combination of a struggle for political power, a struggle over basic resources, or a struggle for political participation in a multi-ethnic state. However, when the catalyst of militarisation is added to this powder-keg, the situation becomes correspondingly explosive, and locked into a vicious circle. As Wadlow explains: "Militarisation is part of a cycle which leads to the impoverishment of the state, to aggravated debt concerns, to an ever narrower political base requiring ever more violence to stay in power."[74]

Externally-sponsored militarisation of Rwanda was a key factor, some would argue the key factor in the intransigence of that state's rulers. Swift militarisation reinforced a chronically hard state, creating a weapons state in which radical, sectarian, militant extremism could flourish. The failure to make continued support, especially military, conditional on human rights or anti-sectarian criteria scuppered the Arusha peace process. The maintenance of French support for the regime despite Habyarimana's subsequent dismissal of the Arusha accord convinced the regime's extremists that such support would always be forthcoming. Christopher Clapham has identified this radicalisation of extremist regimes through external backing:

> [A]n apparently inexhaustible supply of arms and aid from an all-po-
> werful external patron encouraged rulers to suppose that their own he-
> gemonic ambitions were ultimately unstoppable, and that they could
> therefore proceed with the establishment of a monopoly state which need
> take no account of internal opposition or the indigenous characteristics
> of the societies which they governed ... Ultimately, it was not the im-
> ported armaments which conferred power on the government, but the
> indigenous people who had to use them. When they failed, it failed.[75]

During 1991 and 1992 the EU Council of Ministers had adopted eight criteria which should be applied to arms sales by EU member states. The third
of these stipulated that the exporting states should consider, with regard to
the recipient state, "the internal situation in the country, according to the
existence of conflict or tensions within its borders".[76] In June 1997, EU-
wide agreement was obtained during the Netherlands' EU presidency on the
Programme for Preventing and Combating Illicit Trafficking in Conventional
Arms; and during the UK's EU presidency in 1998, agreement was reached
on an EU Code of Conduct on arms exports. However, a major weakness of
the code is that it does not provide any mechanisms for public accountability or parliamentary scrutiny of arms exports, the need for which has been
reinforced by the investigations and report of the Quilès Commission.[77]

The UN International Commission of Inquiry concluded in November
1998 that international embargoes without effective implementation mechanisms are largely ineffective. Controls at the "Demand-Side" – the warring
parties in the developing world – may be deemed ineffective and impractic-
able in conflict situations; controls are therefore imperative at the "Supply-
Side", in countries with active civil societies and existing mechanisms of
democratic scrutiny and public accountability: including the French National
Assembly's Defence and Foreign Affairs committees. Kathi Austin concludes
that: "Clearly, any effort to reduce the violence in the Great Lakes region must
tackle the degree of internal militarization resulting from unimpeded flows of
weapons and foreign military assistance (...) While an international arms
embargo against the entire region would hold the most promise for curbing
arms proliferation, such a measure is opposed by France and the United States
– both of which continue to vie for strategic advantage in the region. Given
the region's high degree of conflict and lack or respect for the rule of law, it
would appear timely and useful to institute better controls on the supply side
of the arms equation".[78]

However, Eavis and Benson note that; "The vast number of light weapons
already in circulation in regions of conflict... means that supply-side initiatives to tackle the problem will not be enough on their own".[79] And in January

2000, a meeting of African observers of arms trafficking passed a resolution at a meeting in the Ugandan capital Kampala which:

> underlined the need for all states, especially those which produce, export or import arms to take the necessary measures to prevent, curb, combat and eradicate the illicit manufacture of and trafficking in firearms, their parts and components as well as ammunition. It also encouraged states to consider measures to enhance and facilitate cooperation and exchange of data and other information among states with a view to preventing, curbing, combating and eradicating the illicit manufacturing of, and trafficking in, firearms.[80]

Such initiatives from within the continent most devastated in recent years by unchecked arms flows may act as a foil to Afropessimists' portrayals of Africa as a victim only, and counter the received Western wisdom that solutions may only be found in the capitals of those Western countries which are also the source of the arms which have so exacerbated Africa's recent crises.

Notes

1. This consideration of arms transfers stems from an earlier paper, "Intervention and accountability: the enduring limits on parliamentary scrutiny of French military operations overseas since the Quilès Commission report", presented to the Security and Intelligence Studies Group panel on Parliamentary Oversight of Security and Intelligence at the PSA Annual Conference, University of Nottingham, 23 March 1999.
2. See Bernard Koucher, *Le malheur des autres*, (Paris, Odile Jacob, 1991). Kouchner is currently UN administrator in Kosovo.
3. "On a ainsi la confirmation de l'implication de la France dans cette tragédie, déjà dénoncée par les ONG. La Commission parlementaire a dû céder à cette pression de la société civile, tout en tentant d'atténuer la responsabilité française. Le détail des ventes d'armes est pourtant éloquent..." Observatoire des transferts d'armements, *La lettre de l'Observatoire* no. 17: 1, March 1999, p. 2.
4. Assemblée nationale, *Rapport d'information déposé par la Mission d'information de la Commission de la défense nationale et des forces armées et de la Commission des affaires étrangères, sur les opérations militaires menées par la France, d'autres pays et l'ONU au Rwanda entre 1990 et 1994*, Paris 15 December 1998; see, www.assemblee-nationale.fr
5. Bureau du Sénat belge, *Rapport de la commission d'enquête parlementaire sur le Rwanda*, Brussels 17 December 1997; see, www.senate.be
6. UN Security Council document S/1998/1096, *Final Report of the International Commission of Inquiry (Rwanda)*, New York 18 November 1998.
7. Jeffrey Boutwell and Michael T. Klare eds., *Light Weapons and Civil Conflict: Controlling the Tools of Violence*, (Oxford, Rowman & Littlefield, 1999), "Introduction" p. 3.
8. Gérard Prunier, *The Rwanda Crisis 1959–1994: History of a Genocide*, (London, Charles Hurst, 1995), p. xii.
9. "[L]es bras qui ont coupé en morceaux hommes, femmes et enfants étaient rwandais. Ce n'étaient pas des bras de pantins. Ce n'étaient même pas des bras armés par nos soins.

Car comble de l'horreur, pour leurs victimes, les tueurs se sont servis de machettes et non pas des armes à feu que nous leur avons livrés abondamment". A. Glaser and S. Smith, *L'Afrique sans Africains*, (Paris, Stock, 1994), p. 35. Smith is *Libération's* Africa specialist, Glaser editor of *La Lettre du Continent*.

10. Stephen D. Goose and Frank Smyth, "Arming Genocide in Rwanda", *Foreign Affairs* 73: 5, September/October 1994, p. 90.

11. Michael T. Klare, "The International Trade in Light Weapons: What Have We Learned?" in Jeffrey Boutwell and Michael T. Klare (eds.), *Light Weapons and Civil Conflict*, p. 20.

12. Neil Middleton, "Rwanda killers armed by West", *Observer*, 9 April 1995; the writer quantified this armoury as follows: "From March 1992 until June 1993, Egypt sold arms, including mortars, long-range artillery, rocket-propelled grenades and landmines to Rwanda in a deal worth about £4 million. It was financed by Crédit Lyonnais, which still has an interest in getting its money back. France also supplied arms and maintenance for French-manufactured armoured cars and helicopters. With straightforward opportunism, South Africa sold automatic rifles, rifle grenades, high-explosive grenades, M26 fragmentation grenades, light and heavy machineguns, grenade launchers and mortars, worth nearly £4 million in total".

13. Kathi Austin, "Light Weapons and Conflict in the Great Lakes Region of Africa" in Jeffrey Boutwell and Michael T. Klare (eds.), *Light Weapons and Civil Conflict*, pp. 31, 34.

14. Many accounts also emphasise Rwanda's post-colonisation culture of obedience; Philip Gourevitch quotes Laurent Nkongoli, vice-president of the Rwandan national assembly: "In Rwandan history, everyone obeys authority. People revere power, and there isn't enough education. You take a poor, ignorant population, and give them arms, and say, 'It's yours. Kill.' They'll obey." Philip Gourevitch, *We Wish to Inform You That Tomorrow We Will be Killed With Our Families*, (London, Picador, 1999), p. 23.

15. See Mel McNulty, "The Militarization of Ethnicity and the Emergence of Warlordism in Rwanda, 1990–94" in Paul B. Rich (ed.), *Warlords in International Relations*, (London, Macmillan, 1999), pp. 81–102.

16. Jean-Marie Kalfèche, "En Afrique, la France n'a plus de politique, seulement des mauvaises habitudes", *L'Express* 4 November 1988.

17. Guy Martin, "Continuity and Change in Franco-African Relations", *Journal of Modern African Studies* 1995, 33:1, p. 6.

18. Robin Luckham, "Le militarisme français en Afrique", *Politique africaine*, 2: 5, février 1982, p. 96.

19. Keith Somerville notes that: "At the Khartoum summit of the Organisation of African Unity in late July 1978, France came under very heavy attack for the role it had played in Zaire, Benin and Sao Tome... President Giscard d'Estaing's calls for a pan-African military force (backed by France and other Western powers) was denounced by President Nyerere of Tanzania as 'the height of arrogance'. He went on to say that 'it is quite obvious, moreover, that those who seek to initiate such a force are not interested in the freedom of Africa. They are interested in the domination of Africa'. (...) Resolutions of the summit and of the earlier OAU Council of Ministers meeting in Tripoli denounced foreign military intervention in Africa and the use of mercenaries to overthrow or threaten governments." Keith Somerville, *Foreign Military Intervention in Africa*, (London, Pinter Publishers/New York, St Martin's Press, 1990), p. 104.

20. Jacques Isnard, "Selon le Congrès américain, la France a été le deuxième exportateur d'armes en 1998", *Le Monde* 10 September 1999.

21. Guy Martin, "Francophone Africa in the Context of Franco-American Relations" in John W. Harbeson and Donald Rothschild (eds.), *Africa in World Politics: Post Cold-War Challenges*, (Boulder CO, Westview Press, 2nd edn. 1995), p. 176.

22. Human Rights Watch Arms Project, *Arming Rwanda: The Arms Trade and Human Rights Abuses in the Rwandan War* (New York, Human Rights Watch, 1994), Section III, "Arms Flows to the Government of Rwanda".

23. Ex-Foreign Legionnaire, interviewed by Stephen Bradshaw for BBC Panorama, "The Bloody Tricolour", broadcast 20 August 1995.

24. The Quilès Commission report tells how: "L'offensive du FPR en juin 1992 déclenche l'envoi d'une deuxième compagnie 'Noroît'. Dans un télégramme du 10 juin 1992, l'ambassadeur à Kigali estime que cette décision jointe à la livraison de munitions et de radars et à la nomination d'un conseiller sont autant de signes de la volonté de la France de ne pas laisser déstabiliser le Rwanda."

25. Unpublished in either the *Journal officiel* (Paris), or the Defence Ministry's *Bulletin officiel des armées*, a copy of the Franco-Rwandan military technical assistance accord of 1975, with its 1992 amendment, was passed to the author by a French journalist, who recovered his copy from the Rwandan Defence Ministry in July 1994.

26. Annexe 2.5, "Accord particulier d'assistance militaire du 18 juillet 1975", Assemblée nationale, *Enquête sur la tragédie rwandaise (1990–1994)*, Tome II, Paris, 1998, pp. 80–85.

27. Steering Committee of Joint Evaluation of Emergency Assistance to Rwanda (JEEAR), *The International Response to Conflict and Genocide: Lessons from the Rwanda Experience*, (JEEAR, Copenhagen, March 1996), p. 67.

28. The Rwandan government army (*Forces Armées Rwandaises* – FAR) numbered 5,200 in 1990 against the RPF's estimated 7,000, and were by all accounts poorly trained and initially short of munitions.

29. "Les services spéciaux français officiels ont bloqué en 90 l'attaque des terroristes du FPR avec l'Ouganda, le travail de la DGSE. Un travail remarquable dont on peut être très fier dans cette première phase de guerre. Il y a eu du côté français des héros que l'on connaîtra jamais, des histoires extraordinaires de types qui ont pris des initiatives folles, qui ont fait des cartons à l'extérieur avec quelques hélicoptères seulement et quelques canons. Il y aurait matière à un livre sur l'héroïsme des Services Secrets au Rwanda, face à l'Ouganda et au FPR... ce qui explique leur haine à l'encontre de la France. L'homme de la rue ne peut sans doute pas comprendre, mais ça a été une belle partie". Captain Paul Barril, former head of the GIGN *(Groupe d'intervention de la Gendarmerie nationale)*, and currently director of the "private security firm" SECRETS (*Société d'études, de conception et de réalisation d'équipements techniques et de sécurité*), one of five constituent companies of *Groupe Barril Sécurité*, interviewed in *Playboy* (French edition, Paris), February 1995.

30. Interviews: Tito Rutaremara, Major Sam Kaka, Major-General Paul Kagame, Kigali October-December 1996.

31. Interview with the author, Kigali, October 1996.

32. "Les autorités françaises ont... tenu à ce que les forces armées rwandaises soient toujours régulièrement approvisionnées en munitions lors des différentes offensives sérieuses menées par le FPR". Assemblée nationale, Mission d'information commune Rapport no.1271, *Enquête sur la tragédie rwandaise (1990–1994)*, Paris 1998, Tome I: Rapport, p. 175.

33. Assemblée nationale, Mission d'information commune Rapport no.1271, *Enquête sur la tragédie rwandaise (1990–1994)*, Paris 1998, Tome I: Rapport, p. 175.

34. "Les livraisons d'armes et de munitions, jointes à l'opération d'assistance opérationnelle menée quelques jours plus tard à partir du 23 février par le Lieutenant-Colonel Didier Tauzin, permettront aux FAR de redresser spectaculairment la situation en une quinzaine de jours face au FPR". Assemblée nationale, Mission d'information commune Rapport no.1271, *Enquête sur la tragédie rwandaise (1990–1994)*, Paris 1998, Tome I: Rapport, p. 176.

35. "La Mission n'entend pas sur ce problème épuiser la réalité du sujet et notamment elle ne prétend pas, s'agissant du trafic d'armes, élucider tous les cas évoqués à travers différents articles ou ouvrages, de marchés parallèles ou de livraisons effectuées au moment des massacres, en avril 1994, ou après la déclaration d'embargo des Nations Unies le 17 mai 1994." Assemblée nationale, Mission d'information commune Rapport no.1271, *Enquête sur la tragédie rwandaise (1990–1994)*, Paris 1998, Tome I: Rapport, p. 168.

36. Jeffrey Boutwell and Michael T. Klare eds., *Light Weapons and Civil Conflict*, "Introduction", p. 3.

37. Michael T. Klare, "The International Trade in Light Weapons: What Have We Learned?" in Jeffrey Boutwell and Michael T. Klare (eds.), *Light Weapons and Civil Conflict*, pp. 18–19.

38. See Belkacem Elomari & Bruno Barillot, *Armes légères, de la production à l'exportation: le poids de la France*, (Lyon, Observatoire des transferts d'armements, September 1999), p. 97.

39. There have been stuctural reforms of these ministries since the election of the Jospin government in June 1997. Current Cooperation Minister Charles Josselin's full title, since the merging of Cooperation and Foreign Affairs in Feburary 1998, is Minister Delegate with responsibility for Cooperation and Francophony. The Military Cooperation Mission is now the responsibility of the Defence Minister, Alain Richard.

40. "31 cessions directes d'armes et munitions au Rwanda ont. . . été réalisées sans respect des procédures". Assemblée nationale, Mission d'information commune Rapport no.1271, *Enquête sur la tragédie rwandaise (1990–1994)*, Paris 1998, Tome I: Rapport, p. 172.

41. "Cela signifie en clair que ces dons non 'autorisés' ont été fait sous la seule autorité de l'armée". Observatoire des transferts d'armements, *La lettre de l'Observatoire*, no. 17: 1, March 1999, p. 3.

42. "Dans un tel contexte de reprise en main, il n'est guère étonnant que certains responsables militaires français aient pu avoir le sentiment de construire une armée, dont il fallait de surcroît s'assurer qu'elle serait régulièrement alimentée en munitions". Assemblée nationale, Mission d'information commune Rapport no.1271, *Enquête sur la tragédie rwandaise (1990–1994)*, Paris 1998, Tome I: Rapport, p. 340.

43. "En valeur, les cessions directes représentent un total d'environ 42 millions de francs". Assemblée nationale, Mission d'information commune Rapport no.1271, *Enquête sur la tragédie rwandaise (1990–1994)*, Paris 1998, Tome I: Rapport, p. 172.

44. African Rights, *Rwanda: Death, Despair and Defiance*, (2nd ed, London, 1995), p. 67.

45. V. Morris and M.P. Scharf, *The International Criminal Tribunal for Rwanda*, New York: Transnational Publishers 1998, p. 52.

46. Statistics from Human Rights Watch Arms Project, *Arming Rwanda: The Arms Trade and Human Rights Abuses in the Rwandan War*, Section III, "Arms Flows to the Government of Rwanda".

47. *Human Rights Watch World Report 1994*, (New York, HRW, December 1993), p. 38.

48. Michael T. Klare, "The International Trade in Light Weapons: What Have We Learned?" in Jeffrey Boutwell and Michael T. Klare (eds.), *Light Weapons and Civil Conflict*, p. 18.

49. Stephen D. Goose (Washington Director of the Human Rights Watch Arms Project) and Frank Smyth (author of the Arms Project's report "Arming Rwanda"), "Arming Genocide in Rwanda", *Foreign Affairs*, September/October 1994.

50. Kathi Austin, "Light Weapons and Conflict in the Great Lakes Region of Africa" in Jeffrey Boutwell and Michael T. Klare (eds.), *Light Weapons and Civil Conflict*, pp. 30, 31.

51. Assemblée nationale, Mission d'information commune Rapport no.1271, *Enquête sur la tragédie rwandaise (1990–1994)*, Paris 1998, Tome I: Rapport, p. 177.

52. See Mel McNulty, "The collapse of Zaire: implosion, revolution or external sabotage?", *The Journal of Modern African Studies*, 37:1, March 1999.

53. Steering Committee of Joint Evaluation of Emergency Assistance to Rwanda (JEEAR), *The International Response to Conflict and Genocide: Lessons from the Rwanda Experience*, (Copenhagen, JEEAR, March 1996).

54. Goose and Smith in *Foreign Affairs* Sept/Oct 1994; they reinforce their point be desribing how: "In March 1993, following the release of a report detailing the massacre of several thousand unarmed Tutsi civilians between 1990 and 1993, Belgium withdrew its ambassador, Johan Swinnen, for two weeks to protest the abuses. In contrast, France apologized for them. Said French Ambassador Jean-Michel Marlaud, 'There are violations by the Rwandan Army, more because of a lack of control by the government, rather than the will of the government.' Hutu leaders got the message that they could get away with genocide facilitated by foreign arms."

55. This non-exhaustive list was suggested by Mehdi Ba – author of *Rwanda, un Génocide français* (Paris, L'Esprit frappeur, 1997) – in his commentary on the Quilès Commission's report, "Rwanda, encore un effort", *Le Nouvel Afrique-Asie*, 113, February 1999.

56. Lt. Col. Rwabalinda erroneously describes the MMC as the "maison militaire de coopération Française" [sic]. Agir ici/Survie, 1er "dossier noir" de la politique africaine de la France, Paris December 1994, Document 1; the documents are also reproduced in Mehdi Ba, *Rwanda: Un génocide français*, (Paris: L'esprit frappeur, 1997), pp. 106–109.

57. However, French attempts to present the interim government as an acceptable partner, or as part of the potential solution, were made impossible by the ongoing genocide. Quilès notes: "C'est en partie en raison de son attitude par rapport au gouvernement intérimaire qu'il lui fut difficile de faire accepter le caractère strictement humanitaire de l'opération Turquoise, puisque certains y voyaient une intention cachée de soutien au régime qui organisait le génocide." Assemblée nationale, *Mission d'information commune Rapport no.1271, Enquête sur la tragédie rwandaise (1990–1994)*, Paris 1998, Tome I: Rapport p. 344.

58. "Toutes les sources militaires que j'ai pu contacter au fil des derniers mois ont catégoriquement nié qu'il y ait eu des livraisons françaises d'armes vers le Rwanda, même pendant toute l'année 1994". Stephen Smith on Radio *France Inter*, 21 August 1995, quoted in Mehdi Ba, *Rwanda, un génocide français*, p. 23. This statement, however, contradicts Smith's own reports from that year, quoted below.

59. "Au Conseil de sécurité de l'ONU, le 17 mai, la France a fait cause commune avec l'ambassadeur du gouvernement intérimaire rwandais (GIR), qui tentait de s'opposer au vote d'un embargo sur les armes à destination du Rwanda – au prétexte que cet embargo ne pénaliserait que les forces 'gouvernementales'. La France s'y opposait parce que le flux des livraisons se poursuivait, avec l'aval de la plupart des militaires, hostiles à l'embargo". Observatoire permanent de la Coopération française, *Rapport 1995*, (Paris, Desclée de Brouwer, 1995), p. 157.

60. Human Rights Watch, *Rwanda/Zaire, Rearming with Impunity: International Support for the Perpetrators of the Rwandan Genocide*, (New York, Human Rights Watch, May 1995), pp. 6–7.

61. Kathi Austin, "Light Weapons and Conflict in the Great Lakes Region of Africa" in Jeffrey Boutwell and Michael T. Klare (eds.), *Light Weapons and Civil Conflict*, p. 36, and Human Rights Watch, *Rearming with Impunity*.

62. Michel Muller, "Trafic d'armes via Paris, pour la dictature rwandaise", *L'Humanité* 31 May 1994; Franck Johannès, "Les Kalachnikov de l'étrange pasteur", *Le Journal du Dimanche* 3 July 1994; Stephen Smith, "Les mystères de Goma, refuge zaïrois des tueurs rwandais", *Libération* 4 June 1994.

63. "[T]outes les sources sur place – y compris des expatriés français bien placés – expriment leur 'certitude' que ces livraisons d'armes ont été 'payées par la France'." Stephen Smith, "Les mystères de Goma, refuge zaïrois des tueurs rwandais", *Libération* 4 June 1994.

64. "Mais une aide en sous-main, par des circuits parallèles, c'est toujours possible. Vous savez, des officines de trafic d'armes à Paris, je pourrais vous en parler..." Stephen Smith, "Les mystères de Goma, refuge zaïrois des tueurs rwandais", *Libération* 4 June 1994.

65. Joint Evaluation of Emergency Assistance to Rwanda, *The International Response to Conflict and Genocide: Lessons from the Rwanda Experience*, (Copenhagen, Steering Committee of the JEEAR, March 1996), Synthesis Report (John Eriksson) p. 54.

66. "La presse a... fait état d'une violation par la France de l'embargo posé par elle le 8 avril et par l'ONU le 17 mai. Il est ainsi reproché à la SOFREMAS, société française d'exploitation de matériels et systèmes d'armement contrôlé par l'Etat d'avoir rompu l'embargo en procédant à des livraisons via Goma au Zaïre. De même, la société Luchaire, dépendant à 100% de Giat Industries, aurait également procédé par ce biais à des livraisons.

Dans son rapport de mai 1995, Human Rights Watch indique avoir appris du personnel de l'aéroport et d'un homme d'affaires local que cinq convois étaient arrivés à Goma en mai et juin 1994 contenant de l'armement et des munitions venant de France et destinés au FAR.

Sur ces différents points, la Mission n'a pas pu recueillir à ce jour d'éléments probants, en dépit des demandes qu'elle a formulées pour obtenir, notamment de l'association Human Rights Watch, copie des documents ou bordereaux relatifs à la SOFREMAS et trouvés au Zaïre dans un bus abandonné près de Goma".

Assemblée nationale, Mission d'information commune, Rapport no.1271: *Enquête sur la tragédie rwandaise (1990–1994)*, Tome I: Rapport, Paris: Assemblée nationale 1998, pp. 176–177.

67. UN Security Council document S/1998/1096, *Final report of the International Commission of Inquiry (Rwanda)*, New York 18 November 1998, para. 73.

68. Stephen D. Goose and Frank Smyth, "Arming Genocide in Rwanda", pp. 92–93.

69. Joint Evaluation of Emergency Assistance to Rwanda, *The International Response to Conflict and Genocide: Lessons from the Rwanda Experience*, p. 12.

70. William Cyrus Reed, "Guerrillas in the Midst" in Christopher Clapham (ed.), *African Guerrillas*, (Oxford, James Currey, 1998), pp. 138, 140.

71. Michael Evans, "Whitehall lapse let UK firm sell arms to Hutus", *The Times*, 22 January 1997.

72. Paul Eavis and William Benson, "The European Union and the Light Weapons Trade", in Jeffrey Boutwell and Michael T. Klare (eds.), *Light Weapons and Civil Conflict*, p. 92.

73. Jeffrey Boutwell and Michael T. Klare (eds.), *Light Weapons and Civil Conflict*, "Introduction" p. 3.

74. René Wadlow, "African States: Security and Conflict Resolution", *Genève-Afrique* 19, February 1991, p. 96.

75. Christopher Clapham, *Africa and the International System: The Politics of State Survival*, (Cambridge, Cambridge University Press, 1996), p. 156.

76. Quoted in *La lettre de l'Observatoire*, no.17:1, March 1999, p. 3.

77. Eavis and Benson note that: "If the aims of transparency and accountability are to be realized, the member states will need to adopt common, rigorous systems of parliamentary scrutiny over their arms exports, including prior notification of sensitive exports to a parliamentary committee (as occurs in Sweden and the United States)". Paul Eavis and William Benson, "The European Union and the Light Weapons Trade", in Jeffrey Boutwell and Michael T. Klare (eds.), *Light Weapons and Civil Conflict*, p. 95.

78. Kathi Austin, "Light Weapons and Conflict in the Great Lakes Region of Africa" in Jeffrey Boutwell and Michael T. Klare (eds.), *Light Weapons and Civil Conflict*, pp. 30, 36.

79. Paul Eavis and William Benson, "The European Union and the Light Weapons Trade", in Jeffrey Boutwell and Michael T. Klare (eds.), *Light Weapons and Civil Conflict*, p. 90.

80. Moses Draku, "Africa to have firearms control centre", Pan African News Agency, 14 January 2000, at: http://www.woza.co.za/africa/jan00/armscentre14.htm

Crime, Law & Social Change **33**: 131–149, 2000.
© 2000 *Kluwer Academic Publishers. Printed in the Netherlands.*

Subcontracting military power: The privatisation of security in contemporary Sub-Saharan Africa

GERRY CLEAVER
School of International Studies and Law, Coventry University, Priory Street, Coventry, CV1 5FB, UK

Abstract. This article seeks to establish a clear difference between the classical view of mercenaries as hired guns and the more recent, business oriented, phenomenon of private security companies. The limitations of the definitions currently used in international law will be explored and their impact on the control of private military forces assessed. The article will then go on to identify the particular circumstances existing in Africa that provide such a fertile environment for the operation of private security companies. The activities of Executive Outcomes and Sandline International Ltd will be used as case studies, particularly their operations in Sierra Leone. Their corporate connections will be highlighted, especially their links to mineral extraction companies, and how these are used to finance their operations by the host countries. Finally, recent attempts to legislate to control the activities of these companies are examined.

Introduction

During the 1990s there has been much debate in both political and academic circles about the role of so-called private security companies and mercenaries in Africa's conflict zones. In some of the literature the terms private security company and mercenary are treated as being synonymous and therefore I intend to devote some space to a discussion of this terminology. It is also important to put the current situation in its historical context especially with regard to Africa's post-independence history. This is a subject that stirs up a great deal of emotion wherever it is debated. It is possible to find passionate arguments for and against the use of private security companies and mercenaries in much of the recent literature on the subject, though it must be said that there is far less of the former than the latter. It is not my intention in this article to adopt any particular moral position but to analyse the facts as I see them.[1]

This article will also examine the circumstances pertaining in Sub-Saharan Africa that facilitate the privatisation of security, as well as examples of recent operations by private security companies and mercenaries. The effectiveness of these interventions will be analysed in the context of the claims made by the advocates of security privatisation and the allegations made by their opponents. Finally, I will consider the reaction of individual states and supranational organisations to this emerging phenomenon and their attempts at "controlling" it.

Definitions

Given that much of the contemporary debate concerning private security companies centres on the legality of their operations and whether or not they should be viewed as mercenaries, it is necessary to examine the definitions of "mercenary" currently in use by the international community. One might be forgiven for believing that arriving at a definition of a mercenary should be a relatively simple task. A mercenary is surely someone who fights wars for money. Whilst this criterion certainly does apply to mercenaries it could also be applied to all professional soldiers and some moralists might argue that all professional soldiers should be considered mercenaries of a sort. For the purposes of this article a more precise definition of what a mercenary is will be required if they are to be distinguished from private security companies.

There have been a number of attempts at defining mercenaries in international law. These include: the 1977 Convention for the Elimination of Mercenarism in Africa, established by the Organisation of African Unity; Article 47 of the 1977 Additional Protocol I of the Geneva Conventions; and the 1989 International Convention against the Recruitment, Use, Financing and Training of Mercenaries. Article 47 of the Additional Protocol to the Geneva Conventions describes a mercenary, inter alia, as someone participating in a particular conflict, specifically recruited for that purpose and motivated purely by personal gain. They also have to have been promised rewards by a party to the conflict in excess of those available to their equivalents in the forces of that party. In addition, to qualify as a mercenary they must not be a national or a resident of the country involved in the conflict or a member of the armed forces of another state on official duty in the state in which the conflict takes place.[2]

Article 47 is generally deemed to apply only to inter-state conflicts and to "wars of national liberation", and therefore it might be argued that civil wars remain outside its provisions. These conflicts are precisely the ones in which the business of private security companies has flourished in recent years in Africa. Article 47 also suffers from a lack of whole hearted support from the major western powers, many of whom are also dragging their feet on ratification of the 1989 International Convention. This latter Convention and its OAU counterpart are more wide-ranging when it comes to the types of conflict covered by their definitions of mercenary activity. To those states which have signed up to these international agreements, mercenaries are criminals, outside the protection of international law and not entitled to be treated as prisoners of war if captured. This status also, de facto, relieves mercenaries of the requirement to govern their activities during any conflict according to the obligations placed on combatants by international law.

Reference to these international conventions does not greatly help clarify matters when consideration is given to the status of private security companies. For the purposes of this article I will join with other writers on this subject in excluding from the term private security company those organisations that merely provide security guards for buildings or individuals, or who are engaged in neighbourhood security schemes to counteract crimes such as burglary, mugging, car-jacking etc.[3] The type of private security company upon which this article will concentrate is that which provides military expertise of a kind more traditionally associated with the armed forces of a nation-state. The activities of these companies are often multifarious and they may well be engaged in the provision of personal security and the protection of static installations. However, what sets them apart is their ability to provide military expertise whether it be technical, logistical, organisational or in actual combat.

Defining these companies and their employees as mercenaries, as laid down within international law is problematical. This is especially the case with Article 47 of the Additional Protocol to the Geneva Convention. As regular employees of a company can these individuals be considered as specifically recruited for any given conflict? When one is dealing with salaried employees of a contracted company can their motivation be said to be one solely of personal gain? In addition, it seems that many categories of advisor employed by these companies cannot be considered mercenaries, as they do not actually participate in combat. If, as they claim they do, these private security companies restrict their employment to legitimate governments, then it is difficult to categorise them as mercenaries, especially if the definition used in international conventions refers to someone engaged in overthrowing the constitutional order. Things become even more complex when these companies operate alongside international forces engaged in a humanitarian intervention. The confusion as to the status of these private security companies is reflected in the reports of the United Nations Special Rapporteur of the Commission on Human Rights, Enrique Ballesteros. While deprecating the development of such companies he admits that within the terms of international law it is not possible to definitively categorise them as mercenaries. Ballesteros makes the point that this is an issue that requires clarification at the international level given that current legislation is open to a variety of interpretations.[4] What is clear is that the continued employment of such companies by governments has serious implications for state sovereignty, especially in Africa.[5]

Background

The use of mercenaries is by no means a modern phenomenon and is nearly as old as organised warfare itself. Historical examples are legion and quoted at length in the literature. It was the rise of the nation-state and the concomitant creation of national armies that led to the demonisation of mercenaries. It became almost dishonourable to be seen as fighting merely for money rather than for one's country and employing "foreigners" in your army was deemed to be, at the very least, an underhand tactic. There is a sizeable element of hypocrisy in all of this as all the European colonial powers employed troops recruited from their colonies, both during the acquisition of empire and in the World Wars of this century.

There were a variety of reasons for the employment of colonial troops but chief among them was that they were generally much cheaper than their European counterparts, often available in greater numbers, and better suited to tropical environments. As a bonus they often turned out to be excellent soldiers. Were these troops mercenaries? Or did their status as imperial subjects mean that they could be counted as members of the "national" forces of the colonial power? A soldier in the King's African Rifles in World War One may have been fighting for Britain, but his imperial masters most certainly would not have considered him to be British. This might be considered a moot historical point, but in the contemporary debate much is made of the foreign origins of mercenaries as being a defining characteristic. What happens if the putative mercenary adopts, or is given, the nationality of the country in which he is fighting? The nationality issue is further complicated if he is an employee of a private company with multinational connections.

The employment of mercenaries by major European powers continues to this day. Both the French Foreign Legion and Britain's Gurkhas are recruited from people who are not citizens of the employing state.[6] Although incorporated into the armies of these two countries and officered by their nationals, these units hark back to an earlier tradition of hiring foreigners to do your fighting for you. Participation in "Blue Helmet" operations has given these units de facto recognition by the United Nations. Since the origins of both these units date back to the first half of the Nineteenth Century then perhaps tradition and longevity have bestowed an element of legitimacy upon them. If in some future tightening of international legislation in this field, these units were to be reclassified as mercenaries, then this might lead to some interesting redefinition of French military interventions in post-colonial Africa.[7]

Prior to the expansion of private security companies in the last decade, mercenary activity in post-colonial Africa was typified by the operations of groups led by such notorious individuals as Mike Hoare, Bob Denard, Rolf Steiner and Costas Georgiou, better known as "Callan".[8] These names and others like them have been associated with all of the continent's hotspots: The Congo, Comoros, Seychelles, Zimbabwe, Benin and Angola, to name but a few. They were used both to prop up regimes and to overthrow them. They were employed in civil wars and struggles for liberation and earned a reputation for brutality that led to their being nicknamed *les affreux* – the terrible ones.

These mercenary activities were by and large funded by means of direct payments to either the individuals concerned or to a "front" company that acted as a recruiting agency. Although this funding may have come directly or indirectly from the resources of the employing state, the direct exploitation of a state's natural resources by the mercenaries themselves or their associates was not part of the bargain. To be sure, mineral exploitation companies may well have benefited from the activities of these mercenaries and even encouraged them. But the connection always remained covert, and was certainly not formalised through any identifiable corporate linkages. In this one respect at least, the activities of today's private security companies differ markedly from those of the earlier "soldiers of fortune".

Although these individuals achieved a certain degree of notoriety, their activities were by no means the only examples of foreign military interference in the affairs of independent African states. African and non-African states intervened both covertly and overtly in the affairs of the newly independent states of Sub-Saharan Africa. A great many of these interventions, whilst reprehensible for many reasons, could not justifiably be termed mercenary. However, one might question the role played by the Cubans in Angola and Ethiopia, for example, or South Africa's use of units such as the famous 32 Battalion in Angola in support of UNITA.[9] African states also "loaned" their troops in support of their political allies.[10] Morocco lent troops to President Mobutu of Zaire in the 1970s when his regime was under threat from Katangan rebels. In turn, Mobutu provided some of the better units of his otherwise disreputable army in support of the Habyarimana regime in Rwanda in the early 1990s. These two examples, out of the many that have been documented, help to counterbalance the impression that might be obtained from some of the literature, that up until the advent of private security companies, African states had relied solely on their own resources for the provision of security.

Typologies

Attempts to produce a typology of contemporary private military activity are made more difficult by the involvement of the same individuals and companies in a variety of different military-related activities at the same time.

However, notwithstanding these problems of classification, it is possible to identify a number of general categories of private military activity in Africa. The first type is the "classical" mercenary, individuals recruited for their military expertise to fight in a specific conflict – for example, the Serbs allegedly recruited by former officers of the French military to fight for Mobutu in 1997.[11] This vain attempt to shore up a collapsing regime ended with the Serbs turning on their erstwhile allies in the Zairean army whilst fleeing from the advancing rebels. Nowadays many mercenaries are employed for their technical knowledge rather than just for their prowess in combat. They are contracted to operate and maintain the more sophisticated weaponry now to be found on all the world's battlefields, such as aircraft, helicopters and artillery. It has been noted that the provision of this type of expertise can be directly linked with contracts to supply such equipment.[12] Increasingly, though, much of this work now also falls into the second general category of privatised security activity, namely the private security company.

The activities of these companies can be further subdivided. Firstly there is actual participation in combat, leading and supporting the forces of the employer state. The best known exponent in this field is Executive Outcomes (EO). Next are the types of activity associated with the enhancement of the capabilities of the employer state. These include the provision of training, especially at the higher command level, military intelligence and analysis, and weapons supply. A major player in this area is the US company, Military Professional Resources Incorporated (MPRI).[13]

Thirdly, as mentioned earlier, private companies are also involved in supplying security for installations and personnel. In addition private companies are increasingly employed to provide logistical support and maintenance facilities, not only for the militaries of individual states, but also for the United Nations. Many western militaries are moving toward the privatisation of the "non-teeth" or "tail end" aspects of military operations, including logistics and base support.[14] This is increasingly the case where forces are deployed abroad in humanitarian operations. This is part of a more general process of divesting the state of activities that are believed to be more properly the province of private companies. The companies involved in the provision of this type of support may not themselves have military origins or structure and are usually divorced from the actual fighting. It may be safely assumed that they would nevertheless be employed to provide some sort of military advantage to the host army, if only to release their own logistics troops for front line duty. In this case they might well find themselves included in any broader definition of mercenary activity adopted by the international community.

Much of the literature concentrates on the activities of companies such as EO and MPRI who are involved in the first two categories of private security company activity, and I will now go on to examine the factors that have led to the creation of an environment in Sub-Saharan Africa in which they have been able to flourish.

The operating environment

In the last decade private security companies have prospered in an international environment of increasing instability and insecurity. Whilst this is a global phenomenon, it is arguable that its most extreme and pernicious manifestation is to be found in Sub-Saharan Africa. The factors leading to the creation of this environment are both international and African in origin.

Africa has suffered from very serious international marginalisation following on from the end of the Cold War. During that conflict Africa became a battleground for the superpowers who conducted their rivalry via proxies such as Cuba and South Africa. The consequences of this rivalry still haunt Africa today, particularly in Angola. Nevertheless, during this period Africa was, to a significant degree, a centre of attention for the superpowers and many African leaders were able to exploit this to the political and pecuniary advantage of both themselves and their countries. However, in the immediate aftermath of the collapse of the Eastern Bloc in 1989 Africa, as one writer has described it, "lost its political worth" and the states of Sub-Saharan Africa became "so much irrelevant international clutter".[15] This political marginalisation has been accompanied by growing economic isolation, with the continent accounting for less than two percent of international trade.

The end of the Cold War saw rising expectations, especially in the West, of a peace dividend. This was to be achieved via the reduction of military forces, and the phenomenon was not just limited to the Western powers. It has led to a reduced military capacity among the Western states and an increasing reluctance to become involved in areas not deemed to be vital to their national interests. Africa usually falls into this category. The reduction in military forces released a great deal of experienced manpower onto the private market and facilitated the growth of private companies, through the availability of this resource as well as through the increasing use of private companies by Western militaries to provide logistical services. This post-Cold War military retrenchment also released a great deal of hardware for private use and international export. In the economically depressed states of Eastern Europe and the former USSR, the arms industries were often the most advanced and competitive segments of the economy. It is therefore understandable that these states should seek to maximise their foreign currency earnings through increased arms exports to the world's trouble spots.[16]

The early years of this decade also saw a dramatic decline in international participation in peacekeeping on the African continent. The debacles in Somalia and Rwanda have effectively crippled the reputation of the United Nations in Africa.[17] The humiliation suffered by US forces in Somalia led to a radical rethink in the US as to its commitment to United Nations peacekeeping operations. This culminated in the issuing of Presidential Decision Directive 25 in May 1994. This laid down a number of criteria which would have to be satisfied before the US would participate in future United Nations peacekeeping operations. Effectively the future use of US combat forces in such operations was ruled out.[18] Without active US participation the other Western powers have been most reluctant to become involved in any United Nations peacekeeping operations in Africa. These developments, combined with mistakes within the United Nations itself, led to the disaster of UNAMIR I in Rwanda.[19] In reality peacekeeping in Africa has been devolved to African states themselves and they are woefully ill-equipped for this task.[20] The US, Britain and France are prepared to provide some assistance to African peacekeeping operations, but at one step removed from the actual participation of their forces.[21] The French have now started to restructure their armed forces and withdraw some of their troops from Africa where they have had a long-term military presence in the post-colonial era.[22] This combination of Western disengagement and limited African capacities has created a security vacuum into which the private security companies have moved.

Within Africa itself a number of factors have contributed to this poor security environment. The post-colonial African state has been characterised by a lack of popular legitimacy for the institutions of state and its political processes. Widespread systemic corruption on the continent has undermined the legitimacy of politicians and the state itself, as well as contributing directly to the poor performance of local security forces. Chronic economic failure, the debilitating impact of structural adjustment policies and fierce competition for ever scarcer resources have created an environment where recourse to violence is often seen as the only way out of a desperate situation. The overthrow of long serving dictators and the effective collapse of some states has added to the overall air of insecurity, while at the same time the military retrenchment in South Africa following the demise of apartheid has created a pool of experienced manpower available for private employment. These political and economic circumstances, together with Africa's underdeveloped natural resources, have created an opportunity for those able to exploit it.

Executive outcomes: The archetypal private security company

EO is probably the most widely known of the private security companies. Part of its notoriety derives from the reports of their apparent "success" in bringing a form of peace to parts of Angola and Sierra Leone. However EO has become the primary target of those who are critical of the activities of private security companies in general. This is largely due to its origins. EO started in 1989 as an incorporated company registered in South Africa and Britain. Its founders, Eeben Barlow and Lafras Luitingh, were former members of South Africa's apartheid-era special forces,. In 1997 both men left EO and the company was then headed by Nick van den Bergh, a former officer in the South African parachute regiment. It appears that his past was a little less controversial than those of his predecessors and thus better for the corporate image.[23]

Most of EO's front line operatives have been recruited from former members of South Africa's special forces units that operated in the apartheid era. These units, such 32 Battalion, Koevoet, Paratroops and Reconnaissance Commandos, were all heavily involved in South African military operations in Namibia, Angola and Mozambique.[24] The Namibian settlement in 1990 and the end of apartheid in 1994 led to the disbandment of these units and the creation of a reserve of potential recruits for organisations such as EO. The officers employed are almost exclusively white, whilst many of the soldiers are of Angolan or Namibian origin. EO does not maintain a standing army as such, but recruits to meet its contractual needs. The common experiences of its recruit base make welding them into an effective force less problematical than with a more eclectic group.

However, it is these origins at the cutting edge of apartheid South Africa's military that have caused such problems for EO's image makers. Many commentators, especially African ones, cannot help but ascribe evil motives to anything done by what have been described as "apartheid's attack dogs". This tends to bring a mixture of emotions to any debate on private security companies in Africa, generally manifesting itself in revulsion at the involvement of these representatives of a pariah system in the affairs of independent Sub-Saharan African states. This is compounded by embarrassment that these states cannot sort out their own security problems without recourse to such people.

The corporate connections of EO are difficult to pin down.[25] Formerly part of a now defunct holding company, Strategic Resources Corporation, EO is closely connected to a number of other private security companies such as Lifeguard Security and Saracen Security. EO also has a business relationship with the Branch-Heritage Group, which is based in the same London office building as agents acting for EO. A former British SAS veteran, Anthony Buckingham, heads the Branch Heritage Group. The group includes a number of mineral extraction companies such as Branch Energy, Branch Minerals, Diamond Works and Heritage Oil and Gas. It also includes the private security company, Sandline International. The mineral companies operate in places such as Angola and Sierra Leone and have employed EO or its affiliates for the purposes of providing security. They have all benefited from the consequences of EO interventions in these two countries. Officially there is no corporate link between EO and the Branch Heritage Group, although they share interests in Ibis Air, often referred to as EO's air force. But the two organisations seem to operate to each other's benefit. The mineral companies provide the introduction for EO which then provides the security environment that allows for the profitable extraction of the minerals that might otherwise be impossible to access. This close association puts the mineral companies at an advantage when negotiating contracts, as they can link their operations to the provision of security. When one looks at the oil and diamond reserves of Angola and the diamonds of Sierra Leone, the sums of money at stake are vast and from the mineral companies' point of view well worth the risk. The cost of employing private security companies is small beer in comparison to the potential rewards, and it is all to the good if you can get the host government to foot the bill.

The origins of EO's activities in Angola are not entirely clear. It appears that the company was initially retained by a number of oil companies in 1992 to protect their installations in the Soyo region of Angola where Heritage Oil and Gas had interests.[26] This area was subsequently overrun by UNITA and in March 1993 EO was contracted by the Angolan government to assist in the recapture of this strategically vital region. Backed by Angolan troops EO operatives, numbering less than 100, recaptured the facilities. Although they were subsequently lost again after EO's departure, this action so impressed the Angolan government that it offered EO a US$40 million dollar one year contract to train its forces. The contract was continuously renewed until January 1996. Over 500 EO personnel were employed, many in combat roles. They are credited with turning around the fortunes of the Angolan government and its military and with forcing UNITA to the negotiating table. EO was principally concerned with recapturing diamond and oil fields, as these are crucial to financing war in Africa. Because many EO personnel had fought with UNITA in the past they had excellent knowledge of their tactics and limitations. EO eventually left Angola after pressure on the Angolans from the US.[27]

EO was called into Sierra Leone by the besieged government of Valentine Strasser in March 1995. Much of the country, including the valuable diamond and rutile mines, was in the hands of the Revolutionary United Front (RUF), headed by Foday Sankoh. The civil war in Sierra Leone was a spillover from the Liberian conflict and was conducted with almost inconceivable barbarity, mostly against unarmed civilians. The government forces had effectively ceased to exist as an organised force and the soldiers and rebels became so indistinguishable as to lead to the coining of a new term, "sobels".[28] All this needs to be borne in mind when placing the actions of, firstly, EO and, later on, Sandline, into context. The RUF were no liberation movement struggling against foreign oppression. They were no better than murderous gangsters who used mutilation as a deliberate weapon against defenceless civilians. Meanwhile, the international community, at both the global and regional level, singularly failed to find a resolution to this conflict.

Between December 1995 and October 1996 EO launched a series of offensives that secured the Freetown area, reoccupied the diamond and rutile mines, and eliminated the RUF bases. They established sufficient security for elections to be held in March 1996 that led to a civilian regime and forced the RUF to sign up to a peace accord in November 1996. The cost to Sierra Leone of the involvement of EO was some US$35 million. This was to be paid in cash by monthly instalments. There is no evidence that EO itself obtained diamond concessions, though Branch Energy did.[29] This was a heavy burden on an economy such as Sierra Leone's. Nevertheless, the security provided was essential for its future well being and in reality was not available elsewhere. It is interesting to note that both UNITA and the RUF made the departure of EO a condition of their agreeing to a peace deal. Both of them subsequently reneged on these deals. A criticism levelled at private security companies in general, and EO in particular, is that they have failed to deliver lasting solutions to the problems of Angola and Sierra Leone. In their defence it must be stated that they never claimed that that was what they were trying to do. They offered particular solutions to specific problems. As for long-term solutions, it is not just private security companies that have failed, so have the United Nations and regional organisations. EO has always claimed that it worked only for legitimate governments. While one might argue over the legitimacy of the MPLA regime in Angola, there is an even bigger question mark over that of Valentine Strasser in Sierra Leone. In Africa the definition of legitimate can be very elastic. Criticism that focuses on this element of their activities might be easier to sustain.

EO has also operated in a number of other African states, including Kenya and Uganda, but these operations have had a much lower profile. The reputation of EO personnel is such that they are sought by many parties to conflict. There are stories that the Mobutu regime in Zaire attempted to recruit ex-EO personnel during its dying days in 1997.[30] Former EO operatives are said to be involved on both sides of the conflict in Angola today. The company itself officially went out of business on 1st January 1999. A statement issued at the

time said that EO no longer saw itself as having a role to play in conflict resolution in Africa. Its closure may be connected with South African legislation
on private security companies, but reports suggest that its offices in Pretoria
remain staffed and that some of its personnel are now employed by Lifeguard
Security. It may well be that this archetypal private security company could
yet reappear under another name.[31]

Sandline: Exposing the conundrum

The furore surrounding the so-called "arms to Sierra Leone affair" had rather
more to do with the machinations of the British political system than with
any deep-seated concern for the fate of a small West African country.[32] Nevertheless the inquiry of the parliamentary Foreign Affairs Committee into the
relationship between the Foreign Office and Sandline International did bring
the role of private security companies in Africa to the attention of the wider
British public. It also exposed the conundrum facing most Western powers,
in this case the British government, when faced with international crises. On
the one hand they feel obliged by the pressures of public opinion to be seen
to be doing something, but on the other they are equally aware that the same
public will rarely countenance the dispatch of national forces to remote and
dangerous corners of the world.

Sandline International is very closely associated corporately with the
Branch Heritage Group, headed by Anthony Buckingham. Another company
in the group, Diamondworks, has extensive diamond mining interests in Sierra Leone, which it took over from Branch Energy in 1996. Sandline is
headed by a former colonel in the British army, Timothy Spicer, and operates
out of offices in London, though it is registered in the Bahamas. It offers
military training, logistics, supplies, planning and threat analysis. It had a
close working relationship with EO with whom it was involved in an abortive
contract in Papua New Guinea in February 1997.[33]

The involvement of Sandline International in the affairs of Sierra Leone came as a result of the overthrow in May 1997 of the democratically-
elected civilian government of Ahmed Tejan Kabbah. His regime was overthrown by an Armed Forces Revolutionary Council headed by Major Johnny
Paul Koroma. This junta immediately allied itself with the RUF, to form
a "People's Army".[34] The military had resented the loss of access to the
diamonds and other economic resources of Sierra Leone that a civilian government had brought. In addition they resented the growing influence of the
Kamajor civilian militia who had been highly effective in assisting EO in
defeating the RUF the previous year. This new alliance between the junta
and the RUF merely made public something that had been suspected for a

long time, namely that elements of the army had co-operated with the RUF to plunder the natural resources of Sierra Leone.

The Koroma junta was internationally isolated but proved immune to diplomatic efforts aimed at its removal. The junta embarked on a series of murders to stamp out opposition and to all intents and purposes behaved in a decidedly criminal manner. Despite this the international community seemed reluctant to actually do anything to remove them. The United Nations passed Security Council Resolution 1132 (1997) imposing an arms embargo on Sierra Leone.[35] However, this can be interpreted as being little more than gesture politics given the state of impotence to which the United Nations has been reduced, especially in Africa, and the ease with which the purveyors of arms evade regulation and border controls.

President Kabbah, in exile in Guinea, was put in contact with Sandline International, allegedly by the British High Commissioner to Sierra Leone, Mr Penfold, who had also relocated to Guinea. Sandline International were contracted to supply weapons and equipment to forces loyal to President Kabbah and also to the Nigerian-led ECOMOG forces who were stationed in Sierra Leone and who were preparing to confront the junta militarily. The arms came from Bulgaria and were shipped via Nigeria and possibly Guinea. The deal was financed to the tune of US$10 million by an Asian businessman, Rakesh Saxena. He has a major interest in Diamondworks which was promised major diamond concessions in return for this finance.[36]

Whether or not the arms supplied by Sandline International helped in the overthrow of the junta is debatable, as ECOMOG forces succeeded in this task, at least as far as Freetown was concerned, by March 10 1998, before the bulk of the arms arrived. Nevertheless the arms, equipment and expertise provided by Sandline International did assist the government of President Kabbah in the following months to extend some control beyond the capital. However the Junta/RUF forces remained undefeated and capable of launching further murderous attacks. The Kabbah government was compelled to sign a peace agreement with the RUF in July 1999 which allows them a significant share of power.

The uproar in Britain over Sandline International and Sierra Leone centred on the extent to which Foreign Office officials and Ministers were aware that Sandline International was in breach of a United Nations arms embargo. There were also arguments as to whether or not the embargo was meant to apply to the forces of the legitimate government. The fact remains that a private security company was instrumental to some degree in the restoration of a democratically-elected government and the removal of a murderous military junta.

Regulating private security companies

In his latest report, the United Nations Special Rapporteur on mercenaries, Enrique Ballesteros, makes the point that current international legislation on the subject is extremely limited in its effectiveness.[37] The only current international legislation in force is Article 47 of the 1977 Protocol I Addition to the 1949 Geneva Conventions. However this legislation does not attempt to ban mercenary activity as such but, as we have seen merely defines the legal status of mercenaries. The International Convention against the Recruitment, Use, Financing and Training of Mercenaries was adopted by the United Nations General Assembly in December 1989. In order for it to enter into force it needs to be ratified by 22 states. At the time of writing, nearly a decade later, it has only been ratified by 19.[38] All this international legislation is riddled with loopholes, especially with regard to private security companies, which are not catered for in the above treaties. As Ballesteros points out, the interest of the international community would appear to lie in the regulation of the activities of these companies. He argues that these companies are usurping responsibilities that are the obligations of states, namely defence and security, and that in permitting and often encouraging this, for whatever reasons, states are undermining their own legitimacy.[39]

The United Nations Special Rapporteur seems to imply that there are no circumstances in which a state ought to resort to the use of private security companies for the provision of security. This rather absolutist view appears to be based on a belief that they employ mercenaries, whose use is universally detestable, and that the price of these companies is usually met from the precious natural resources of states already in dire economic straits. Nevertheless, in what appears to be tantamount to an admission that private security companies can be useful, Ballesteros pointedly calls for their activities to be regulated, not outlawed.[40]

In 1998 South Africa enacted the Regulation of Foreign Military Assistance Act which sought to place limits on the activities of private security companies based in that country. Essentially companies who were based in South Africa and who wished to provide military services abroad would in future need the permission of the South African government. Such permission could be refused if the proposed activity conflicted with South Africa's international obligations, would lead to human rights infringements in the host country, cause or exacerbate instability, support terrorism, worsen regional conflicts, be against South Africa's national interest, or be unacceptable for any other reason.[41] This legislation is obviously aimed at organisations such as EO. Though they persistently stated that they saw no difficulties in complying with the Act, shortly after its introduction they closed their Pretoria offices, possibly with the intent of relocating to somewhere where the legislative environment was more conducive to their activities.

In October 1999 it was reported that the British government was considering the introduction of legislation to regulate the activities of private security companies based in the UK.[42] Britain is not a signatory to the 1989 United Nations Convention on Mercenaries, suggesting that it believes it is impractical to outlaw the activities of private security companies. The British Foreign Office has studied the South African law and a spokesman stated that the government had, "decided to initiate a thorough and open debate on the problem (of private security companies) and the options for dealing with it both nationally and internationally."[43] The act of engaging in mercenary activity in a foreign state at peace with Britain is already outlawed by the Foreign Enlistment Act of 1870, which will have to be repealed to accommodate any new legislation. A Green Paper on the proposals is promised for 2000, and these moves would appear to indicate some form of official admission as to the potential usefulness of private security companies, notwithstanding the embarrassment caused by the Sandline affair. In support of this belief Donald Anderson MP, chairman of the House of Commons Foreign Affairs Committee, has been quoted as saying that, with regard to private security companies, "in some cases there is a legitimate role for their work, particularly when they are involved in the protection of workers abroad." [44]

An indirect form of regulation may come from the increasing international awareness that it is natural resources that help fund the activities of private security companies, mercenaries and rebel movements alike. This is particularly the case with diamonds. Africa produces diamonds of exceptional quality and size and many are relatively easy to mine.[45] This is especially so in Angola and Sierra Leone. The diamond trade is one of the most heavily regulated in the world and dominated by one company: De Beers. Their London based Central Selling Organisation keeps the price of diamonds artificially high by maintaining a large stockpile.[46] Nevertheless, rebel groups such as UNITA have very successfully used illegal diamond mining to fund their military campaigns, often to the tune of hundreds of millions of dollars per year.[47] On October 3 1999 a campaign called "Fatal Attractions" was launched to get the diamond-buying public to question the source of their purchases and boycott illegally mined diamonds.[48] De Beers quickly followed with an embargo on all Angolan diamonds not from approved government sources.[49] The impact of such policies may be limited as they will be difficult to enforce. However, it does demonstrate a growing awareness that it is Africa's natural resources that are the ultimate attraction for freebooters of all persuasions, whether they be private security companies, multinational corporations, or mercenaries. If governments especially can be dissuaded from selling off the "family silver" to pay for security then maybe the climate for private security companies will be less amenable. This seems to be unlikely in the short term and especially when one considers that the employment of EO by the government of Sierra Leone was given tacit approval by the IMF.[50]

Conclusions

The present circumstances in much of Sub-Saharan Africa provide a fertile environment for private security companies, mercenaries, and rapacious mineral companies. International companies want access to Africa's natural resources and desperate governments need to raise revenue from their exploitation. In regions of insecurity the personnel and equipment needed for these industries need protection. The local security forces are simply not up to the task and so the private sector steps in. It is the resource-rich regions that are the centres of conflict – Angola, Sierra Leone and the Democratic Republic of the Congo, to name but three. Africa's enormous economic, political and social problems are leading to increasing levels of conflict on the continent. The wider international community has effectively abandoned any idea of intervening militarily in Africa's conflicts, regardless of the humanitarian suffering. Different standards are applied to Africa than are applied to the former Yugoslavia. It is unpleasant, it may even be racist, but it is a fact. The United Nations is in no position to intervene either. It is financially crippled and its actions hamstrung by a reliance on American support for effective action. Its actions in Somalia and Rwanda have also fatally undermined its credibility in Africa.

African peacekeeping resources are limited and the track record of African peacekeeping operations is at best patchy.[51] The present Nigerian government seems disinclined to continue in the role of regional policeman for West Africa and this must cast into doubt the future of ECOMOG as a regional intervention force.[52] In many cases it is the states' own security forces that are part of the problem. In Sierra Leone the army united with the RUF rebels to unseat the democratically-elected government. This again was about control of valuable resources, in this case diamonds. When a government has ineffective or unreliable security forces, and the international community either cannot or will not intervene, where else can it turn to in a crisis other than to private security companies?

Mercenaries of all types abound in Africa today. From the old-fashioned soldiers of fortune, to skilled technicians operating expensive imported equipment, to the private security companies, their services are much in demand.[53] The demand comes not just from desperate African governments or rebel groups. Multinational corporations use them to protect their interests and facilitate their access to Africa's natural wealth, in some cases they have developed very close and mutually beneficial working relationships. Foreign governments also see them as a useful substitute for intervention by their own forces.

Private security companies are driven by profit, they are not charitable institutions. They do not claim to be able to solve all of a state's problems but are employed for a specific task, and in many cases they are remarkably effective given their small numbers. In order to pay for them states have to draw on whatever resources they have, and this often means mining concessions. But before private security companies are universally condemned for this impact on African economies, questions have to asked about the involvement of African states in the affairs of their neighbours. For example, Zimbabwe's intervention in the Democratic Republic of the Congo has far more to do with the exploitation of that country's natural resources by the Zimbabwean elite than any deeply felt affection for Laurent Kabila.[54]

As the pronouncements of international organisations appear increasingly as ineffective window dressing and sanctions become something of a joke, governments might well view the possibilities provided by private security companies with favour. However the stigma still attached to such companies means that governments and their officials prefer to keep such relationships away from public scrutiny. Much of the criticism of private security companies is justified but a lot is predicated on there being a viable alternative to their employment available to desperate African governments. This is just not the case. In an ideal world there would be no need for the services of private security companies. Unfortunately contemporary Sub-Saharan Africa is a far from ideal world.

Notes

1. Of the recent literature, the most useful general overviews are: Thomas K. Adams, "The New Mercenaries and the Privatization of Conflict", *Parameters* (US Army War College Quarterly) Summer 1999. Accessible at;
   http://carlisle-www.army.mil/usawc/parameters/99/sum mer/adams.htm; David Isenberg, "Soldiers of Fortune Ltd: A Profile of Today's Private Sector Corporate Mercenary Firms", paper for the Center for Defense Information, Washington, DC, November 1997, accessible at: http://www.cdi.org; David Shearer, "Private Armies and Military Intervention", *Adelphi Paper 316* (Oxford, Oxford University Press/International Institute for Strategic Studies, 1998).
2. Shearer, "Private Armies", p. 17.
3. Adams, "the New Mercenaries", p. 1.
4. Enrique Ballesteros, United Nations Special Rapporteur, "Report on the question of the use of mercenaries as a means of violating human rights and impeding the exercise of

the right of peoples to self determination", United Nations Document E/CN.4/1998/31, 27.1.98, paras 67–92.
5. Ibid.
6. Britain still recruits for the Royal Gurkha Rifles in Nepal and many nationalities are to be found within the ranks of the French Foreign Legion.
7. The Foreign Legion has been heavily involved in many of France's military interventions in Africa, particularly in Chad and more recently in Rwanda in 1994.
8. Shearer, "Private Armies", p. 15. See also Peter Tickler, *The Modern Mercenary: Dog of War or Soldier of Honour?* (Wellingborough, Patrick Stephens Ltd, 1987), and Mike Hoare, *Congo Mercenary* (London, Robert Hale Ltd, 1991).
9. 32 Battalion was largely made up of Angolans led by South African officers and NCOs.
10. See Roy May and Arnold Hughes, "Armies on loan: Toward an explanation of transnational military intervention among Black African states", in S. Baynham (ed.), *Military Power & Politics in Black Africa* (London, Croom Helm, 1986).
11. "Des ex-gendarmes de l'Elysee participeraient au recrutement de mercenaires pour le Zaire", *Le Monde*, 8.1.97; "Mercenaries bark but don't bite", *New African*, April 1997.
12. Adams, "The New Mercenaries", p. 3.
13. See MPRI's website at http://www.mpri.com
14. Rhys Dogan and Michael Pugh, "From Military to Market Imperatives: Peacekeeping and the New Public Policy, paper presented at the British International Studies Association Conference, University of Durham, 17–18.12.96.
15. See S.Decalo, "The Process, Prospects and Constraints of Democratisation in Africa", *African Affairs* 1992, p. 91.
16. "Eastern Europe's Arsenal on the Loose: Managing Light Weapons Flows to Conflict Zones", BASIC occasional paper, 26.5.98. Accessible at: http://www.bacisint.org. See also, Al Venter, "Arms into Africa", *New African*, January 1999.
17. See Roy May and Gerry Cleaver, "African peacekeeping: Still dependent?", *International Peacekeeping* Summer 1997, 4(2): 1–21.
18. Ibid.
19. Ibid.
20. See, Gerry Cleaver and Roy May, "Peacekeeping: The African Dimension", *Review of African Political Economy*, Dec. 1995, 22(66): 485–497; Gerry Cleaver and Roy May, "African Perspectives: Regional Peacekeeping", in Roy May and Oliver Furley (eds.), *Peacekeeping in Africa* (Aldershot, Ashgate, 1999), pp. 29–48.
21. See Roy May and Gerry Cleaver, "African peacekeeping: Still dependent?'; Gerry Cleaver, "The African Crisis Response Initiative", paper presented at the biennial conference of the African Studies Association of the UK, University of London 14–16.9.98.
22. *West Africa*, 28.7–3.8.97, p. 1196 and p. 1199; "Gabon, France discuss military bases", Pan African News Agency 30.7.97.
23. Shearer, "Private Armies", p. 41. See also, Isenberg, "Soldiers of Fortune Ltd."; "Africa's new enforcers", *The Independent*, 16.9.96; "Corporate dogs of war who grow fat amid the anarchy of Africa", *The Observer*, 19.1.97.
24. Unlike the other units mentioned, Koevoet was a highly effective counter-insurgency unit of the South West Africa Police. See Helmoed-Roemer Heithman and Paul Hannon, *Modern African Wars 3: South West Africa* (Osprey Men at Arms, No. 242, London, Osprey Publishing, 1991).
25. See Shearer, "Private Armies", and Isenberg, "Soldiers of Fortune Ltd."
26. Shearer, "Private Armies", p. 46.
27. See Isenberg, "Soldiers of Fortune Ltd."

28. Alfred B. Zack-Williams, "Dimensions on West African Conflicts", paper presented at the ASAUK Symposium "Vulnerabilities", Coventry University, 16.9.99.

29. David J. Francis, "Mercenary Intervention in Sierra Leone: Providing National Security or International Exploitation?", *Third World Quarterly* 1999, 20(2): 319–338, 326.

30. Peta Thorneycroft, "Mobutu couldn't afford South African mercenaries", *Weekly Mail & Guardian* 18.7.99 at: http://www.sn.apc.organisation/wmail

31. See Adams, "The New Mercenaries". Also, Sophie Pons, "Executive Outcomes to close on its own terms," *Daily Mail & Guardian*, 11.12.99, at: http://www.mg.co.za

32. See, Select Committee on Foreign Affairs, *Sierra Leone*, 2nd Report Session 1998–99, HC–116, at: http://www.parliament.the-stationery office.co.uk/pa/cm199899/cmselect/

33. See Isenberg, "Soldiers of Fortune Ltd"; Enrique Ballesteros, "Report on the question of the use of mercenaries as a means of violating human rights and impeding the exercise of the right of peoples to self determination", United Nations Document E/CN.4/1999/11, 13.1.99.

34. Francis, "Mercenary Intervention in Sierra Leone", p. 327.

35. Ballesteros, E/CN.4/1999/11, para. 27.

36. Francis, "Mercenary Intervention", p. 328.

37. Enrique Ballesteros Report on the question of the use of mercenaries as a means of violating human rights and impeding the exercise of the right of peoples to self determination. United Nations Document A/54/326 7/9/99. Paragraph 52.

38. Ibid, para. 73.

39. Ibid, para. 66.

40. Ibid, para. 62.

41. Regulation of Foreign Military assistance Bill, South African Ministry of Defence (B54-97), para 6.

42. "Cook to lift ban on mercenaries", The Sunday Times, 3.10.99.

43. Ibid.

44. Ibid. See also, "Double edged Sword: The case for a pragmatic assessment of mercenary forces", *The Times*, 5.5.98.

45. "Rough Diamonds", *The Guardian* (Education Supplement), 7.9.99.

46. Ibid.

47. Ibid.

48. "Diamonds traded for guns lose their sparkle", *The Sunday Telegraph*, 3.10.99.

49. "De Beers ban on gem sales hits UNITA", *Daily Telegraph*, 8.10.99.

50. See Isenberg, "Soldiers of Fortune Ltd".

51. See Gerry Cleaver and Roy May, "African perspectives: regional peacekeeping".

52. "Nigerian troops announce Sierra Leone pullout", BBC World Service, 21.10.99. via http://news.bbc.co.uk

53. A.J. Venter, "Security in the Badlands", *Combat and Survival* Dec. 1999, 11(9).

54. "Zimbabwe losses add up in Congo", BBC World Service, 25.11.99. via http://news.bbc.co.uk

Crime, Law & Social Change **33:** 151–190, 2000.

Examining international responses to illicit arms trafficking

OWEN GREENE
Department of Peace Studies, University of Bradford, Bradford, BD7 1DP, UK

Abstract. Concerns about illicit trafficking in small arms and light weapons have moved rapidly up the international agenda since 1996. Within about three years a range of international responses to this problem, and to the closely related issue of small arms proliferation, have developed at sub-regional, regional and international level – in Africa, Europe and the Americas as well as globally. This article examines the development and design of each of the main initiatives in this issue area. It analyses the different ways in which the problems have been framed in each agreement or programme, and the significance of linkages between them. These recent developments are judged to be substantial. Despite the regional and institutional variations, the shared normative and programmatic elements appear to be sufficient to support the development of winning global coalitions – able to establish a co-ordinated international action programme even if not actually to prevent illicit trafficking in the foreseeable future.

Introduction

Efforts to prevent and combat illicit trafficking in conventional arms are now high on the international agenda. Since 1997, they have been the focus of high-profile initiatives by several regional organisations, including the European Union (EU), Organisation of American States (OAS), Mercosur, Organisation of African Unity (OAU), Southern African Development Community (SADC), and the Economic Community of West African States (ECOWAS). At the global level, two of the most prominent UN negotiating processes at the turn of the century relate to the development of an international "protocol against the illicit manufacturing of and trafficking in firearms, their parts and components and ammunition" and preparations for an international conference on "the illicit trade in small arms and light weapons in all its aspects' to be held in 2001.

International talk about combating illicit arms trafficking is not, of course, new. For several decades, States have found it relatively easy to agree in principle that illicit arms trafficking is a "bad thing", and that all States should do their best to prevent it. Numerous UN resolutions have been agreed to that effect. Such declarations have often been regarded with weary cynicism. It is an open secret that many governments are deeply implicated in much of the illicit arms trade, either by facilitating covert supply to proxies and allies or by turning a "blind eye" to the diversion into the black market of legal arms transfers from or through their territory. In any case, governments lack the capacity to do more than limit purely criminal activities, and international declarations have not obviously stimulated governments to devote more resources to crime control.

This article examines the recent surge of international activities aiming to enhance co-operation to combat illicit arms trafficking, and the extent to which they are of real interest and significance. One question is the extent to which the regional and international programmes and instruments that are being established are themselves significant in relation to the design and development of international agreements. In many ways, they appear to break new ground. International norms, rules and institutions are being developed in a range of issue areas where there is little history of substantial international co-ordination. Such issue areas include: regulating legal arms transfers; arms brokering; marking and tracing of firearms; weapons stockpile management and destruction; and arms collection from civilians. The article examines recent development of international co-operation in these issue areas at global and regional levels, as they relate to illicit trafficking in conventional arms.

However, the recent development of activities to tackle illicit arms trafficking is also interesting from a number of other perspectives. It is important to assess the extent to which recent international activities are really associated with changes in the patterns of States' interests and concerns relating to covert or illicit flows of conventional arms. That is, does the increased diplomatic activity reflect a real increased interest of governments to tackle illicit arms trafficking? If it does, regional co-operation has some prospect of being effective in some regions, and claims that a powerful coalition is developing for action at a global level are re-inforced.

The topic is also interesting in relation to the development of linked or "nested" international regimes. The relationship between various local, national regional and international institutions and agreements is inevitably complex in this area. Co-operation to combat illicit arms trafficking is thus an interesting case study of the challenges and trade-offs involved in establishing mutually-re-inforcing arrangements at these different levels.

More fundamentally in this context, there are also questions relating to the linkage between issue-areas. It is widely recognised that illicit arms trafficking cannot effectively be tackled through a narrowly focused regime to prevent or combat arms smuggling by criminals. A more comprehensive approach is needed. But this implies further international challenges.

Thus, international co-operation to combat illicit arms trafficking needs to be embedded in broader efforts to combat transnational criminal networks and to prevent and reduce excessive accumulation and spread of small arms and light weapons. The agenda for tackling such "small arms proliferation", for example, is broad. It includes: preventing and combating illicit trafficking; enhancing controls on legal arms transfers and stockpiles; enforcement of arms embargoes; development, peace-building and governance in conflict-prone and war-torn societies; disarmament in the implementation of peace agreements; civilian weapons collection programmes; and arms stockpile management and destruction of surplus weapons.

The article focuses on international initiatives to tackle illicit trafficking in firearms, small arms and light weapons. It is in this area that many of the most important recent regional or global responses have developed. It therefore does not deal with international efforts to prevent illicit trafficking in other military goods, such as sensitive dual-technologies for weapons of mass destruction or international concern, important though these are.

The article is organised as follows. The next section briefly outlines the character and dimensions of the problem of illicit trafficking in conventional weapons, and particularly small arms and light weapons, to provide necessary context. The following sections examine in some detail the recent regional responses, followed by an examination of global initiatives, particularly within a United Nations framework. The final section provides a concluding assessment, and a discussion of the prospects for establishing a co-ordinated international action programme.

Characterising the illicit arms trade

The term "illicit arms trade" is concise but unduly narrow. The issue area includes all forms of illicit transfers of arms, ammunition and associated materials. More broadly, most recent international initiatives in this area also address illicit manufacture, acquisition, possession, use and storage of such arms and materials.[1]

The complex of problems involved in the illicit transfer, manufacture, possession and use of arms is not well monitored or understood. However, it is clearly multi-dimensional. It is driven by demand from a variety of types of client. These include: embargoed governments; armed groups involved in war, banditry and insurgency; terrorists; criminals and criminal organisations; and also citizens who want arms for self defence or cultural reasons but cannot obtain gun licences. The illicit arms trade is (wittingly or unwittingly) sourced from government arsenals, legal producers and gun holders, war booty, arms caches in areas of conflict; as well as by illicit manufacturers. In fact, the source of a large proportion of illicit conventional arms is government disposals of "surplus" arms or thefts from insecure government stockpiles.

There are broadly three types of trafficking processes.[2] Firstly, much of the trafficking is carried out through small-scale transactions by individuals or small firms that deliberately break the law by illegally transferring arms to illicit recipients, or by displaced people carrying guns for protection. Secondly, higher-value or more difficult illicit shipments of arms often involve corrupt officials, brokers or "middle-men" motivated mainly by profit. These often use well-established networks and channels also employed for smuggling other illicit goods. But the users of arms and their sympathisers are also often directly involved in arms trafficking. Thirdly, governments themselves, or at least agencies of States, are involved. Not only do they often turn a blind eye to the two types of trafficking outlined above, but they also deliberately facilitate covert flows of arms to their proxies or allies, or to embargoed or suspect destinations for profit.

A large proportion of the illicit arms trade is in civilian firearms and small arms and light weapons. Broadly, the term "small arms" refers to conventional weapons produced (if not used) for military purposes that can be carried by an individual, including pistols, rifles, sub-machine guns, assault rifles and grenades. Light weapons can be carried on a light vehicle, and operated by a small crew. They include heavy machine guns, light mortars, and shoulder-fired anti-tank or anti-aircraft missiles.[3]

Firearms, small arms and light weapons are relatively amenable to illicit trafficking. By definition, they are easily portable. Compared to "heavy" weapons systems such as tanks or aircraft, they are also relatively easy to conceal. They have relatively low cash value, and small shipments of small arms are often not regarded as "strategic" by state authorities, in contrast for example to sensitive components or technologies for missiles or weapons of mass destruction.[4] Small arms can be transported by individuals or light vehicles, hidden in small storage places, and smuggled in shipments of legitimate cargoes. Moreover, many types of small arms and light weapons require minimal maintenance and logistic support. Therefore they can be operated relatively easily. They are also durable. A cache of submachine guns, for example, may be readily useable after years of storage.

Importantly, small arms and light weapons are more widely traded and held, both legally and illegally, by non-state groups than are heavy weapons. Only national armed forces or large rebel armies normally operate major weapons such as tanks and aircraft. In contrast, small arms and light weapons are also widely held and used by the police, bandits, criminals, and ordinary citizens, and are appropriate for every type of violent conflict: not only inter-state or civil war, but also communal conflicts, crime and social violence. Thus these weapons are desirable to all of the main types of clients for illicit arms.

Although governments have been able to agree that illicit transfers of arms, ammunition and military equipment are a "bad thing", the definition of "illicit transfers" has long been contested. It has always been clear that it includes arms smuggling by criminals in clear contravention of the laws of every state whose territory is involved. But what about transfers authorised by only some of the States concerned, or "covert" state-sponsored supplies to rebel groups?

Throughout the Cold War, the two superpowers and their allies were reluctant to agree that supplying arms to friendly non-state "freedom fighters" was necessarily illegitimate. Governments of post-colonial and developing countries have been inclined to agree, when it came to the question of whether it was wrong in principle to support arms transfers to bodies such as the African National Congress, Palestine Liberation Organisation, or "anticolonial" resistance groups. In this context, there has been a tendency to confine intergovernmental initiatives on illicit transfers to vague declarations or partisan understandings of what is "illicit".

Since the mid-1990s, there has been progress towards a relatively inclusive international definition of what is meant by "illicit". In 1996, the UN Disarmament Commission agreed that "illicit arms trafficking is understood to cover that international trade in arms which is contrary to the laws of States and/or to international law".[5] Article 2 of the draft International Firearms Protocol defines "illicit firearms trafficking" as "The import, export, acquisition, sale, delivery, movement or transfer of firearms, their parts and components and ammunition from or across the territory of one State Party to that of another State Party without the authorisation of or in violation of the legislation or regulations of any one of the States Parties concerned".[6]

These are still contested definitions. Some governments continue to argue that the Firearms Protocol's definition should apply only to transfers between non-State groups and civilians, or even be confined to transfers by transnational criminal organisations.[7] There is also continuing debate about the extent to which transfers implicated in breaches of international humanitarian or human rights law are included.

As the international debates have become more substantial, it has proved awkward to try to define illicit arms trafficking as a specific issue area for the purposes of developing effective international responses. It frames the problems both too narrowly and too broadly. Illicit arms trafficking is deeply embedded in the broader problems of: international crime and corruption; excessive and destabilising transfers and accumulations or arms; and insecurity and gun control in conflict-prone societies. Thus international responses to illicit arms trafficking need to be part of more comprehensive international efforts in these broader issue areas.

However, the problem of illicit arms trafficking also needs to be divided into narrower issue areas, around which efforts to strengthen international co-operation can more effectively be mobilised. These include co-operation for: individual criminal investigations involving weapons; preventing and combating transnational arms trafficking by criminal or terrorist organisations; enforcement of arms embargoes; preventing diversion of legal arms shipments to unauthorised recipients (including governments); preventing illicit or covert flows of arms to areas in conflict; and collecting and destroying unlicensed arms after conflicts.

The character and success of international initiatives to address illicit arms trafficking problems depends substantially on the ways in which the issue is framed (for example, as an issue of crime or international security). To some extent, this is determined by the regional context. It is not surprising that in the late 1990s the problem of illicit arms trafficking in Central Africa has generally been framed as an international security issue, while in Americas it has primarily been addressed as a problem of combating transnational criminal organisations. However, as will become clear, it is also a matter of diplomatic "art" and agenda-setting processes.

We now examine the recent regional and international responses to the problems of illicit arms trafficking.

Regional responses

Although illicit arms trafficking takes place on a global scale, each region and sub-region experiences and perceives the problem in different ways. Moreover, countries are typically most affected by and concerned about the problems in their immediate neighbourhood. Thus developing co-operation at a sub-regional and regional level is a particular priority.

Since the 1996, substantial regional initiatives to combat and prevent illicit arms trafficking have developed in Africa, Europe and the Americas. Below we examine these in turn.

In other regions, specific regional co-operative agreements on this issue are so far either weak or absent. This is not to imply that Asian or Pacific States do not co-operate with others to combat illicit arms trafficking. But where they do so it is primarily through bilateral co-operation amongst enforcement or intelligence agencies, or through international institutions such as Interpol and relevant UN programmes. Some distinctive regional arrangements for police co-operation in this problem area are beginning to emerge in East Asia through ASEAN and the ASEAN Regional Forum consultations.[8] But they have yet to become substantial or distinctive.

For regional co-operation to develop in this relatively new and sensitive issue area, participating countries must not only recognise shared interests and concerns but also there must be political leadership and a degree of commitment. Moreover, it is easier to start developing co-operative approaches in a new issue area if there are already in place some institutional frameworks for agenda-setting and some functioning regional mechanisms or organisations. These can be used, adapted or developed as required, without the challenges and delays involved in arranging special high-level meetings or establishing entirely new institutions.

In practice, regional and international processes have become closely inter-related, in this as in most other issue areas at the end of the 20th century. Global institutions such as the United Nations, and also inter-regional partner-ships, can also be used to support the development of sub-regional initiatives, even in the absence of strong local institutions.

Africa

Much of Sub-Saharan Africa has experienced intense problems of insecurity, conflict, criminality and violence during the 1990s. In most regions, small arms and light weapons are widely available. Destabilising flows of illicit or covert arms are a major problem. Most of these flows take place sub-regionally and from one part of Africa to another, drawing on earlier arms supplies during the Cold War and the residues of past conflicts. Nevertheless, there is also high demand for additional arms from outside Africa.

These arms have not in themselves caused the conflicts and crime in which they are used. The multiple crises in much of Sub-Saharan Africa have a range of underlying causes, relating for example to weak and/or oppressive states, wrenching economic and social change, deprivation, and complex social and political divisions. However, wide availability and flows of arms have ex-acerbated and prolonged conflicts, facilitated warlordism and banditry, and contributed to violent crime.

At the regional and international level, the problem of illicit arms traf-ficking in Africa has primarily been considered in the context of: excessive and destabilising accumulations and flows of arms (particularly small arms and light weapons); UN sanctions breaking; and an obstacle to post-conflict peace-building and reconstruction. In Post-Cold War Africa, the United Na-tions and the wider international community have had a direct interest and involvement in addressing each of these issues. Thus they have played an in-fluential role in the development of regional as well as international responses to illicit arms trafficking in these contexts.

The Organisation of African Unity (OAU) is the main regional organ-isation. African governments have generally been diplomatically careful at least to try to associate their initiatives relating to illicit arms trafficking with OAU Resolutions. Since the mid-1990s, the OAU has sought to increase its capacity to contribute to efforts to prevent conflicts and tackle security and tackle security problems. Nevertheless it remains a slow-moving institution, with relatively little capacity in these issue areas.

In June 1998, the OAU adopted a decision on the proliferation of small arms and light weapons, stressing the role the OAU should play in co-ordinating efforts to address this problem in Africa and requesting the OAU Secretary-General to prepare a comprehensive report on this issue.[9] On 14 July, 1999, the Assembly of Heads of State and Government of the OAU adopted a Decision on the Illicit Proliferation, Circulation and Illicit Trafficking of Small Arms and Light Weapons that, *inter alia*, calls for a co-ordinated African approach to the problems addressed by the decision, and requested the OAU Secretariat to organise a continental experts preparatory conference on this matter. The Conference was due to take place in the spring of 2000. It is expected to play a significant role in developing common ground amongst African States, in preparation for the forthcoming international conference on illicit trafficking in small arms and light weapons in all its aspects to be held in 2001 (the 2001 Conference).

However, it is at the sub-regional level that the most significant recent initiatives on illicit arms trafficking have developed in Africa.

West Africa

It was in West Africa that the first sub-regional initiative on illicit arms trafficking after the Cold War was taken. It began in 1993 as an initiative by Mali; developed in 1996 as a co-operation between the UN and Sahara-Sahel countries, and in 1998 became a programme of the Economic Community of West African States (ECOWAS), supported by the UN and many international donors.

In October 1993, newly elected President Konare of Mali requested the UN Secretary-General to provide assistance in the collection and control of illicit small arms in his country. The widespread availability of such weapons was undermining security and obstructing the implementation of the 1992 "Pacte Nationale" peace accord between the Mali government and the Tuareg rebels. This was a precedent-setting request for the UN: it was a request for practical support for weapons reduction and control inside a State where a UN peace mission was not already in place.

It was not until August 1994 that a UN Advisory Mission was sent to Mali to investigate. The mission concluded that a so-called "security first" approach was needed: Mali needed capacity-building assistance with legal systems, policing, border controls and weapons collection, to create a secure

environment in which demobilisation and post-conflict reconstruction programmes could proceed.[10] The UN initiated a programme, co-ordinated by
the UNDP, to provide such security assistance, accompanied with guarantees and monitoring systems to ensure that is was not misused by internal
security services that were themselves in need of reform. The international
engagement helped to re-inforce the implementation of the Pacte Nationale.
In an important act of political symbolism, Tuareg rebels participated in a
high profile weapons destruction event sponsored by the government and the
UN. Some 3,000 weapons were burned in an event known as the "Flamme de
la Paix" in Timbuctu in March 1996.[11]

Efforts were made to extend this programme to a sub-regional level. A UN
Mission to the Sahara Sahel was established. In 1996 this mission reported
that the proliferation of illicit light weapons posed a serious threat to all
States in the Sahara Sahel.[12] The government of Mali, the UN Department
of Political Affairs, UN Development Programme and the UN Institute for
Disarmament Research (UNIDIR) jointly convened a sub-regional conference, to examine common problems and identify ways to develop regional
co-operation to tackle light arms proliferation and promote conflict prevention and post-conflict reconstruction. The Conference on "Conflict Prevention, Disarmament and Development in West Africa" was held in November
1996 in Bamako, Mali. Government ministers, relevant government agencies
(military, police, judiciary, etc), civil society groups, outside experts, and
representatives of UN agencies and several donor countries all participated.
A fragile consensus was achieved to develop a sub-regional programme not
only to co-operate on combating illicit arms trafficking and possession, but
also to establish a sub-regional moratorium on legal arms transfers of light
weapons.

The emergence of a proposal for a sub-regional moratorium on the import,
export, and manufacture of light weapons at the 1996 Bamako conference
took many by surprise, including most Sahara-Sahel governments. It was supported by the argument that the region already had a destabilising surplus of
such weapons. Moreover, continued legal transfers would undermine efforts
to tackle illicit trafficking, in the context of vague and poorly enforced laws on
weapons transfers and possession, insecure military stockpiles, banditry, and
continued risk of conflict. Nevertheless, without strong informal persuasion
by UN representatives and the support of President Konare of Mali and some
donor countries, it is doubtful that the proposal would have emerged.

Henceforth, however, the moratorium proposal was the focus for a co-
ordinated programme of meetings during 1997–98 to sensitise and persuade
Heads of State to support the proposal. Politically, West African governments
were gradually persuaded that a declaratory moratorium would help to catch

international attention and mobilise wider international assistance. Importantly, donors agreed that declaration of a three–year moratorium would be accompanied by a "Programme for Co-ordination and Assistance on Security and Development" (PCASED). This programme would provide capacity-building aid to help to strengthen local agencies and institutions, assist with weapons collection and control, and associated peace-building activities.

Attention also shifted from the "Sahara-Sahel" to the Economic Community of West African States (ECOWAS). At the 1996 Bamako conference, non-Sahel countries like Liberia and Cote D'Ivoire, were invited as observers, but some ECOWAS governments including Nigeria were not even represented. It was important to involve such countries, and also to embed the initiative in the main existing sub-regional institution. This helped to attract support from countries like Nigeria and Ghana that had a wider stake in promoting ECOWAS. It also had the effect of marginalising Sahel countries outside ECOWAS. Algeria was probably content to be left out of an initiative of which it was deeply sceptical. But Chad and Cameroon, which retained a lively interest and concern, were unfortunately left out in their allocated "Central African" sphere.

After repeated delays, a moratorium was officially declared by the ECOWAS heads of state and government at their meeting in Abuja on 30–31 October 1998. They declared a Moratorium on the Importation, Exportation and Manufacture of Light Weapons.[13] It is due to run for least three years, after which progress will be reviewed. This declaration enabled implementation of the Programme for Co-ordination and Assistance for Security and Development (PCASED) to begin in earnest. A plan of action for its implementation was agreed by ECOWAS Foreign Ministers in Bamako on 24 March 1999, together with a code of conduct for the implementation of the ECOWAS Moratorium.[14]

The ECOWAS Moratorium, combined with the PCASED programme, attracted wide international attention. The UN urged other sub-regions to consider taking similar initiatives.[15] Predictably, however, implementation has proved to be a challenge. It rapidly became clear in 1999 that there was substantial confusion about the terms of the Moratorium. In several ECOWAS countries, the military and the arms transfer licensing authorities were apparently unaware that their government had declared the Moratorium.

In practice, some arms supplier countries played a key role in establishing procedures for implementing the Moratorium. Faced with applications for licenses for arms transfers to ECOWAS countries, they referred the application to the ECOWAS Secretariat, asking whether ECOWAS had granted a special exemption to permit this transfer.[16] This triggered ECOWAS consultations, leading either to the withdrawal of the application or to the elaboration through precedent of agreed ECOWAS guidelines for exemption. In one case, for example, Ghana was permitted to import military equipment for use in a military training exercise, provided that the equipment was monitored and returned to supplier after the exercise was completed.

This is an important illustration of the ways in which international engagement has been vital for the development and implementation of the ECOWAS moratorium (and the associated PCASED programme). Following the ad-hoc efforts to promote implementation noted above, some donors aimed to strengthen ECOWAS' capacity to implement its initiative more systematically. In October 1999, the UK sent consultants to report on what needed to be done in this respect. In December 1999, ECOWAS Heads of Government agreed to implement the main recommendations, including the establishment of a new ECOWAS Department of Political Affairs, Defence and Security, with responsibility for implementing the Moratorium.[17]

However, the pressure was not all in one direction. For example, in 1997 and again in 1998, participating West African governments directly called on the arms supplying states of the Wassenaar Arrangement to respect and support the West African Moratorium. The "Wassenaar Arrangement" was established in 1996 as the new multilateral conventional arms supplier regime to replace COCOM. At the time, members of the Wassenaar Arrangement were not clear that it was part of the Arrangement's role to be a partner in the development of arms transfer moratoria. Politically, however, they felt obliged to respond positively.[18] Support for the ECOWAS Moratorium henceforth became a recognised part of the on-going concerns of the Wassenaar Arrangement.

The PCASED Programme has become an important paradigm for co-operative programmes between donors and regions suffering from widespread illicit arms trafficking and excessive flows and availability of small arms. The main donors to this or closely associated projects include Belgium, Canada, France, Germany, Japan Netherlands, Norway, Sweden, Switzerland, the UK and the USA, as well as the UNDP which has a key co-ordinating role. Since 1999, the European Union has a whole has also supported PCASED.

It is instructive in this context to review the main programme elements of PCASED.[19] They include activities to:

- Establish a culture of peace
- Support Training Programmes for military, security and police forces
- Enhancing weapon controls at border posts
- Establish a regional light weapons data-base and register
- Collect and destroy surplus and unauthorised weapons
- Facilitate dialogue with arms supplier countries (Wassenaar Arrangement etc.)

- Revise national legislation and administrative procedures
- Mobilise resources for the PCASED objectives and activities
- Enlarge membership of the ECOWAS Moratorium

Thus, for example, support for developing appropriate national legislation and administrative procedures to control small arms and light weapons is a core element of the PCASED programme. In this element, the main PCASED aims include:

- Review, update and harmonise national legislation and regulations of small arms and light weapons bearing on civilian possession, use and transfer;
- Ensure the use of legal instruments, such as export and import permits and end-user certificates to control illegal transfers and proliferation;
- Harmonise different national legislation with a view to developing a regional convention on light weapons that would touch on control and reduction as well as humanitarian law issues;
- Set up National Commissions on light weapons issues that would co-ordinate and develop policy relating to these questions. Concomitantly, there would be the emergence of the necessary administrative framework for the regular management of these issues.

Other elements of the PCASED programme re-inforce this one: training and capacity-building of customs, police, the judiciary and security forces; reform of the police and security structures to meet the real needs of the people of the countries involved and to build trust between the police and security forces and communities; collecting surplus weapons; and building and maintaining data-bases.

In spite of the important precedents set in West Africa, it is important to emphasise that the problems of illicit arms trafficking and associated problems remain intense in the region. Several ECOWAS countries continue to be implicated in covert arms shipments, particularly during 1998–99 to the complex of conflicts involving Sierra Leone and Liberia. Moreover, the PCASED programme is only at the early stages of implementation, and ECOWAS is some way from developing adequate institutional capacity to promote and ensure such implementation. Nevertheless, it remains a substantial regional response in a difficult context, with real potential for future development.

Southern Africa
The region of Southern Africa is certainly severely affected by the wide availability and flow of small arms light weapons and illicit arms trafficking, and by the problems associated with them.[20] These have been required and used in numerous civil wars, inter-state conflicts, as well as in banditry and crime.

Indeed, covert arms supply was an important component of struggle between South Africa and the "front-line states" during the Apartheid era. With the end of civil wars in Namibia and Mozambique, and transition from apartheid towards democratic elections and an ANC government in South Africa, it became possible to envisage a Southern African sub-regional response to illicit arms trafficking.

South Africa joined the Southern African Development Community (SADC) in 1994. In practice, it took some time for the illicit arms trafficking issue to rise on the agenda of SADC, the main sub-regional organisation. Other issues dominated the agenda in the mid-1990s. Moreover, it took time for relevant SADC institutions to be put in place. The SADC Organ for Politics, Defence and Security was established in 1996, within which the most important committee for our purposes is the Inter-State Defence and Security Committee (ISDSC).[21] The ISDSC has three sub-committees, for defence, public security and state security, where relevant ministers from SADC countries meet to address concerns relating to regional peace and security. In practice, these bodies were highly politicised in the late 1990s, and hampered by rivalry between President Mugabe (who chaired the Organ for Politics, Defence and Security) and President Mandela.

In practice, the first initiatives in Southern Africa relating to illicit arms started in 1995 through bilateral and trilateral co-operation between South Africa and its neighbours. The new South African government, and particularly the South African police, became intensely concerned about arms flows into South Africa from neighbouring states. As violent crime and personal insecurity increased in South Africa, and political violence continued in Kwa-Zulu Natal, demand for small arms grew. Illicit trafficking of arms into South Africa became profitable and widespread, particularly from arms caches left over from the wars in Mozambique and Namibia, and from arms pipelines associated with the wars in Angola and Central Africa.

As a partial response, South Africa and Mozambique (with the co-operation of Swaziland where appropriate) began a series of joint weapons destruction operations in Mozambique. These were known as "Operations Rachel", and involved joint operations between South African and Mozambican police (with military support) to find and destroy hidden arms caches, often on the basis of information from local communities in Mozambique. Between October 1995 and June 1996 four such Operations Rachel were conducted.[22] They succeeded in destroying some 12,000 firearms, 6,350 anti-personnel mines, 7,000 mortars, 300 launchers and cannons, 1,260 hand grenades, and over 3,300,000 rounds of ammunition. Although this probably constituted only a small proportion of the hidden weapons, these are substantial numbers. Just as importantly, close working relationships developed between the police of

South Africa, Mozambique and Swaziland. These operations were resourced on shoestring budgets from South Africa. But with donor support forthcoming in 1999, they are continuing into 2000 and beyond.

It was not until 1998 that initiatives were taken to develop a genuinely sub-regional programme on small arms proliferation and illicit arms trafficking. As in West Africa, support from outside the region played an important role. In this case, the European Union decided to promote co-operation with Southern Africa as part of its new EU Programme for Preventing and Combating Illicit Trafficking in Conventional Arms. As part of its EU Presidency in early 1998, the UK government sponsored a workshop in May 1998 in South Africa, organised by Saferworld (UK) and the Institute for Security Studies (South Africa), on "Developing Controls on Arms and Illicit Trafficking in Southern Africa".[23]

The workshop brought together relevant officials from Southern African and EU countries, as well as the EC Commission and representatives from Interpol, the Southern African Development Community (SADC) and the Southern African Regional Police Commissioners Co-ordinating Organisation (SARPCCO). It aimed to explore and develop a regional response to light arms proliferation and illicit arms trafficking, and also to identify ways in which the EU could assist in its implementation.

The workshop participants agreed a document entitled "A Southern African regional action programme to tackle light arms proliferation and illicit arms trafficking".[24]

This document was subsequently endorsed at the SADC-EU Ministerial Meeting in November 1998.[25] It sets out a detailed agenda for action in four key, and interrelated, areas:

- combating illicit arms trafficking (by strengthening laws, regulations and operational capacity; improving marking and record-keeping systems to trace illicit arms; and improving national and regional information exchange);
- strengthening regulation of, and controls on, the accumulation and transfer of civilian firearms and small arms and light weapons (and associated ammunition and explosives);
- promoting the removal of weapons from society and the destruction of confiscated or "surplus" arms, and developing programmes to reverse "cultures of violence";
- enhancing weapons-related transparency, information exchange and consultation in Southern Africa, through measures to increase public transparency and to improve confidential information exchange between police, customs, and legal authorities in the region.

In each of these areas, the action programme not only detailed proposed national and regional measures to be taken by Southern Africa countries and sub-regional bodies, but also identified ways in which the EC and EU Member States could most usefully provide assistance in their implementation.

The challenge in 1999 was to properly establish a SADC programme and the framework for co-operation with the EU and other donors, and also to begin implementation. At its meeting on 13–14 August 1999, the SADC Council took the official decision to establish a co-ordinated SADC framework for the "Prevention and Combating of Illicit Trafficking in Small Arms and Related Crimes".[26] Importantly, it agreed that the Southern African Regional Police Chiefs Co-operation Organisation (SARPCCO) should be the implementation agency for SADC policy on small arms and cross-border crime prevention. It further established a Working Group to work out SADC policy in this area and develop an SADC regional action programme.

Thus, in contrast to West Africa, police co-operation has been established as the main institutional framework for SADC countries to co-operate in combating and preventing illicit arms trafficking. In fact, there is a relatively long history of police co-operation in Southern Africa. Since the 1970s, there were conferences of Front Line Chiefs of Police, and limited co-operation on police operations developed.[27] The Southern African Regional Police Chiefs Co-operation Organisation (SARPCCO) was established in August 1995. It has a Permanent Co-ordinating Committee, and a Secretariat consisting of one or two officers from each member state based at the INTERPOL Sub-Regional Bureau in Harare, Zimbabwe. Its joint operations are underpinned by an international agreement amongst participating states signed in October 1997: the "Agreement in respect of Co-ordination and Mutual Assistance in the Field of Crime Combating".

Most importantly, during the late 1990s SARPCCO established itself as a relatively effective organisation, conducting substantial joint operations to tackle: motor vehicle thefts, drug trafficking, trafficking in precious stones and metals; trafficking in endangered species and their products; illegal immigrants and forged travel documents, and commercial and economic crime. Combating firearms trafficking was one of SARPCCO's tasks from the beginning, and during 1998–99 this emerged as a priority.

To promote elaboration and implementation of a regional action programme, in September 1999 there was a second EU-SADC workshop in South Africa, sponsored by Finland as part of its EU Presidency together with the UK, and once again organised by Saferworld and the ISS. SARPCCO and all members of the new SADC Working Group participated, and a number of priority areas for practical projects (and EU support) were identified.[28] These included information-exchange and training programmes to combat illicit trafficking; co-operation in safeguarding and destruction of confiscated weapons and improvements in arms stockpile management; developing co-ordinated policies on legislation on firearms control and arms transfers; supporting Operation Rachel type operations and voluntary community-based weapons collection programmes; and public education projects. By early 2000, official EU-SADC co-operation on such projects had yet to be established, but some individual projects were starting to be funded on a bilateral and ad-hoc basis.

Alongside these developments, in 1999 the SADC Legal Sub-Committee began negotiations to draft a SADC "Protocol on the Control of Firearms, Ammunition AND Other Related Materials".[29] These negotiations made rapid progress, and agreement had virtually been achieved by January 2000. It is intended that the Protocol, which will be legally binding, will be signed at the SADC Council Meeting in summer 2000. The draft provisions of the Protocol have wide scope, covering state-owned as well as civilian firearms. In addition to establishing minimum standards for national firearms legislation, firearms marking, and operational co-operation to combat illicit trafficking and destroy confiscated arms, the draft protocol includes provisions for the disposal and destruction of surplus state-owned firearms, voluntary weapons collection programmes and public education.[30]

By the beginning of 2000, therefore, a Southern African sub-regional response to illicit arms trafficking was developing rapidly. At key stages in 1998–99, the EU and other donors (the USA and Canada also became involved) helped to stimulate this response through sponsored workshops and the promise of donor support. However, much of the initiative has been driven by SADC governments and agencies, as well as by pressures from Southern African non-governmental groups. South Africa and Mozambique were particularly important in stimulating a regional response, together with the institutions for police co-operation. In practice, Angola and the Democratic Republic of Congo are not yet involved in these efforts, although they are SADC members: they are overwhelmed by the problems of civil war.

It is noteworthy that, in spite of the focus on SARPCCO and police co-operation, the sub-regional response to illicit arms trafficking aims to have a wide scope, addressing wider issue of small arms proliferation and state-owned weapons as well as criminal access to firearms. However, it remains to be seen whether SARPCCO institutions will be able to mobilise co-ordinated actions by all of the agencies that need to be involved. For example, the customs service and the judiciary have little substantial involvement with SARPCCO activities. One problem is that border guards and customs officers in much of Southern Africa focus on ensuring payment of appropriate duties and do not typically regard themselves as having an important role in combating illicit trafficking. It remains to be seen whether further sub-regional institutions need to be established for customs officers, for example, to address such problems.

East Africa

In comparison with West and Southern Africa, sub-regional responses elsewhere in Africa remain undeveloped. However, there has been significant recent progress in East Africa. There have been major flows of arms throughout East Africa, due to the multiple conflicts in the Horn of Africa, Sudan and the Great Lakes region. Moreover, Kenya and its neighbours have experienced increasing gun-related crime, banditry and cattle rustling. These concerns have pushed the issue of illicit and uncontrolled flows of arms, particularly small arms, high on the political agenda.

Since the mid-1990s Kenya, Uganda and Tanzania gradually developed operational co-operation amongst police, customs and border control officials within the framework of the East Africa Co-operation arrangement.[31] In the first instance, this co-operation developed in relation to problems such as trafficking in stolen cars. The operational co-operation remained low profile, in part because of higher-level political tensions.

However, during 1999, the political atmosphere improved considerably. The governments of Kenya, Uganda and Tanzania decided to launch a new East African Community (EAC). Kenyan President Arap Moi made a speech calling for sub-regional action in October 1999. On 30 November 1999, the three Presidents signed the Treaty establishing the new EAC at a ceremony in Arusha, Tanzania. The way was opened for rapid progress.

At the same time the Inter-Governmental Authority on Development (IGAD), the primary sub-regional organisation for the Horn of Africa, decided to try to develop sub-regional initiatives in this issue area. It is interested to promote both police co-operation to combat illicit trafficking and a security-building approach to engage with the problem of reducing arms flows to conflict zones and managing disarmament in the context of demobilisation programmes.

In this context, it was striking during the autumn of 1999 that East African states sought to build directly on the earlier initiatives in West and Southern Africa. Due to the ECOWAS precedent, the possibility of an East Africa moratorium on the import, export or manufacture of arms even appeared to be on the agenda, in spite of the unpromising context of the war between Eritrea and Ethiopia and civil wars in Sudan and Somalia.

Perhaps more promisingly, Southern African precedents were also actively explored. Interestingly, East Africa countries already have an Eastern Africa Police Chiefs Conference process, in direct analogy to that of SARP-CCO. East African representatives joined a meeting of the SADC Legal Sub-

Committee in January 2000, to learn the possibilities for rapidly developing their own sub-regional protocol to prevent and combat illicit arms trafficking.[32] In February 2000, IGAD co-sponsored a preliminary sub-regional workshop in East Africa to explore the opportunities further. In another parallel with the Southern African process, this workshop was supported by Norway and some EU states, and the two NGOs ISS and Saferworld again helped with its organisation, along with the Nairobi-based Security Research and Information Centre (SRIC). On 12–15 March 2000 Kenya held a meeting of foreign ministers from 10 countries in the Horn of Africa and the Great Lakes region, resulting in the 'Nairobi Declaration' on the problem of the proliferation of illicit small arms and light weapons in the Great Lakes region and the Horn of Affrica. Building on this, these countries then aimed to establish a 'regional action programme' similar to that of Southern Africa.

Europe

The states of Europe and the former Soviet Union are collectively major suppliers of arms and ammunition. This is clear both from official data-sources on legal transfers, including the UN Register of Conventional Arms and the US Congressional Research Service, and from unofficial sources such as the SIPRI arms transfers database.[33] Reliable information on illicit arms flows is relatively scarce. Nevertheless, it is clear that a large fraction of illicitly held or traded weapons have at some stage been exported from European countries, often many years ago.

After the Cold War, military restructuring and downsizing have made vast stockpiles of arms available for release on the market. Many of these have entered the illicit trade. This has particularly been a problem in ex-Warsaw Pact countries, where large arms stocks have been combined with a wide need for hard currency and at least a partial breakdown of internal and border controls during a prolonged and difficult transitional period. Unauthorised sales and thefts from government storage facilities and armed forces has also been a major problem, facilitated by corruption, poor monitoring and record-keeping, and inadequately paid personnel. There is also evidence that substantial quantities of weapons pass illicitly in transit through European countries, or are traded by "third-party" brokers based in their territories. Some governments have also been guilty of tolerating covert arms transfers to one or more favoured parties in armed conflicts, in the Balkans, Caucasus or in Africa.

Europe is perhaps the continent with the most highly developed and dense complex of regional and sub-regional institutions, on which responses to illicit arms trafficking could be developed. Thus it is no surprise that European initiatives relating to illicit arms trafficking are amongst the most fully developed. However, these initiatives are mainly concentrated in the EU and its Associate Countries. There few no substantial sub-regional initiatives in Eastern Europe and Central Asia. Moreover the Organisation for Security and Co-operation in Europe (OSCE) and NATO have only recently begun to develop regional initiatives to address this problem area.

The OSCE

In principle, the Organisation for Security and Co-operation in Europe (OSCE) appears to be well adapted to provide a framework for addressing the complex challenges posed illicit arms trafficking and small arms proliferation. It is an established security-building organisation, which explicitly recognises the importance of a comprehensive approach to security, in which internal conflicts and problems are a legitimate focus of collective concern not least because they may endanger regional security. Moreover, the OSCE has a widely recognised track record in developing and strengthening collective principles and norms in response to complex challenges.

In practice, the issue of small arms proliferation and illicit arms trafficking emerged on the OSCE agenda some time after United Nations had developed a leading role in the issue area. As discussed below, by 1997 important UN processes were established to develop relevant consensual international norms and recommendations. In this context, many OSCE countries doubted whether the OSCE could make a distinctive contribution in this area.

In practice, there was also a distinct lack of political will to enter such potentially sensitive areas. The conflicts in the Balkans, Caucasus and parts of Central Asia meant that some OSCE Member States had a sensitive interest in covert arms supplies, and the OSCE operates by consensus. Nevertheless, several governments continued to try to find ways to place aspects of the problem of small arms and light weapons proliferation on the OSCE agenda. On 9–10 November 1998, Canada, Norway, the Netherlands and Switzerland, in co-operation with the NGO BASIC, co-sponsored an international workshop on the issue at the OSCE in Vienna. A number of recommendations and areas of potential comparative advantage for the OSCE were identified at the Workshop.[34] These included information exchange mechanisms and elaboration of guidelines to reduce the risk of diversion of legal arms transfers and to promote surplus weapons destruction.

However, the crisis in Kosovo frustrated attempts to focus attention on this issue at the OSCE summit in Oslo in December 1998. Nevertheless, during 1999 the issue was discussed at the OSCE's Forum for Security Co-operation (FSC). In December 1999, the OSCE summit in Istanbul accepted the FSC's recommendation to "conduct a working group study of the various proposals relating to small arms and light weapons made by OSCE Member States, with the aim of agreeing on a set of specific measures that may be taken". It also agreed that a seminar should be convened by March 2000 to examine this set of proposed measures. The outcomes of this meeting remained unclear at the time of writing, but the prospects for rapid progress on OSCE initiatives in this area did not seem good.

NATO and the Euro-Atlantic Partnership Council

The Euro-Atlantic Partnership Council (EAPC), the political forum of the members of the North Atlantic Treaty Organisation and the Partnership for Peace programme, has included the issues of small arms and light weapons in its 1998–2000 Action Plan. In accordance with this Action Plan, the EAPC Council in April 1999 established an Ad-Hoc Working Group on Small Arms. Between March and June, this Ad-Hoc Working Group identified three subjects for further detailed study: stockpile management and security; "best practices" with respect to national export controls; and disarmament of small arms and light weapons in the context of peace-keeping operations.[35]

In the autumn of 1999, the Ad-Hoc Working Group held detailed consultations, involving some outside experts, to identify practical programmes in each of the above areas. A range of options were identified. Because of its close links with NATO and the Partnership for Peace Programme, the EAPC has potentially strong comparative advantages in promoting practical projects relating to defence and security institutions.

Significantly, many states expressed particular interest in developing projects relating to weapons stockpile management and security. On 2–3 December 1999, the Netherlands and Bulgaria co-hosted an international workshop at its Foreign Ministry to explore these options further.[36] Stockpile security touches on the critical issue of reducing thefts and losses from military, police or other official weapons stockpiles. Stockpile management is closely linked to this, but also addresses problems relating to the safe management and disposal of stocks of weapons that have become surplus to requirements. Many countries of the former USSR confront real problems with the security, management of weapons stored on their territory. There was wide interest in developing joint training programmes through NATO and Partnership for Peace programmes, to disseminate good practice and help to establish collective guidelines in this area.

Further, discussions on bilateral projects seemed promising. Moldova, Georgia and Albania were amongst the countries expressing interest in obtaining assistance from NATO countries in tackling some of these problems. For example, Moldova is concerned about large quantities of obsolete and unstable arms and ammunition left in their territory after the break-up of the

USSR. Assistance with securing or destroying such stocks may be mobilised through the EAPC process.

Thus, during 1999, NATO/EAPC moved from doing nothing in this area to a situation where there were real prospects of it establishing co-operative and practical projects to tackle one of the main sources of illicit arms: insecure weapon stores and military units, and surplus military equipment.

The European Union

European Union initiatives on illicit arms trafficking and the proliferation of small arms and light weapons did not start in earnest until 1997. Since then, however, the EU has taken a series of substantial measures. In June 1997, the EU Council established the EU Programme for Combating and Preventing Illicit Trafficking in Conventional Arms. In June 1998, the EU Code of Conduct on Arms Exports was adopted. On 17 December 1998, the Council of the European Union adopted a legally binding Joint Action on the EU's contribution to combating the destabilising accumulation and spread of small arms and light weapons. In May 1999, the EU Development Council passed a resolution stating that EU Commission development assistance funds may be used to assist countries to tackle problems associated with illicit arms trafficking and small arms proliferation.

The EU Programme for Preventing and Combating Illicit Trafficking in Conventional Arms set the framework within which the EU's efforts subsequently developed in this area. The Netherlands took the lead in establishing the EU Programme, during its Presidency of the EU in the first half of 1997. It was motivated by a concern to develop a comprehensive EU programme to address light weapons proliferation. At the time, however, some EU states were reluctant to agree to a programme which explicitly focused on restraining legal as well as illicit arms accumulations and transfers, and which singled out small arms and light weapons for attention. The Netherlands government thus decided to aim for an EU programme on illicit arms trafficking, recognising that in practice there were close links between the two issue areas. The process by which the initiative was developed displayed similar characteristics to those of all subsequent EU measures in this area. In particular, there was close co-operation between "like-minded" EU governments and some policy research experts and NGOs such as Saferworld.

The EU Programme for Preventing and Combating Illicit Trafficking in Conventional Arms was agreed at the Amsterdam summit in June 1997. It involved political commitments, without binding financial or legal obligations. The Programme provides a framework for EU action in three main areas:[37]

I. Strengthening collective efforts to prevent and combat illicit trafficking in arms from and through the European Union, including developing enhanced information exchange and improving co-ordination and co-operation amongst intelligence, customs and law enforcement agencies.

II. Taking concerted action to assist other countries in preventing and combating illicit arms trafficking. Assistance to these countries could include: establishing or strengthening their legal and administrative systems for regulating and monitoring arms possession and transfers; enhancing their capacity to enforce such regulations (for example through helping to resource and train adequate number of police and customs officials); and promoting national and sub-regional co-operation amongst police, customs and intelligence services.

III. Taking concerted action to assist countries in regions affected by small arms proliferation and illicit trafficking, especially in post-conflict situations and in regions with only minimal security and stability. Such actions could include: helping to suppress illicit circulation and trafficking in arms; supporting the integration of former combatants into civilian life and the removal of weapons from circulation through measures such as weapons collection, buy-back and destruction programmes schemes.

The Programme is thus relatively comprehensive in scope, focusing on ways in which the EU could support other countries and regions as well as on preventing illicit trafficking from or through the EU itself.

As far as Part I of the EU programme is concerned, most EU states were in need of improved co-ordination even at a national level. Regulating the possession and flow of small arms requires co-ordination amongst a variety of government agencies, since such weapons may be held or used for a relatively wide range of purposes, such as hunting, self defence, display, crime, policing, commercial or military exports, or equipping the armed forces. The different agencies involved tended not to operate in different spheres, and there were serious gaps in co-ordination. To address such problems, in 1997 the Belgian government established a specific central co-ordination unit, with mechanisms to ensure systematic information-exchange and consultation amongst relevant policy-making and operational bodies. In 1998, the Netherlands and the UK established similar inter-departmental committees on small arms and illicit trafficking. The EU Programme helped to stimulate these national improvements, and encourage the wider dissemination of good practices amongst other EU and Associate states.

The first EU activity specifically designed to promote implementation of Part I of the EU Programme was organised by the UK in February 1998 during its EU Presidency. A "European Conference on Trafficking in Arms" was held in London, in which national officials from police, customs, and intelligence agencies, foreign and interior ministries as well as legal experts and Interpol representatives participated. It aimed to promote the co-ordination amongst EU and Associate countries of operational and enforcement mechanisms to tackle illicit weapon trafficking. The meeting was a useful initial step: before the meeting many of the officials reportedly had not even met or discussed the issues with their counterparts from other EU states, let alone co-ordinated their activities closely. This was even more the case with respect to officials from Central Europe.

The meeting identified a number of needs, including arrangements for better information-exchange and databases and improved systems for identifying and tracing illicit arms. However, except in one area, there was little systematic follow-up during the remainder of the year. The exception related to arms trafficking to terrorists. An EU working group examined proposals in this area through 1998, resulting in an EU Council Recommendation on arms trafficking.[38] This included a ten-point programme for information-exchange, co-operation and adoption of best practice amongst relevant national intelligence and enforcement agencies.

In summer 1998, the EU Associate Countries of Central and Eastern Europe publicly aligned themselves with the EU programme, as well as with the 1998 EU Code of Conduct on Arms Exports. The EU Code of Conduct consists of eight criteria which EU states agreed to apply in the decisions on issuing arms export licenses, together with some information exchange and consultation mechanisms relating to their implementation. A important focus of some subsequent ad-hoc workshops was to strengthen links between EU officials and their Central and Eastern European counterparts and discuss priorities for strengthening arms export controls and preventing diversion of arms transfers to illicit or unauthorised use.[39]

Implementation of Parts II and III of the EU Programme for Combating and Preventing Illicit trafficking in Conventional Arms are concerned with developing partnerships between the EU and countries that are severely affected by illicit arms trafficking and proliferation of small arms and light weapons. In early 1998, the UK Presidency selected Southern Africa as the main initial focus for such efforts, resulting in the co-operation programmes discussed above in relation to Southern Africa. EU countries' support for the West African initiatives (see above) also came within the framework of the EU Programme.

In addition, the EU decided to support a UN weapons collection programme in district in central Albania. In 1997, hundreds of thousands of small arms, including semi-automatic rifles, were looted from police and army stores throughout Albania during the public disturbances after the collapse of pyramid-selling schemes. In June 1998, a UN Mission aimed to develop a gun-collection programme to Albania, and recommended an approach which linked voluntary gun-collection with local development aid projects.[40] In January 1999, the UN launched its first pilot project within this programme, in the district of Gramsch. This is co-ordinated by the UNDP, but depended greatly on the support of the so-called "Group of Interested States" convened on German initiative to support practical disarmament measures around the world.[41] The EU agreed to help to fund the UN's Gramsch project. It insisted that the collected weapons and ammunition were destroyed, rather than returned to insecure Albanian military stores. In practice, EU states also provided technical assistance, particularly in the safe disposal on large amounts of unstable ammunition that was recovered.

By the autumn of 1998, the international context had changed, and all EU states were now prepared to develop a collective programme that went beyond illicit arms trafficking to encompass efforts to prevent and reduce the destabilising accumulation and spread of small arms and light weapons. On 17 December, the EU Council adopted a "Joint Action on the European Union's contribution to combating the destabilising accumulation and spread of small arms and light weapons".[42] The objectives of the Joint Action are (i) to combat and contribute to ending the destabilising accumulation and spread of small arms and light weapons, (ii) to contribute to the reduction of existing accumulations of these weapons to levels consistent with countries' legitimate security needs, and (iii) to help regions suffering from problems associated with excessive accumulation and spread of small arms to tackle them. In 1999, all EU Associate states, EFTA (European Free Trade Area) member states, and the government of South Africa aligned themselves with this 1998 EU Joint Action.

The first substantive part of this EU Joint Action sets out a set of principles and measures to which the EU and its member states not only commit themselves but also promise to promote their adoption by the rest of international community. Article 3 focuses on prevention measures. For example, exporting countries should commit themselves to supply small arms only to governments (or their licensed procurement agents) in strict accordance with the EU Code of Conduct and with appropriate end-use guarantees, while all countries should import and hold small arms only to a level commensurate with their legitimate self-defence and security requirements. Article 4 focuses on ways to reduce existing accumulations of small arms. For example, assistance should be provided, where appropriate, to countries requesting support for controlling and eliminating surplus small arms in their territory, particularly where this may help to prevent arms conflict or in post-conflict situations. Article 5 focuses on commitments to try to include weapons collection and destruction provisions in peace agreements or international peace missions.

The second main part of the Joint Action is primarily concerned with the ways in which the EU should promote adoption of the above principles and measures. Most importantly, it clarifies that EU funds and resources should be provided for projects aimed at promoting and implementing them. This is further re-inforced by the May 1999 EU Development Council Resolution on "combating the excessive and uncontrolled accumulation and spread of small arms and light weapons as part of the EU's emergency aid, reconstruction and development programmes".[43] The makes it clear the funds managed by the EU Commission should also be used for these purposes.

During 1999, the EU's co-operation programmes with Southern Africa, West Africa and Albania continued, and extended to include Cambodia. An EU Fact-Finding Mission was sent to Cambodia in July 1999. On the basis of its recommendations, the EU allocated funds for a project in Cambodia. This is to help to strengthen and extend the Cambodian government's weapons collection programmes, support the development of appropriate legislation and regulations governing firearms possession and the transfer or sale of military equipment, and promote good practice in stockpile management and destruction.

In summary, between 1997 and 1999, the EU developed a series of substantial programmes to help to combat and prevent illicit arms trafficking and proliferation of small arms and light weapons. In practice, the contribution to such efforts in Africa and elsewhere is more visible than they are to restricting supplies from and through the EU itself, where the effects are harder to observe. It does seem clear, however, that the EU programmes and guidelines helped to raise awareness and restraint amongst national export licensing authorities and enforcement agencies.

The Americas

During the 1980s, covert supplies of arms and ammunition were delivered on a large scale to military groups fighting in the civil wars and insurgencies that took place in Latin America, and particularly Central America.[44] As these conflicts ended, the war-torn societies and the international community confronted the problems of banditry and social violence associated with the wide availability of arms, particularly small arms and light weapons, amongst civilians. Nevertheless, regional responses to illicit arms trafficking in the Americas have primarily emerged in the context of programmes to combat drug trafficking and transnational organised crime.

For many years, regional efforts to combat drug trafficking in the Americas were mobilised around US government concerns to combat and prevent drug supplies. Along with the processes of production and distribution of drugs, however, came high levels of criminal violence and gun use. The criminal organisations involved acquired large arsenals of illicit arms, to protect their territories and operations. Armed opposition groups in countries such as Colombia and Peru were also deeply involved in trafficking arms and drugs. Many of the weapons came from the USA, where sophisticated firearms could be bought relatively easily due to its liberal gun laws. They could then be shipped to Latin American countries, often taking advantage of opportunities to divert legal exports of civilian firearms to unauthorised destinations.

Concerns about illicit arms trafficking moved up the political agenda of the members of the Organisation of American States (OAS). Moreover, in 1994 the USA resumed active participation in the OAS, after a period of over 25 years in which it had not attended OAS summit meetings. The 1994 Summit of Heads of States of the Americas re-oriented the organisation to meet new challenges, including economic and trade issues, terrorism and drug trafficking.

Mexico, Colombia and others emphasised the links between drugs and arms trafficking. They succeeded in including firearms in the agenda of Inter-American Drug Abuse Control Commission (CICAD) – one of the OAS's Commissions. As a result, in 1996 the OAS established an expert group on firearms and explosives within CICAD. This had the task of determining "applicable measures for effecting inter-country co-operation for controlling illicit transnational movements of arms and explosives related to drug trafficking with a view to preparing model regulations in this field".

In September 1997, the expert group finalised its recommendations for CICAD "Model Regulations for the Control of the International Movement of Firearms, their Parts, Components and Ammunition", which were agreed in Lima, Peru, in November 1997.[45] They are not legally binding. But they provide guidelines for national regulations. They include detailed guidelines on licensing procedures; systems for ensuring authenticity of shipping documents, pre-notification procedures for shipments and transit routes, and national responsibilities relating to record-keeping, information exchange and consultation.

Alongside this process, negotiations began in early 1997 for an OAS Convention against illicit firearms trafficking and manufacture. In May 1997, the US president Clinton and Mexican President Zedillo declared that they would work together for the success these negotiations. Agreement was achieved remarkably rapidly. In November 1997, the governments of the Organisation of American States (OAS) signed the Inter-American Convention Against the Illicit Manufacturing of and Trafficking in Firearms, Ammunition, Explosives and their Component Parts.[46] The agreement came into force in 1998 (after two ratifications), and by October 1999 had been ratified by nine of the 31 signatory States.[47]

The stated purpose of the OAS Convention is: "To prevent, combat, and eradicate the illicit manufacturing of and trafficking in firearms, ammunition, explosives, and related materials" as well as to "promote and facilitate co-operation and exchange of information and experience among States Parties". The OAS Convention sets out a range of substantial commitments, control mechanisms, legal requirements, and co-operation procedures. These include:

- instituting legislative measures to criminalise illicit manufacturing and trafficking, as well as offences deemed to facilitate such activities;
- marking firearms at the time of manufacture and import, identifying the name of manufacturer, the place of manufacture, and serial number to facilitate identification and tracing;
- establishing an effective and more standardised system of export, import and international transit licenses;
- strengthening controls at export points;
- exchanging information in areas such as: authorised producers, dealers, importers, exporters and carriers of firearms, ammunition, explosives, and other related materials; and scientific and technological information for prevention, detection and investigation;
- exchanging experience and training in areas such as identification, detection, tracing and intelligence gathering;
- providing mutual legal assistance to facilitate investigation and prosecution of illicit activities and establishing illicit weapons activities as extraditable offences.

There is also provision for a consultative mechanism to review implementation and further elaborate guidelines and best practices as appropriate.

The CICAD Model Regulations and the OAS Convention are mutually reinforcing. Their primary focus is to strengthen controls on legal firearms transfers and manufacturers, to reduce the scope for diversion for illicit or unauthorised purposes. The scope of the OAS Convention is restricted to civilian transfers of firearms. Transfers between States and for purposes of national security are not covered. Nevertheless, it is important to recognise that it has a wide definition of a firearm, to include virtually all arms that can fire projectiles. It is also legally binding, which may improve implementation and compliance.

Nevertheless, it takes time to implement the detailed regulations and systems required by the OAS Convention and the CICAD Model Regulations. By the end of 1999, some OAS States had largely incorporated the obligations into their national practices, including Brazil, Mexico, Canada and the USA (although the latter two States had not yet ratified the Convention). But most developing country members of the OAS had not yet managed to do so. For example, systems for marking all firearms on import were not yet in place in most countries.

In June 1999, the OAS General Assembly adopted a resolution requesting CICAD to continue to provide assistance to OAS member States to promote compliance with the OAS Convention. There have also been sub-regional efforts. For example, Paraguay is a known centre for illicit arms trafficking in South America. Partly in order to promote implementation in this neighbour-hood, on 24 July 1998, Mercosur members (Argentina, Brazil, Paraguay and Uruguay) and Associated States (Bolivia and Chile) signed the Memorandum of Understanding that created a Joint Register Mechanism of Buyers and Sellers of Firearms, Explosives, Ammunition and Related Materials. This is at least evidence of political will amongst key Mercosur countries to promote effective implementation to the extent that they can.

International and global responses

As discussed in the Introduction, it is possible to trace international efforts to combat illicit trafficking in conventional arms back many years; at least as far back as the League of Nations. However, during the Cold War, global co-operation on arms trafficking was largely limited to declarations. INTERPOL provided an international mechanism for co-operation on criminal investigations by the Police. But even in this case, INTERPOL systems for tracing stolen firearms were relatively rudimentary until the 1990s. As far as the United Nations is concerned, it was not until the Cold War was drawing to a close that General Assembly resolutions on illicit arms trafficking began to have much significance. In this section, we briefly outline international developments from 1990–97, and then examine key recent international responses to illicit arms trafficking.

The United Nations 1990–98

In 1988, the UN General Assembly adopted Resolution 43/75I. This brought together the substance of previous UN documents relating to the potentially destabilising effects of arms accumulations and transfers, and to illicit and covert arms trafficking. It also established a UN Group of Governmental Experts, which met from 1989 to develop ways and means of promoting transparency in arms transfers, and to consider the issue of illicit arms. The Group reported in July 1991.[48] Its most important recommendation was for an international register of arms transfers, which led to the establishment of the UN Register of Conventional Arms. It also recommended some general norms and good practices for States to combat and prevent illicit arms trafficking, including: adequate national legislation; effective arms transfer licensing systems, border controls and customs authorities; and international information exchange.

The Group's recommendations formed the basis of General Assembly resolution 46/36 H in 1992, which amongst other things called upon the UN Disarmament Commission (UNDC) to consider establishing guidelines for international arms transfers. This started an important process for developing agreed norms, on legal arms transfers as well as on illicit arms trafficking. After difficult negotiations, the UNDC finally achieved consensus on a set of guidelines and recommendations in 1996.[49] Though limited, these continue to help to provide an internationally agreed set of norms, as a basis for international discussions in this contested area.

In the meantime, the changed international context meant that the UN had become much more intensely involved in international peace-keeping and peace-building operations, including difficult humanitarian interventions in the context of internal conflicts, pre-emptive deployments of troops, and missions to monitor and implement peace-agreements. As a result, the UN had increasingly to deal with the problems associated with the wide availability and flows of small arms, and to try to manage the processes of disarming, demobilising and re-integrating former combatants. Moreover, with the end of the Cold War, the problems of transnational crime, drug trafficking and terrorism also rose higher on the international security agenda.

As discussed in the previous section, in response to a request from Mali in 1993, the UN became involved in supporting Mali in its efforts to assist in the collection and control of illicit arms. Stimulated by this, in 1995, the UN Secretary-General issued a report, *"Supplement to An Agenda to Peace"* – an addendum to his 1992 *Agenda for Peace* – in which he highlighted the problems of light weapons proliferation and internal conflicts, and the need for "micro-disarmament" programmes to tackle them.[50] After the ensuing debates, it proved possible to secure agreement in the General Assembly to Resolution 50/70 B, sponsored by Japan, which proposed a UN study on the significance of small arms and light weapons in conflict situations in which the UN is involved.

More specifically, a UN Panel of Governmental Experts was to be established in 1996 to prepare a report on:

(a) the types of small arms and light weapons actually being used in conflicts being dealt with by the United Nations;

(b) the nature and causes of the excessive and destabilising accumulation and transfer of small arms and light weapons, including their illicit production and trade;

(c) the ways and means to prevent and reduce the excessive and destabil-
    ising accumulation and transfer of small arms and light weapons, in
    particular as they cause or exacerbate conflict.

The UN Panel held three sessions between June 1996 and July 1997, together
with three regional workshops (in South Africa, El Salvador and Nepal). Its
report was published in summer 1997,[51] and accepted by majority vote by the
UN General Assembly in December 1997. The 1997 Report of the UN Panel
of Experts made some 23 recommendations to help to prevent and reduce
excessive and destabilising accumulations and transfers of small arms and
light weapons.

Alongside these developments the UN also began a process aimed at promoting controls on civilian firearms, for the purposes of crime prevention and
public safety. In 1995, the Commission on Crime Prevention and Criminal
Justice, one of the subsidiary bodies of the UN Economic and Social Council
(ECOSOC) requested the Centre for International Crime Prevention, based
in Vienna, to carry out an international study of firearm regulation. One of
the primary motivations for the study was concern about transnational illicit
trafficking in firearms.

The UN "International Study on Firearm Regulation" was released in
May 1997.[52] Between September 1997 and January 1998, a series of four
regional workshops were held in Slovenia, Tanzania, Brazil and India to
consider the study and discuss the possibility of establishing agreed international guidelines. The wide variety of national norms and laws relating to
the sale, ownership, possession and use of firearms by civilians meant that
agreements on domestic firearms regulations did not seem to be a promising
approach. However there was wide interest in co-operative action to combat
transnational illicit trafficking in firearms.

An international protocol against firearms trafficking

In April 1998, the ECOSOC Commission on Crime Prevention and Criminal
Justice adopted a resolution calling for a "legally binding international instrument to combat illicit manufacturing of and trafficking in firearms, their
parts and components and ammunition within the context of a United Nations
Convention against Transnational Organised Crime.[53] Having just signed the
1997 OAS Convention, OAS member States were particularly strongly in
favour of such an international firearms protocol. Moreover, a consensus in
support of the proposal had developed amongst the G-8 states by early 1998,
which was formally expressed at the G-8 summit in Birmingham, UK, in
May 1998. Following a UN General Assembly resolution to the same effect

in December 1998, negotiations for a Firearms Protocol formally began in January 1999, with a view to completion before the end of the year 2000.

At the time of writing, the negotiations are still underway. Nevertheless, by the end of January 2000, the main components of the draft protocol were becoming reasonably clear.[54] Most fundamentally, the initial draft of the protocol was based largely on the 1997 OAS Convention. It has retained this basic character through subsequent revisions. Thus the Firearms Protocol will be a legally binding agreement, supplementary to a UN Convention on Transnational Organised Crime. It will apply to all classes of firearms, but not to State-to-State transactions or transfers for purposes of national security. The definition of a "firearm" may not be as wide as in the OAS Convention, but will probably at least include any barrelled weapons that will expel a shot, bullet or projectile, excluding pre-1900 antiques.

The main articles of the Draft Firearms Protocol include the following. Each State Party must ensure that activities prohibited by the Protocol are criminalised by the adoption of appropriate national legislation. It must confiscate all illicitly manufactured or trafficked firearms, and ensure that such confiscated weapons do not fall into civilian hands. For the purposes of identifying and tracing firearms, States Parties shall require that appropriate markings identifying the name of the manufacturer, place on manufacture, and serial number, are applied at the time of manufacture and on each import.[55] They shall ensure that reliable records containing information required to identify or trace the firearms are maintained for at least ten years. They shall establish or maintain effective systems for licensing exports or imports of firearms, in accordance with a set of guidelines and minimum standards established in the Protocol.

To prevent theft or diversion, States Parties shall ensure the security of firearms at the time of manufacture, import, export or transit, maintain effective border controls, and strengthen transborder co-operation amongst police and customs. They shall exchange information on issues including: authorised producers, dealers, importers and exporters of firearms; means of concealment and trafficking routes used by criminal organisations; legislative experiences, and ways and means of combating money-laundering. They shall co-operate in tracing lines of supply and diversion points for firearms that may have been illicitly manufactured or trafficked, including providing prompt and accurate responses to requests for assistance in such tracing. State Parties shall identify a national contact point, and establish an international focal point to facilitate implementation. It is also possible that the Protocol will include provisions for the registration and licensing of arms brokers. All of the obligations outlined above relate to parts and components and ammunition as well as to the firearms themselves.

Toward an international action programme on small arms and light weapons

The negotiations for an international Firearms Protocol are explicitly targeted against illicit trafficking in civilian firearms by criminals. However, as discussed above, most illicit arms originate from legal producers or government stockpiles. In many circumstances, particularly in regions of conflict or war-torn societies, illicit arms trafficking is closely linked with excessive and destabilising flows and accumulations of small arms and light weapons, including those in which governments are involved. In parallel with the Firearms Protocol negotiations, international discussions developed on these wider agendas relating to internal or international security, peace building and disarmament.

In December 1997, the UN General Assembly agreed, by resolution 52/38 J, to establish a UN Group of Governmental Experts on Small Arms. This UN Group of Experts was established in early 1998, and consisted of representatives of 23 States, including all five of the permanent members of the UN Security Council and key states from each of the main regions. It was asked to report on the implementation of the recommendations in the 1997 Report of the UN Panel of Experts, and make recommendations for further actions. It was also asked to make recommendations on the objectives, scope, and agenda of an international conference on the illicit arms trade in all its aspects, which was to be convened by 2001 (the 2001 Conference).

This new UN Group of Governmental Experts was essentially an international negotiating body tasked with achieving a politically-binding agreement on recommendations to States and international organisations to prevent and reduce destabilising flows and accumulations of small arms and light weapons. A consensus report by the Group would almost certainly be accepted by the UN General Assembly. Moreover, international momentum was now developing towards agreeing substantial international responses to small arms proliferation and associated illicit arms trafficking. In this context, many States (including China, France and the UK) which had not participated in the previous Panel of Experts felt obliged to engage more closely with the issues and carefully negotiate the content and formulation of any recommendations.

After meeting over a period of 15 months, the UN Group of Governmental Experts finalised a consensus report on 1 August, 1999.[56] It was subsequently endorsed by the UN General Assembly. In summary, the 1999 Report reviewed in detail progress towards implementing each of the recommendations of the 1997 Panel of Experts, concluding that some progress had been made in specific areas but in most cases there had been insufficient implementation. The Group made a range of further recommendations, to the UN, other international and regional organisations, and States. For example, these included:

- All States should ensure adequate safeguards on weapons stores to prevent loss or theft;
- International assistance should be provided where requested to efforts to collect and safeguard weapons or destroy surplus or confiscated weapons;
- All States should ensure that they exercise control over all arms brokering activities performed in their territory or by dealers registered in their territory, even in cases where the arms do not enter their territory;
- All States should ensure that they have laws, regulations and procedures in place to exercise effective control over the production or transfer of small arms and light weapons in their areas of jurisdiction. Applications for export authorisations should be assessed according to strict national criteria for all weapons, including second-hand or surplus arms.
- All small arms and light weapons should be reliably marked during the production process with information enabling authorities to identify the country of manufacture, the manufacturer and serial number. All necessary measures should be adopted and enforced to prevent the manufacture, stockpiling or transfer of inadequately marked weapons. All inadequately marked weapons that are collected or confiscated should be expeditiously marked or destroyed;
- The UN, and Member States in a position to do so, should promote and support initiatives to disseminate useful or successful practices relating to stockpile management and storage, weapons collection, and destruction of surplus arms;
- The UN and other international or regional development assistance organisations (such as the World Bank) should intensify and co-ordinate their activities in adopting an "integrated and proportional approach to security assistance and development aid" in regions where conflicts come to an end and where serious problems relating to small arms proliferation have to be dealt with urgently.

In addition to these and other recommendations of the 1999 Report of the UN group of Governmental Experts on Small Arms, several other recent documents also help to provide a basis for the next stage of developing co-ordinated and sustained international action on small arms proliferation and illicit arms trafficking. After three years of discussions, in April 1999 the UNDC adopted some new "Guidelines on conventional arms control/limitation and disarmament, with particular emphasis on the consolidation of peace".[57] These guidelines relate, for example, to the speedy reduction and removal of surplus arms through weapons collection and destruction in conflict-prone or war-torn areas.

The 1999 Report of the UN Group of Governmental Experts on Small Arms and the 1996 and 1999 UNDC guidelines the now form the main basis for international efforts to develop co-ordinated and sustained international actions against illicit arms trafficking and small arms proliferation. The main focus of international negotiations in this area during 2000–2001 will be the international conference on illicit trafficking in small arms and light weapons in all its aspects, to be held in 2001 (the 2001 Conference).

The first Preparatory Committee for the 2001 conference was due to be held from 28 February–4 March 2000. The objectives and scope for this conference remain contested. However there is broad consensus that its main objectives are to:

- strengthen or develop norms and standards at the global, regional and national levels that would re-inforce and further co-ordinate efforts to prevent and combat the illicit trafficking in small arms and light weapons in all its aspects;

- develop agreed measures to prevent and combat illicit arms trafficking and small arms proliferation in war-torn or conflict-prone regions;

- mobilise political will and raise awareness in the international community;

- promote responsibility by States with regard to arms transfers.

It is widely hoped that the 2001 Conference will not only achieve agreements at a high political level on relevant on sets of general norms and standards, but also on a number of politically binding agreements and programmes in specific areas. These may include: regulating arms brokering activities; marking and tracing small arms and light weapons; international mechanisms to support responsible stockpile management and destruction of surplus weapons; and information exchange arrangements.

In fact modest international mechanisms to mobilise support for practical measures such as weapons collection and destruction have recently been started. In March 1998, an open-ended "Group of Interested States" was established to mobilise such support on request. Chaired by Germany, this group has since supported a number of projects, including a workshop in Guatemala to learn from Central American experiences with weapon collection, a weapons collection project in Albania, and weapons destruction in Liberia in November 1999. To help to support such efforts, a Trust Fund for the Consolidation of Peace through Practical Disarmament Measures was established by the UN Secretary-General in August 1998. Similarly, the UNDP Trust Fund for Support to Prevention and Reduction of the Proliferation of Small Arms was established in November 1998 as a result an initiative by Norway. These are small funds, however, and as yet mechanisms to match resources with those that need them are inadequate.

The UN Security Council

Finally, the UN Security Council (UNSC) has become progressively more concerned about the enforcement of its mandatory arms embargoes, and associated issues relating to illicit arms trafficking. In 1998, the UN Secretary General submitted a report to the UNSC on Africa, which highlighted the problems caused by illicit arms trafficking and small arms proliferation in the region.[58] For example, in Resolution 1196 (1998), the Council expressed its willingness to consider all appropriate measures to assist the effective implementation of UN arms embargoes, including inquiries into arms trafficking routes, deployment of monitors at borders and points of entry, and follow-up of possible specific violations.

Similarly, in 1995 and again in 1998, the UNSC established an International Commission of Inquiry on arms flows to the Great Lakes region of Central Africa. In May 1999, the Security Council decided to establish two expert panels to collect information and investigate reports relating to the violation of the measures imposed against UNITA with respect to arms and related material, petroleum and petroleum products, diamonds and the movement of UNITA funds.[59] In a precedent-setting initiative, systematic efforts were made by the UNSC to exert pressure against such violations by UNITA in the autumn of 1999, with some effect. Overall, the UN Security Council is becoming more active in the enforcement of its mandatory arms embargoes, but has yet to establish effective mechanisms that enforce embargoes rather than investigate violations.

Concluding remarks

In 1996, there were few international or regional co-operative measures to prevent or combat illicit trafficking in conventional arms. By the beginning of the year 2000, the situation has changed very substantially. Much has been achieved over the last three years. There are substantial regional initiatives in Europe, Sub-Saharan Africa and the Americas. Important progress has been made towards establishing agreed norms and guidelines at the international level in this challenging issue area. A powerful international coalition of concerned states, regional and international organisations, experts and NGOs is developing to use these to mobilise international action.

There are good prospects for an international protocol against trafficking in firearms to be agreed before the end of 2000, in the framework with the UN Convention against Transnational Organised Crime. The forthcoming 2001 Conference (the "international conference on illicit trafficking in small arms and light weapons in all its aspects" due to take place in 2001) now provides an international focus for efforts to establish an international action programme to tackle small arms proliferation and illicit arms trafficking.

Does this recent surge of initiatives indicate increased political will to prevent and combat illicit trafficking in conventional arms "in all its aspects"? In some regions, this does appear to be the case. With the end of the Cold War, powerful states have reduced interests in maintaining covert arms supplies to allies and proxies. It has become easier for concerned groups to make plausible arguments to governments that they have an interest in conflict prevention and post-conflict peace building. As transnational crime and terrorism rise on the political agenda, so too do concerns to combat arms trafficking. Democratic governments are increasingly sensitive to public concerns, and aware that decisions to authorise dubious arms transfers may well come back to haunt them politically.

However, the surge of recent initiatives on illicit arms trafficking and small arms proliferation remains consistent with a more cautious assessment. The complexity of the issue area offers many opportunities for coalitions of a few concerned states, international organisations and public pressure groups to frame proposals so that they are hard to resist in principle. Once such proposals are on the agenda in an established regional or international forum, they can be pursued to some agreement. But it will require sustained and co-ordinated implementation before those involved in illicit arms trafficking may be greatly inconvenienced, particularly with respect to small arms and light weapons for which there are so many sources of supply and opportunities for concealment.

By the same token, however, there appears to be the potential for a "winning coalition" to be developed by 2001 in support of an international action programme, which establishes some strong international norms together with mechanisms to support worthwhile co-operative efforts and regional and national initiatives. For example, a combination of key members of the OECD, OAS, EU and Associated Countries, and SADC, together with a few other concerned States, amounts to a powerful potential coalition of States. Similarly, a substantial NGO coalition also appears to be in formation, with the establishment of the International Action Network on Small Arms (IANSA).[60]

Perhaps the major challenge over the next five years is for these groups to co-ordinate and clarify useful shared objectives, so that these can be achieved and institutionalised before the present high levels of international awareness and concern give way to other priorities.

Notes

1. See, for example, the scope of *the Report of the UN Group of Governmental Experts on Small Arms*, (UN Document A/54/258, United Nations, 19 August 1999), and of the *Draft Protocol against the Illicit Manufacturing of and Trafficking in Firearms, Their Parts and Components and Ammunition*, (United Nations: UN Document A/AC.254/L.147/Add.3, 27 January 2000).

2. See, e.g. A. Karp, "The Rise of the Black and Grey Markets", in R. Harkavy and S. Neuman (eds.), *The Arms Trade: Problems and Prospects in the Post Cold War World*, in *The Annals of the American Academy of Political and Social Science*, 1994 (535), 175–189; or M. Klare, "The Subterranean Arms Trade: Black Market Sales, Covert Operations and Ethnic Warfare" in A. Pierre (ed.), *Cascade of Arms: managing conventional arms proliferation*, (Cambridge, Mass; Brookings, 1997), pp. 43–74.

3. The 1997 *Report of the UN Panel of Governmental Experts on Small Arms* (United Nations: Document A/52/298; 27 August 1997) provided a more refined and precise definition, which has become internationally accepted. This distinguishes between small arms, which are weapons designed for personal use, and light weapons, which are designed for use by several persons serving as a crew. The category of small arms includes: revolvers and self loading pistols, rifles and carbines, submachine guns, assault rifles, and light machine guns. Light arms include heavy machine guns, hand-held under-barrel and mounted grenade launchers, portable anti-aircraft guns, portable anti-tanks guns, recoilless rifles, portable launchers of anti-aircraft missile systems, and mortars of calibres less than 100 mm. Ammunition and explosives form an integral part of small arms and light weapons used in conflict.

4. Shoulder-fired anti-aircraft missiles or anti-tank missiles have emerged as an exception to this, as concerns have increased during the 1990s about access by terrorists or insurgent groups to sophisticated systems such as the US Stinger and UK Blowpipe missiles.

5. United Nations Disarmament Committee, "Guidelines for international arms transfers in the context of General Assembly Resolution 46/36 H of December 1991", *Official records of the General Assembly, Fifty-first Session, Supplement No 42* (United Nations: A/51/42, annex 1, 1996) paragraph 7.

6. *Draft Protocol against Illicit manufacturing . . .*, (A/54/258), passim. Note that, at the time of writing, amendments to this definition remained under discussion.

7. For example, Pakistan made this argument in the Firearms Protocol negotiations and also, together with Qatar, Oman, the Sudan and Syria, argued that the definition should not prevent arms transfers to groups involved in struggles for self-determination or who might need them for self-defence. See footnote 47 of *Draft Firearms Protocol*, ibid.

8. ASEAN Regional Forum intersessional group on confidence-building measures consideration of the issue of "preventing and combating illicit trafficking in conventional arms".

9. The decision was taken at the thirty-fourth meeting of the OAU Council of Ministers, held in Ouagadougou, Burkina Faso, from 4 to 7 June 1998; OAU Council of Ministers CM/Dec.432 (LXVIII), Proliferation of Small Arms and Light Weapons Doc.CM/2057 (LXVIII) Add.2.

10. *Report of the Mali Advisory Mission*, (New York: United Nations, 1994).

11. R. Poulton and I. Ag Youssouf, *A Peace of Timbuktu: democratic governance, development and African peacemaking*, (Geneva: UNIDIR; 1998).

12. *Sahara-Sahel Advisory Mission Report* (New York, United Nations, 20 September 1996).

13. *Declaration of a Moratorium on importation, exportation and manufacture of light weapons in West Africa*, Economic Community of West African States, twenty-first Ordinary Session of the Authority of Heads of States and Government, Abuja, 30–31 October 1998.

14. *Plan of Action for the Implementation of the Programme for Co-ordination and Assistance for Security and Development (PCASED)*, adopted by ECOWAS Foreign Ministers in Bamako on 24 March 1999, and the *Code of Conduct for the Implementation of the Moratorium on the Importation, Exportation and Manufacture of Light Weapons*, adopted by ECOWAS Heads of States and Government in December 1999. See United Nations document A/53/763-S/1998/1193, 18 December 1998, for details of the Programme for Co-ordination and Assistance for Security and Development (PCASED).

15. See e.g. *Report of UN Panel of Experts on Small Arms*, (United Nations: Document A/52/298; 27 August 1997).

16. Interviews with relevant national officials, June and October 1999.

17. Personal Communication, Foreign and Commonwealth Office, London, December 1999.

18. Public Statement of the Wassenaar Arrangement, Vienna, 10 December 1997.

19. *Programme for Co-ordination and Assistance for Security and Development,* Economic Community of West African States, 1998.

20. See, e.g. C. Smith and A. Vines, *Light Arms Proliferation in Southern Africa*, London Defence Studies No 42, (London: Centre for Defence Studies, 1997); V. Gamba (ed.), *Society Under Siege,* (South Africa, Institute for Security Studies, 1997) Volume I.

21. H. Solomon and J. Cilliers, "The Southern African Development Community and Small Arms Proliferation", in V. Gamba (ed.), *Society Under Siege: licit responses to illicit arms* (Pretoria, Institute for Security Studies, 1998), pp. 75–93.

22. See M.Chachiua, *Operations Rachel 1996–1999*, ISS Monograph Series No 38, (South Africa: Institute for Security Studies; June 1999), for a detailed discussion of these operations.

23. EU-Southern African Conference on "Developing Controls on Arms and Illicit Arms Trafficking in Southern Africa", Saferworld/Institute for Security Studies, Midrand, South Africa, 3–6 May 1998.

24. *Southern Africa Regional Action Programme on Light Arms and Illicit Arms Trafficking*, (London: Saferworld/ISS; May 1998).

25. Joint Communiqué on the Ministerial Conference between the European Union (EU) and the Southern African Development Community (SADC), Vienna, Austria, 3–4 November 1998.

26. SADC Council Decision, Prevention and Combating of Illicit Trafficking in Small Arms and Related Crimes, 13–14 August 1999.

27. F. Msutu, Head of Interpol Sub-regional Bureau for Southern Africa, "Building the Capacity to Combat Illicit Trafficking of Firearms in Southern Africa", paper presented at seminar hosted by Belgian Ministry of Foreign Affairs, *Implementing the EU Programme for Preventing and Combating Illicit Trafficking in Conventional Arms: a Programme of Action*, Palais d'Egmont, Brussels, 30 November–1 December 1998.

28. A. McLean and E. Clegg (eds.), *Towards implementation of the Southern Africa Regional Action Programme on Light Arms and Illicit Trafficking,* Report of Seminar, 8–9 September 1999 Pretoria, South Africa (Pretoria: Institute for Security Studies; 1999).

29. Interviews, O. Mokou, Director National Point of Contact SADC, South Africa, September 1999; O. Mangwana, National Point of Contact SADC, Zimbabwe Ministry of Foreign Affairs, in Pretoria, September 1999.

30. Interview, L. Dlamini, Chair, SARPCCO Legal subcommittee, Vienna, January 2000.

31. Interviews with Tanzanian, Kenya and Uganda police officials: Cape Town, 1997; Tanzania Police official, Midrand, 1998.
32. Personal Communication, L. Dlamini, Vienna January 2000.
33. For further information on the UN Register of Conventional Arms, see for example, the annual reports of the UN Secretary-General on the UN Register of Conventional, and also the Bradford Arms Register Studies series of publications, including example M. Chalmers and O. Greene, *A Maturing Regime?: the UN Register in its sixth year*, BARS Working Paper No 6, (Bradford, Bradford University, January 1999). The US Congressional Research Service publishes annual reports on arms transfers, see for example, R. Grimmett, Conventional Arms Transfers to the Third World 1991–98, Congressional Research Service, Library of Congress, Washington DC 1999. The Stockholm International Peace Research Institute (SIPRI) publishes their findings on the international trade in major conventional arms annually, most recently in *SIPRI Yearbook 1999: armaments, disarmament and international security*, (Oxford: SIPRI/Oxford University Press, 1998).
34. *Small Arms and Light Weapons: an issue for the OSCE?*, Report of a workshop organised by the Governments of Canada, Norway, Netherlands, and Switzerland, in association with BASIC, Hofburg Palace, Vienna 9–10 November 1998 (London: BASIC, 1999).
35. *Work Programme on Ways in Which the EAPC Might Contribute to the Challenge of Small Arms and Light Weapons*, (Brussels, NATO/EAPC Unclassified EAPC(PC-SALW)WP (99) 1 (revised); 25 June 1999); EAPC/PFP and the Challenge of Small Arms and Light Weapons (Brussels: NATO/EAPC Unclassified EAPC(C)D(1999)23; 4 November 1999.
36. Seminar on *Strengthening Management, Security and Transparency of Small Arms and Light Weapons Stockpiles*, The Hague, 2–3 December 1999.
37. EU Council, *EU Programme for Preventing and Combating Illicit Trafficking in Conventional Arms*, June 1997.
38. EU Council, *Council Recommendation on Arms Trafficking*, Brussels, 24 November 1998.
39. For example, On 2 October 1998, the Austrian Foreign Ministry and Saferworld co-hosted a conference in Vienna to review the challenges of preventing and combating illicit arms trafficking from or through the EU and Associate Countries. See O. Greene, *Tackling Illicit Trafficking in Conventional Arms; strengthening collective efforts by EU and Associate Countries,*, Saferworld Report, (London: Saferworld, April 1999).
40. Report of the Evaluation Mission to Albania, 11–14th June 1998, (New York, United Nations, 1998).
41. See, for example, "Recent Disarmament Steps reviewed By Group of Interested States", UN Press Release DC/2623 (New York: United Nations, 18 December 1998).
42. EU Council, *Joint Action adopted by the Council on the basis of Article J.3 of the Treaty on European Union on the European Union's contribution to combating the destabilising accumulation and spread of small arms and light weapons*, (Brussels, EU Council, 17 December 1998).
43. EU Development Council, *Resolution on combating the excessive and uncontrolled accumulation and spread of small arms and light weapons as part of the EU's emergency aid, reconstruction and development programmes*, EU Document No 109/2/99 Rev 2 (DEVGEN), 6 May 1999.
44. See, for example, M. Klare and D. Andersen, *A Scourge of Guns: the diffusion of small arms and light weapons in Latin America*, Federation of American Scientists, USA, 1996.
45. OAS CICAD Drug Abuse Control Commission, *Final Report of the Group of Experts on the Control of Arms and Explosives Related to Drug Trafficking*, CICAD/AREX/doc.5/97 (Washington DC: OAS, 1997).

46. Organisation of American States, *Twenty-fourth Special Session*, AG/doc.7 (XXIV-E/97) rev.1, (Washington DC: OAS, 13 November 1997).

47. The nine states to have ratified by October 1999 are: Bahamas, Belize, Bolivia, Brazil, Ecuador, El Salvadore, Mexico, Panama, and Peru.

48. Report to the UN Secretary-General, *Study on Ways and Means of Promoting Transparency in International Transfers of Conventional Arms*, UN General Assembly Document A/46/301 (New York: United Nations, 1991).

49. UN Disarmament Committee, "Guidelines for international arms transfer. . ." 1996, passim.

50. UN Secretary-General Boutros Boutros Ghali, *Agenda for Peace: a Supplement*, (New York, United Nations, January 1995); see also UN Secretary-General Boutros Boutros Ghali, *Agenda for Peace*, (New York: United Nations, 1992).

51. *Report of the Panel of Governmental Experts on Small Arms*, 1997 passim.

52. United Nations International Study on Firearms Regulation (New York, United Nations, 1998). (first released as released as Economic and Social Council, Crime Prevention and Criminal Justice Division, E/CN.15/1997/L.19, United Nations Office in Vienna, 30 April 1997).

53. Economic and Social Council, Crime Prevention and Criminal Justice Division, E/CN.15/1998/L.6/Rev 1, (Vienna, United Nations Office in Vienna, 28 April 1998).

54. The latest version of the draft protocol available was UN document A/AC.254/L.142/Add.3, (Vienna, United Nations, 27 January 2000).

55. The question of whether firearms must be marked on each import remained open at the time of writing.

56. Report of the UN Group of Governmental Experts on Small Arms, UN Document A/54/258, (New York: United Nations, 19 August 1999).

57. UN Disarmament Commission "Guidelines on conventional arms control/limitation and disarmament, with particular emphasis on the consolidation of peace in the context of General Assembly resolution 51/45 N", *Report of the UN Disarmament Commission*, General Assembly Document A/54/42, (New York, United Nations, May 1999).

58. UN Secretary-General, *Report on the causes of conflict and the promotion of durable peace and sustainable development in Africa*, UN Document A/52/871 – S/1998/318, (New York, United Nations, 13 April 1998).

59. UN Security Council Resolution 1237 (1999) and documents S/1999/837, (New York, United Nations, 30 July 1999); S/1999/829 (New York: United Nations, 28 July 1999).

60. The International Action Network on Small Arms is a global network of over 300 non-governmental organisations from all regions. It was established in October 1998, to facilitate NGO action. See, International Action Network on Small Arms, *Founding Document* (London, IANSA, 1998).

Transforming Social Inquiry, Transforming Social Action

New Paradigms for Crossing the Theory/Practice Divide in Universities and Communities

Edited by:
Francine T. Sherman
Boston College Law School, MA, USA
William R. Torbert
Boston College School of Management, MA, USA

KLUWER INTERNATIONAL SERIES IN OUTREACH SCHOLARSHIP 4

Transforming Social Inquiry, Transforming Social Action advances both the theory and practice of a new paradigm of social inquiry and social action that no longer dichotomizes 'pure research' at 'ivory tower' universities from 'messy' political action in 'real world' communities. Emanating from conversations and projects associated with the Boston College Center for Child, Family, and Community Partnerships, the book provides new models of interdisciplinary collaboration across the theory–practice divide. *Transforming Social Inquiry, Transforming Social Action* is an invaluable resource for foundation and government officials as well as college and university administrators interested in exploring new approaches to teaching and research that take students and faculty into communities and into the various forms of action learning and ethical reflection.

2000
320 pp.
Hardbound,
Price: NLG 290.00 / GBP 86.25   USD 125.00

ISBN 0-7923-7787-7

http://www.wkap.nl

Kluwer academic publishers

P.O. Box 322, 3300 AH Dordrecht, The Netherlands
P.O. Box 358, Accord Station, Hingham, MA 02018-0358, U.S.A.

Crime and Morality

The Significance of Criminal Justice in Post-Modern Culture

By:
Hans C.J. Boutellier
Ministry of Justice, The Hague, and Vrije Universiteit, Amsterdam, The Netherlands

Over the last twenty-five years the significance of criminal justice has dramatically changed. In a 'post-modern' culture, criminal law serves more and more as a focal point in public morality. The 'discovery' of the victim of crime can be seen as the marking point by which criminal justice got its central position in the maintenance of social order. It is the result of a general 'victimalization' of today's morality.

This ingenious book - according to Michael Tonry - combines insights from criminology, sociology and moral philosophy. It is especially inspired by the work of Richard Rorty, who stresses the sensibility for suffering as the major source of morality in post-modern times. It describes the arousal of attention for victims and the development of crime prevention. More specifically, it analyzes child sexual abuse and prostitution.

This 'illuminating' book will be an eye-opener for theorists in criminology and moral philosophy, but will also be an inspiring work for policy makers in the area of criminal justice.

Contents:
Preface; *M. Tonry.* Foreword to the Translation. **1.** Morality, Criminal Justice and Criminal Events. **2.** Morality and Criminal Justice Policy. **3.** Morality and Victims. **4.** Victimalization of the Sexually Abused Child. **5.** The De-victimalization of the Prostitute. **6.** Solidarity or Virtuousness: Rorty versus MacIntyre. **7.** Criminality and Liberalism: Some Closing Comments. References.

2000
196 pp.
Hardbound
Price: NLG 190.00/GBP 66.00/USD 115.00

ISBN 0-7923-6091-5

http://www.wkap.nl

Kluwer academic publishers

P.O. Box 322, 3300 AH Dordrecht, The Netherlands
P.O. Box 358, Accord Station, Hingham, MA 02018-0358, U.S.A.